REIGNITING CURIOUSITY AND INQUIRY IN HIGHER EDUCATION

REIGNITING CURIOUSITY AND INQUIRY IN HIGHER EDUCATION

A Realist's Guide to Getting Started With Inquiry-Based Learning

Stacey L. MacKinnon and Beth Archer-Kuhn

Foreword by Alastair Summerlee

STERLING, VIRGINIA

COPYRIGHT © 2023 BY STYLUS PUBLISHING, LLC.

Published by Stylus Publishing, LLC.
22883 Quicksilver Drive
Sterling, Virginia 20166-2019

Library of Congress Cataloging-in-Publication Data
The CIP data for this title has been applied for.

13-digit ISBN: 978-1-64267-444-6 (cloth)
13-digit ISBN: 978-1-64267-445-3 (paperback)
13-digit ISBN: 978-1-64267-446-0 (library networkable e-edition)
13-digit ISBN: 978-1-64267-447-7 (consumer e-edition)

Printed in the United States of America

All first editions printed on acid-free paper
that meets the American National Standards Institute
Z39-48 Standard.

Bulk Purchases

Quantity discounts are available for use in workshops and for staff development.

Call 1-800-232-0223

First Edition, 2023

I would like to dedicate this book to my daughter, Ireland, whose passion for learning during toddler and early childhood was the inspiration behind The Curiosity Project and my foray into inquiry-based learning (IBL). I hope you always keep the light of your curiosity and imagination burning brightly! Also, to my beloved papa, William McLeod, for instilling in me the joy of curiosity, inquiry, reading, and writing during the 5 short years we had together. To my husband, Robert, who believes in all my dreams and to our Emma who is finding her passion in learning and in life through asking questions. To my wonderful students at the University of Prince Edward Island, especially those 147 who became learning facilitators for multiple semesters over the past 10 years. I have learned so much from you! And lastly, to my former student Rory, who challenged me to "stop assuming we can't and just for a minute imagine what it would look like if we could expand The Curiosity Project into first year and beyond." Here we go!
—Stacey L. MacKinnon

I would like to dedicate this book to the people who first helped me to understand IBL (Michael Potter, Pierre Boulos, Erika Kustra, Center for Teaching and Learning, University of Windsor), the people who allowed me to practice IBL (undergraduate, graduate, and doctoral students at University of Windsor and University of Calgary), the students (Kloie Picot, Savannah Finnessey, Jackie Liu, Lavender Huang, Emilie Maine, and many, many more), and social work faculty (Yeonjung Lee, Jennifer Hewson, Victoria Burns) who joined me in exploring IBL scholarship of teaching and learning research, and all the faculty and sessional instructors who showed interest in my research symposiums and lunch-and-learn sessions to help get you started utilizing this pedagogy.
—Beth Archer-Kuhn

CONTENTS

PART THREE: HOW DO I GET MY STUDENTS STARTED WITH IBL-HE?

PART FOUR: HOW DO I BUILD THE SUPPORTIVE RELATIONSHIPS THAT ALLOW IBL-HE TO THRIVE?

PART FIVE: WHAT DOES SUCCESSFUL IBL-HE LOOK LIKE IN THE END?

This book is timely and prescient.

It provides a hands-on, practical guide to evolutionary changes in methods of pedagogy that can be used by individual instructors and faculty or taken in larger chunks to change the approaches to teaching and learning across courses and programs in higher education. It will be a valuable asset to teachers and learners alike.

Its importance is underscored by the challenges faced by instructors and faculty in making change in academic pedagogy.

Making change in higher education has always been difficult. After all, the academy has weathered change and pressures before and prides itself on gradual evolution rather than revolution. And this includes the approaches to teaching.

But employers, students, and parents are demanding change like never before. The advent of social media, ubiquitously available information through the internet, the rapidly changing pace of societal change through continued automation, and the pandemic require seismic shifts in ways of thinking and working.

Inquiry-based learning (IBL) is a vital tool in making that adaption. It has roots in the hierarchy of learning strategies. Anyone who watches and supports young children learning immediately grasps the fundamental principle that each child finds her or his way to complete any task—whether it is manual or mental. Moreover, the person encouraging the child to learn appreciates that it is vital to encourage the child to try, supports the learner when they fail, and mentors them to persevere until they are successful. This is a perfect allegory of the ideal way to learn. It is messy, it takes time, but the old adage "practice makes perfect" applies. And it is a model of learning that works throughout life.

Deep learning is characterized by exploration, discovery, failure, resilience, triumph, feedback, reflection, and satisfaction. And there are three more subtle nuances: confidence that it is possible to triumph with patience and persistence; a thirst for knowing more and a realization that learning never stops; and understanding that collaboration and interaction with others hastens the process. And these are the essential elements in IBL.

For eons, we have known this is the way that children learn but somewhere, something went wrong in our approach to education. As learners grow up, we switched from this age-old model of effective learning to a didactic approach. This approach personifies the opposite; passive, rote learning that focuses on content not process.

At many levels, delivering content and listening to experts pontificate about complex issues is appealing. On the surface, it is efficient, but there are negatives; it reinforces the hierarchy of "I know and you don't," it diminishes diversity "there is only one right way to think about things," it limits innovation, and it demotivates rather than encourages the learner to take action for their own learning: "Achievement is measured by scoring high marks, not simply the personal reward of knowing."

The didactic, passive learning paradigm has become engrained in higher education and such social constructs are remarkably difficult to change.

But change they must—not only to improve the learning skills of students but to foster diverse ways of thinking and penetrate the hierarchy of intellectual dominance of the predominantly older faculty.

Setting the scene for the concept of IBL and the rationale for its approach, MacKinnon and Archer-Kuhn lay out the pathway for exploring the various aspects of this approach to learning in their book. These include explaining why a fundamental shift in the balance of power in the learning environment is required for success from both the learner and the faculty perspective; different approaches to design; and the concept of balance between more traditional content delivery and focus on process. The discourse leads to a rehearsal of the practical questions that face instructors and faculty considering introducing IBL with examples of the types of approach, ways to lead students gently through the process, breaking the reliance on the "authority voice," and empowering the student to engage effectively with research and different research methodologies.

Once the stage is set, the authors continue with chapters that underscore the importance of three critical characteristics for effective deep learning: reflection, feedback, and building collaborative and cooperative relationships. Reflection on what worked and did not work is vital and a component of higher levels of thinking—an aspect that is commonplace in life after higher education but is sadly often lacking with didactic approaches. Feedback, while part of reflection on "how did I perform," is critical to appreciate your own communication skills and abilities. Again, our current approaches to education focus on achieving grades, not whether or how one's actions and insights are understood and appreciated (or not) by others. However, such behaviors are critical for professional life after higher education. Finally, understanding community and the abilities and challenges of others is a vital component for success.

Among other unique features in the book, the final section on making effective and meaningful connections and measuring success (and even defining success) is not only vital to understand how IBL can be integrated into current educational strategies but also provides an evolutionary, nonthreatening partner to other approaches to pedagogy which will ensure its persistence.

Finally, the book provides the motivation for faculty and instructors in rehearsing the case that IBL does not simply improve the morale, confidence, and deep learning experiences for students; there is evidence that such approaches seed academic and professional transformation.

From my own experiences introducing and maintaining a specific approach to IBL, the last chapter of the book speaks to the long-term impact on the learner and the faculty member. I started to include IBL learning in my teaching practice more than 30 years ago. It is not uncommon for me to hear from past students over that time—they reflect on various aspects of their experiences, but one feature is absolutely persistent—they learned that lifelong connections, learning, and innovation pervade their definition of success in their careers.

Alastair Summerlee

Former President and Vice Chancellor of Guelph University;

Professor Emeritus in Biomedical Sciences;

3M National Teaching Fellow; Past Chair

of the Board of the World University

Service of Canada (WUSC);

Executive Director of FundtheFood

ACKNOWLEDGMENTS

We would not have been able to explore inquiry-based learning in higher education in such depth and detail without the ongoing support of the Faculty of Social Work at the University of Calgary, the Taylor Institute for Teaching and Learning, the University of Prince Edward Island, and the Social Sciences and Humanities Research Council. They have each allowed us the opportunity to grow in our own knowledge, teaching, and research practice and to contribute to the knowledge of many students, faculty, and the growing scholarship of teaching and learning literature.

We would also like to acknowledge Alastair Summerlee, who so graciously agreed to write a forward for this book. With 40-plus years implementing IBL in higher education as a professor, researcher, and administrator, we could think of no better person to take on this task.

INTRODUCTION

The Matter of Inquiry-Based Learning in Higher Education

Stacey L. MacKinnon and Beth Archer-Kuhn

Welcome to *Reigniting Curiosity and Inquiry in Higher Education: A Realistic Guide to Getting Started With Inquiry-Based Learning!* As university professors, we are by nature curious inquirers. Stacey L. MacKinnon is an associate professor of social psychology at the University of Prince Edward Island (UPEI), while Beth Archer-Kuhn is an associate professor in the Faculty of Social Work at the University of Calgary. When a sabbatical opportunity brought us together through the Taylor Institute for Teaching and Learning, our mutual passion for curiosity-driven learning and exploration of inquiry-based learning (IBL) approaches began a research collaboration that has expanded the way we, and others, look at teaching and learning.

While working on our own IBL scholarship of teaching and learning (SoTL) projects, we joined together with the support of a grant from the Taylor Institute for Teaching and Learning to explore "risk and trust" in inquiry-based learning in higher education (IBL-HE). In November 2018, with support from a Social Sciences and Humanities Research Council (SSHRC) Connection Grant, we gathered 32 professors, students, researchers, and educational developers from across Canada, the United States, and the United Kingdom for Reigniting Curiosity and Inquiry in Higher Education: A Working Conference. We spent 3 days intensely discussing the available research and shared our own experiences with university students asking (or not asking) questions. In the end, the group concluded that encouraging research on IBL-HE is slowly beginning to emerge and universities have already begun promoting experiential, inquiry-based approaches to learning explicitly in their courses, curricula, and institutional identities (e.g., McMaster University, University of Calgary, University of Michigan, University of Colorado, University of British Columbia, Emory University, Elon University, Queen's University, University of Prince Edward Island).

As instructors on the front lines, we need a realistic view of how IBL works in higher education (HE) contexts, the challenges we face in incorporating IBL into our classrooms, and what we can do to support the mindsets and skills transfer needed for students to take the lessons of IBL-HE with them after graduation.

The field lacks a research-based, practical resource that will inspire people to incorporate more inquiry into students' learning but also guide them through the pitfalls and challenges students and professors face when bringing meaningful inquiry into our classrooms.

This is that resource.

Fortunately, we can begin to build our IBL-HE practice with the encouragement of a wealth of research on the success of IBL as a pedagogy in K–12 classrooms. IBL is very effective in enhancing students' ability to inquire, research proficiently, and solve problems—the top three characteristics that employers seek in employees (Coplin, 2012). IBL can help students critically evaluate the information they receive (Archer-Kuhn, Lee, Hewson, & Burns, 2020; Hairida, 2016). IBL enhances content retention (Archer-Kuhn, Lee, Finnessey, et al., 2020; Richmond et al., 2015); increases the motivation to learn (Wang et al., 2015); improves overall learning and self-confidence (Wall et al., 2015); and is generally enjoyed by students (Ural, 2016), leading to greater student engagement (Archer-Kuhn, Wiedeman, & Chalifoux, 2020; Smallhorn et al., 2015).

While this is reassuring, we cannot automatically assume that our incoming college and university students have experienced IBL in the past (most have not) or that IBL works in the same way in higher education as it does in K–12. The postsecondary experience presents a unique constellation of circumstances that make taking intellectual risks, such as engaging in IBL, more challenging to achieve. These circumstances include

- short semesters (4 months to 1 week)
- larger classes (30–100-plus students)
- high-stakes and outcome focus, in which students and professors feel the pressure of goal achievement in the service of career development (Boyle & MacKinnon, 2016; Shin & Jung, 2014)
- unrealistic expectations and negative stereotypes of what learning in higher education will/should be (Bunce et al., 2017; MacKinnon, 2017)

Research into IBL in HE is comparatively limited. The majority of it appears in academic journals that are discipline specific and often focus on professional programs (e.g., engineering, preservice teaching, nursing, business). The research tends to focus on very specific projects rather than the fundamentals of IBL as a whole (see Summerlee, 2018, for an exception), and the emphasis tends to be on grades and retention as the key outcome variables (e.g., England et al., 2017; Kogan & Laursen, 2014).

Rather than a firm set of step-by-step instructions, we view IBL-HE as a very flexible pedagogy guided by a set of eight fundamental principles that include having a curiosity mindset; being student-driven; focusing on collaboration not competition; balancing content and process (metacognition); scaffolding; reflecting and critical reflection; embracing the discomfort of new learning (managing anxiety; building trusting relationships; and developing peer, instructor, and external support); and expecting to learn from your students. Unlike specific "how-to" stepwise pedagogies, these principles can be applied in any discipline, at any level of higher education.

We emphasize the importance of both students and instructors developing a learning mindset grounded in curiosity as a key component for knowledge transfer and application of inquiry skills. If we want our students to carry their knowledge and skills forward into other classes, as well as their personal and professional learning experiences, then we need to reignite and strengthen their "desire to inquire" by grounding our classroom learning experiences in students' curiosity as well as modeling our own. To our knowledge, there is no other book currently on the market that addresses why and how to engage in IBL in HE, both pedagogically and with a focus on developing a curious, inquiring mindset to facilitate knowledge transfer and use across the life span.

The purpose of this book, therefore, is to give higher education instructors at any career stage, and in any discipline, a realistic guide to incorporating curiosity- and inquiry-based learning into their classrooms, not only as a pedagogical tool, but also as a mindset, attitude, or "desire to inquire" that can be developed and strengthened, resulting in greater likelihood of lifelong and life-wide learning. The chapters reflect our many years of experience in planning, implementing, mentoring, and researching curiosity and IBL in HE in our own fields and across disciplines. The content also reflects knowledge garnered from SoTL research, including our own published works. We hope they will encourage you to consider your IBL-HE explorations as rich soil for SoTL investigation and publication as well.

The realistic focus of this book is also unique, in that it gives hope and room for growth over multiple iterations of IBL in the higher education classroom rather than expectations that it either "works or it doesn't," or "if it worked once it will work the same way next time." The reality is that there aren't "10 easy steps to success in IBL by tomorrow," and if you are doing it right, it should shift and change from class to class, course to course, or cohort to cohort as your students change and you learn more about how to navigate their curiosity and inquiry.

In our experience, IBL-HE is a distance event, not a 100-yard dash. We encourage you to take your time and go at your own pace with IBL-HE, taking the time to reflect on what is working and what needs adjustment. We have each experimented with IBL-HE in different ways, including as an activity in a course, as an assessment task, and as the basis for an entire course. To support understanding and implementation of IBL-HE, each chapter in this book integrates stories and vignettes of the practical application of IBL-HE. Additionally, our website includes a number of resources we recommend to support you in navigating and developing your own IBL-HE pedagogy. Whether you start small with an activity in a course (structured) and scaffold your IBL-HE practice into something much larger such as the whole course (structured and guided) as Beth has done or you jump right in to open IBL as a major project and figure it out as you go as Stacey did, the key is to recognize that wherever you start, good IBL practice is about always reflecting, always evolving. That's part of what makes IBL-HE so engaging, not only for students but for us as instructors as well!

This book is divided into six parts. Part One consists of two chapters (1–2) that lay out our view of IBL-HE as appropriate for use in any discipline and at any level when guided by a set of fundamental principles (chapter 1) and the importance of grounding IBL-HE in the first of those fundamental principles, the development or reigniting of a curiosity mindset for both students and instructors (chapter 2).

Part Two consists of three chapters (3–5), each of which addresses a foundational decision you as the instructor will have to make in designing your IBL-HE experience. These include how you can start from scratch or adapt assignments you already use to be more IBL-oriented (chapter 3), how much IBL you want to incorporate into your practice as you get started and how structured/scaffolded you want these IBL experiences to be for your students (chapter 4), and what kinds of assessment options IBL-HE lends itself to (chapter 5).

Part Three consists of four chapters (6–9), each of which addresses practical ways to get your students engaged in IBL-HE. These include how to get students to participate and ask questions (chapter 6), how to help them choose research methods for IBL-HE projects (chapter 7), the learning process (metacognition) and what you and your students should reflect on (chapter 8), and how to provide the type of feedback students need for success in IBL-HE (chapter 9).

Part Four consists of four chapters (10–13), each of which addresses the importance of building the kind of supportive relationships that encourage

IBL-HE to thrive. These include building trust in the IBL-HE classroom (chapter 10), incorporating the community into your IBL-HE practice (chapter 11), finding mentoring and communities of practice for yourself and your students (chapter 12), and developing institutional support for successful IBL-HE (chapter 13).

Part Five consists of four chapters (14–17), each of which discusses in depth the big picture goals of IBL-HE, what successful IBL-HE looks like, and the outcomes that you can expect to see in your classroom. These include increased student engagement and pride in learning (chapter 14), increased social justice focus in and even out of the classroom (chapter 15), academic and personal transformation (chapter 16), and strengthening of the lifelong and life-wide learning mindset (chapter 17).

We end the book with several detailed examples of IBL-HE projects using different levels of structure and scope, which you can use for inspiration in designing your own learning experiences. These include "Structured Controversy" (a structured one-time activity that is a great first step in the IBL process; Appendix A), "The Curiosity Project" (an open IBL major semester-long project; Appendix B), "First Year Inquiry Studies" (a full-semester IBL course scaffolded from structured to guided, to open inquiry; Appendix C), and "IBL in Block Week and Group Study" (scaffolded, structured, guided, and open IBL, but in a shorter time frame; Appendix D). Appendix D is presented in a table to reveal the interaction of course content with the IBL-HE process by class (day/week) and how to situate assessment tasks throughout the course. Appendix E is a collection of other helpful resources we have found; you can find many others by visiting our website.

Each chapter opens with the key points or messages. Throughout each chapter you will find personal stories and anecdotes, examples, and discussions of issues. Because this book is designed to get you started, we not only address the questions you may have but include questions at the end of each chapter that you will want to reflect on in order to jump-start your IBL-HE adventure!

Ultimately, this book is intended for those who value work that is well researched, both empirically and through iterative experience, and who are interested in hearing the authors' voices echoing through. We see this book as the closest we can get to inviting each and every reader to sit at our table, have a cup of tea or coffee, and become part of our curiosity and inquiry community of practice. To that end, you will hear both of our voices emerge throughout this book. Our contributions to this book are reflected in our side-to-side authorship rather than a traditional hierarchy. Some chapters we wrote individually based on our experience and expertise; others we wrote collaboratively, as they are issues we have grappled with together over the past

5 years. You will also hear the voices of IBL colleagues and students from a variety of disciplines and institutions. We hope it will inspire you to want to pursue curiosity- and inquiry-based practices in your classrooms, to understand the reality that encouraging curiosity and inquiry is a challenge on a number of levels but worth it, and to share with you the ways we have developed to move over and beyond those "speed bumps," facilitating the kind of knowledge and attitude transfer necessary for lifelong and life-wide learning.

Remember, fostering curiosity through inquiry-based teaching, when done well, is never "finished." This is a constantly evolving process of asking questions (learning from the students where they are); reflecting (figuring out how to support students to find their way); and providing meaningful feedback so that students might find answers to their inquiry questions and spark new ideas. This book includes useful strategies for implementation, as well as why IBL can work, and how sharing curiosity and inquiry with students can make higher education professors even better learners and leaders themselves.

So, pull up a seat, grab your mug, and remember we are excited to hear your voice join ours via our website as you begin your journey into IBL-HE. Now let's talk about *Reigniting Curiosity and Inquiry in Higher Education*!

Cheers,

Stacey and Beth

Postscript: A Bit About What Brought Us Here

Stacey L. MacKinnon: Jumping Into IBL

My interest in IBL initially emerged in 2010 from my experience of watching my toddler explore her world and take great pride in her discoveries. I had already been a very successful professor for 7 years at that point, and as I returned to the classroom after maternity leave, I wondered how it was that higher education students, who had likely been as curious as she was when they were children, became so uninvested in their own learning. Was it possible to reignite that curiosity and stoke their "desire to inquire"?

In 2011, I began by designing The Curiosity Project for my 2nd-year social psychology course, jumping straight into open inquiry and refining the learning experience as the term and years progressed. As The Curiosity Project grew and developed, I noted that many of my students initially lacked either the skills of inquiry or the willingness to ask questions and be reflective, so in 2015, I began designing a nondiscipline-specific course for 1st-year students that would explicitly teach them the inquiry skills and attitudes necessary to become an effective inquiring learner in a hands-on environment full of opportunities for practice and growth. This marked the birth of UPEI 1020 Inquiry Studies as one of the three choices for a required course on our campus.

At the same time, I began working toward turning my 3rd- and 4th-year classes into IBL-HE experiences, a task made much easier by the fact that so many of my students from The Curiosity Project were seeking out more IBL-HE opportunities and were willing to experiment with me on ways to further incorporate IBL into our learning experiences. In 2019, I took The Curiosity Project and my 4th-year inquiry-based course online and found that the change in medium was not an issue in continuing our learning through IBL. My next focus is introducing more elements of IBL-HE into my 250-plus student introductory courses both in person and online.

Rather than formal training, my initial learning about IBL-HE was almost exclusively garnered in the moment, reading, talking with colleagues and students, and experimenting in my classes. My journey through IBL-HE has indeed been my own curiosity project! As my interest grew, I began attending workshops and conferences focusing on IBL, and within a short period of time, I began leading those workshops myself. I also developed a close relationship with the Right Question Institute and not only learned from them but have shared my work on inquiry in higher education with their members across many disciplines and levels of education. I am a lifelong and life-wide learner whose work in creating IBL-HE experiences and researching IBL-HE in the classroom has become a life's work. I wish you the joy I have experienced and continue to experience in working with students in IBL-HE classrooms!

Beth Archer-Kuhn: Learning About IBL

During my doctoral studies, I understood that if I wanted to excel as an academic, I would not only need to learn to develop excellence in research, but also to be skillful as an instructor. To this end, and starting in 2011, I enrolled in six courses where I earned levels 1 and 2 of the University Teaching Certificate (UTC) program. These courses focused on theoretical knowledge, course design, and practical skills of teaching at a postsecondary level. It was here that I was first introduced to IBL. As a requirement of one of the courses, we were asked to choose a specific teaching and learning strategy and teach it to the class. Our group chose IBL, and since none of us had experience with IBL, we first had to learn about it. Through this first exposure, I could see immediately how I might begin to introduce IBL into my, then, sessional teaching.

In my teaching over the next several courses, I used an activity in the course called "Structured Controversy" (Archer-Kuhn, 2013). It is not quite an IBL activity, since the topics are chosen for the students and the activity is not solely student-driven learning, yet, as a teaching and learning strategy, Structured Controversy has some components of IBL (begins broadly, then narrows; students learn critical questioning habits of mind; collaborative learning increases diversity of thoughts, negotiation) and can help prepare students for IBL. The level of student engagement with Structured Controversy was inspiring, and I wanted to learn more about implementing IBL. After utilizing it as a favorable class activity, I shifted it to an assessment task. Student excitement, engagement, and critical thinking, all outcomes of the Structured Controversy, encouraged me to pursue further learning of IBL.

Over the past 10 years, IBL has become my preferred pedagogical method. This book will take the reader through the ways in which I have implemented IBL at all levels of degree programs, including Bachelor of Social Work (BSW), Master of Social Work (MSW), and PhD, using face-to-face courses on campus, in community, during study abroad, and virtually online. I relate these teaching strategies to student outcomes that I have identified through my SoTL research. I will illustrate how this approach to IBL-HE, although somewhat different than Stacey's approach, still uses the same IBL fundamental principles and focuses on key student outcomes we have identified as our goals: encouraging a curiosity-based mindset, learning and practicing inquiry skills, focus on process, writing to learn, critical analysis, interdependent learning, and an opportunity to apply these mindsets and skills to real-world issues.

Two final thoughts: One, as we complete this first of what we hope to be a series of books on IBL-HE, I am thrilled to know that the Faculty of Social Work at the University of Calgary has made a decision to shift their pedagogy in social work field education to IBL. What a wonderful opportunity for the students and indeed the whole faculty to encourage a growth mindset. Two, I have noticed over the last 10 years that IBL is not for everyone. Indeed, it is a lot of work! Yet, for those interested in supporting students to be lifelong learners, those who want to encourage students not what to learn but how to decide what to learn and how to go about that learning, then IBL-HE may be the pedagogy you have been seeking.

PART ONE

FUNDAMENTAL PRINCIPLES AND MINDSETS OF IBL-HE

One of the things that differentiates this book from many others is that we focus on the key questions you need to ask yourself when designing inquiry-based learning in higher education experiences rather than laying out a prescription for "how to." This means that when you focus on incorporating the fundamental principles of IBL-HE, as laid out in chapter 1, into your classroom, there are many correct ways, or said another way, there are no "wrong ways," to do it. Sometimes things work smoothly the first time; other times they may not, but IBL-HE is an iterative process for both students and instructors, so we can model the curiosity and inquiry that we want to see in classes by being open to making changes as we go.

In chapter 1, we share what is known about the student and instructor experience with IBL as foundational knowledge and to help clarify from where the fundamental principles derive. Then we discuss in detail what we believe to be the eight fundamental principles of IBL-HE, based on our research and our practical experience, and why these principles are so important in developing curiosity while engaging in IBL.

In chapter 2, we highlight the importance of viewing IBL-HE as so much more than a pedagogical tool by discussing the vital role of curiosity in the classroom and in life. By modeling and encouraging a curiosity-based mindset, we increase the likelihood that our students will take the skills they acquire in our classrooms into other courses and the rest of their life.

These eight fundamental principles and the curiosity mindset are embedded in every other chapter in this book. As you read, think about how you already embody these principles in your classrooms and be open to considering new avenues for inquiry!

I

EIGHT FUNDAMENTAL PRINCIPLES OF INQUIRY-BASED LEARNING

Beth Archer-Kuhn and Stacey L. MacKinnon

What to Expect

- How we understand IBL
- Theoretical orientation
- Student and instructor experiences across disciplines
- Eight fundamental principles of IBL-HE
- Situating IBL-HE

IBL is not a traditional teaching approach to learning. It is a learner-centered, student-led approach to inquiry (Saunders-Stewart et al., 2012), whereby students design and lead their own inquiry process, with support from the instructor (Ellis, 2016). You can already see in this one simple sentence how the roles have been shifted. The students lead and the instructor supports. Depending on the type (level) of IBL (structured, guided, open), instructor support can vary from a significant amount to much less. As a pedagogy, IBL is best situated within the constructivist paradigm, whereby knowledge is constructed from experience (Apedoe & Reeves, 2006; McKinney, 2014; Spronken-Smith & Walker, 2010), and students gain a deeper level of content understanding through engagement (Teater, 2011). IBL involves critical examination and deconstruction of knowledge creation (Cochran-Smith & Lytle, 2001; Levy, 2012), while also shifting power between student and teacher (Little, 2010). As such, it positions students as coconstructors of knowledge rather than passive recipients (Apedoe & Reeves, 2006; Buckner & Kim, 2014). In HE, IBL can contribute to developing the critical thinking skills required for professional competence and ethical practice.

Several universities have engaged in large-scale IBL initiatives. For example, in Canada, McMaster University has been establishing IBL as a core pedagogy since 1979 (Justice, Rice, Roy, et al., 2009). At UPEI,

11

The Curiosity Project has been developing over the past 10 years, while at the University of Calgary, IBL is being explored within several departments, including both the Faculty of Social Work and the Behavioural Sciences Department. The University of Calgary (2018) has also included IBL in its 5-year education plan, signaling a significant commitment to IBL implementation. Other universities engaging with IBL include the University of Sheffield and University of Gloucestershire in the United Kingdom; Marymount University, Miami University, and Virginia Wesleyan College in the United States; and several in New Zealand (Lee, 2012). With such interest in this pedagogical approach in HE, we believe understanding how to do this well is important for those interested in pursuing IBL-HE, and we share our experiences and understandings in this book as a guide for getting started.

In this chapter, we discuss how we understand IBL, the theoretical orientation, and eight fundamental principles that are present in IBL-HE regardless of your discipline. These principles include the importance of fostering curiosity while engaging in IBL-HE [FP1]; being student driven [FP2]; focusing on collaboration not competition [FP3]; balancing content and process/metacognition [FP4]; scaffolding, choice, and growth [FP5]; reflecting, including critical reflection [FP6]; embracing the discomfort of new learning including managing anxiety, building trust relationships, and peer, instructor, and external support [FP7]; and expecting to learn from your students [FP8]. Please note that this numbering does not indicate level of importance or an order for discussion but rather serves as a reference tool, as you will find these fundamental principles indicated throughout the entirety of this book as their relations (and interrelations) unfold. Let's start by examining the answer to the question "What is IBL-HE?"

How We Understand IBL-HE

There is no fully agreed-on definition for IBL in the research literature. Our teaching practices with IBL-HE are consistent with Spronken-Smith et al. (2011), who describe IBL as an umbrella term that

> encompasses a range of teaching approaches in which learning is stimulated by a question or issue, learning is based on constructing new knowledge and understanding, the teacher's role is one of facilitator, and there is a move toward self-directed learning. (p. 15)

IBL can be described, then, as a set of instructional practices intended to develop higher-order intellectual and academic skills among students. Utilizing

IBL, students seek knowledge through practice in an inquiry-based process (Justice, Rice, Roy, et al., 2009). Unlike traditional teaching and learning methods, whereby instructors drive the learning process, IBL involves student decisions related to question/problem formulation, research and investigation of ideas, critical engagement with literature, and a synthesis of findings (Ellis, 2016). IBL is, nevertheless, also a demanding pedagogy for instructors in their teaching practice.

IBL has been described as a flexible teaching and learning approach without a specific formula (Lee, 2012). We view this flexibility as a strength, in that it allows IBL to be incorporated into small tasks, larger projects, or as a guiding principle for full curricula (Lee, 2012). In this way, instructors can choose how they wish to incorporate IBL into their HE environment. You may want to dip your toe in and try IBL as an activity in a course, or perhaps you want to jump right in and design the entire course utilizing IBL. The approach has less to do with your discipline and depends more on your level of comfort with the unknown and your ability to shift your mindset. Indeed, we are seeing this pedagogy across a range of contexts in HE, such as fieldwork (Yesudhas et al., 2014); undergraduate and graduate courses (Aditomo et al., 2013); and throughout many disciplines, such as science and math (Laursen et al., 2014), psychology (MacKinnon, 2017), and arts/ humanities (Levy, 2012).

Theoretical Orientation

As instructors, we enjoy observing and actively supporting the growth that students achieve with IBL. Situated within the constructivist tradition, IBL recognizes multiple ways of knowing and positions students as coconstructors of knowledge (Apedoe & Reeves, 2006; McKinney, 2014; Saunders-Stewart et al., 2012; Spronken-Smith et al., 2011; Woolf, 2017; Yesudhas et al., 2014). Critical questions arise, such as what is valued as knowledge, who creates it, and who has access to it. Critical thinking requires that these questions be raised and deconstructed (Cochran-Smith & Lytle, 2001).

In that vein, it is important to note that not everyone supports IBL-HE; however, its critics often work under erroneous assumptions based on the lack of agreement on its definition, as the debate between Kirschner et al. (2006) and Hmelo-Silver et al. (2007) shows. Kirschner et al. (2006) argue that constructivist learning pedagogies are ineffective and do not take into account empirical evidence, which has found that minimally guided instruction does not work over the long term. They posit that IBL ignores what is known about human cognitive architecture and memory, that if instructional practice does not impact a student's long-term memory, then nothing has been gained. Hmelo-Silver et al. (2007) argue that Kirschner et al. (2006) mistakenly grouped several pedagogies and practices together, thereby concluding that the process of IBL involves minimal guidance. Hmelo-Silver et al. (2007) cite two weaknesses with the critique by Kirschner et al. (2006). First, they suggest that IBL is the same as discovery learning, and second, their critique ignores the key practice of scaffolding (Hmelo-Silver et al., 2007; Lazonder & Harmsen, 2016). Scaffolding refers to a variety of techniques that are used to support students in understanding and engaging with complex material (Levy, 2012), which generally begins with intensive support and guidance, progressively tapering off until the student is working independently (Spronken-Smith & Walker, 2010). This process supports students in learning complex material while managing a challenging cognitive load [FP5]. In contrast to Kirschner et al.'s conclusion, IBL has a wealth of evidence to support the pedagogy (Hmelo-Silver et al., 2007).

Consistent with constructivism, instructors will notice almost immediately, as we have in our teaching practice, that IBL aims to change the relationship and, in doing so, the power between student and teacher (Levy, 2012; Saunders-Stewart et al., 2012). This shift in practice results in shared power (Saunders-Stewart et al., 2012). Traditionally, teachers transfer information and knowledge to students, and students receive it. This didactic relationship limits student questioning and leaves little space for student engagement (Buckner & Kim, 2014). IBL promotes and fosters students' engagement as partners in knowledge creation; as such, their direct and active role is encouraged (Little, 2010). This partnership in knowledge creation strikes us as critical in HE.

We found some interesting studies in HE that reveal the student and instructor experiences of IBL. The following is a summary of what is currently available across the disciplines. For each of the student and instructor experiences, we provide a vignette to describe the experience in detail.

What Do Students Experience Utilizing IBL?

Within our own classrooms and beyond, we wondered, "What do students experience utilizing IBL?" Our own and others' research has explored student and instructor perspectives about IBL in HE. Woolf (2017) in kinesiology and Archer-Kuhn, Lee, Finnessey, and Liu (2020) in social work collected data on how students perceived an IBL approach. Initially, students reported feeling overwhelmed with the nontraditional format. In both studies, researchers witnessed anxiety and the persistent need for guidance at the outset of the course. However, as time went on, student anxiety and support demands eased, shifting instead to students feeling motivated and sharing their excitement. A similar sequence occurred for MacKinnon (2017) in social psychology, who discovered that student apprehension dissipated over time, with students reporting that they enjoyed the freedom to learn and reflect that they experienced with IBL. At the end of their project, MacKinnon (2017) found that students indicated they would take a similar program (IBL) again and would recommend it to others. Importantly, IBL requires a culture dedicated to learning, with appropriate, available support, whereby students can be better oriented and prepared (Ellis, 2016; McKinney, 2014; Spronken-Smith et al., 2011). Also recommended and deemed critical to student success in these inquiry spaces are information literacy, technology usage, critical examination of literature, and scaffolding (Ellis, 2016; Spronken-Smith et al., 2011; Yesudhas et al., 2014).

Little (2010) explored student experiences at the University of Sheffield's Center for Inquiry-Based Learning in the Arts and Social Sciences (CILASS), where students indicated that as a result of the IBL process, they felt they had a greater and more active role in their learning. However, the author also found that students were initially reluctant to engage or take risks and were unsure about the change in teaching style. For some students, trusting an unfamiliar teaching approach results in caution. Other studies, as well, have documented student resistance to innovative inquiry (Gormally et al., 2009) and to taking greater responsibility for learning (Lee, 2012). McKinney (2014) reiterates that a culture of learning created with IBL strategies should include information literacy (how to discover and use information to create new knowledge).

These findings are consistent with other research that states greater student support is required through the IBL process, such as help with finding related literature, using technology, and critically examining the literature (Yesudhas et al., 2014). Lazonder and Harmsen (2016) say that students do better with inquiry when they receive several forms of guidance from instructors. In particular, scaffolding is relevant, since students who progressively learn, attending to increasingly complex tasks and developing self-direction, are more likely to succeed (FP 5; Spronken-Smith et al., 2011). Additionally, Ellis (2016) found that students who reported a positive experience with IBL tended to utilize technology in a meaningful way, perceived a manageable workload, and integrated their learning experience throughout the course.

We found generalist skill acquisition identified in the literature as an IBL outcome, including enhanced critical thinking (Aditomo et al., 2013; Caswell & LaBrie, 2017; Holaday & Buckley, 2008; Hudspith & Jenkins, 2001; Woolf, 2017); problem-solving (Justice et al., 2009); reflective practice (Gilardi & Lozza, 2009; Kirwan & Adams, 2009; Woolf, 2017); and collaboration skills (Justice et al., 2009). Specific skill acquisition has been noted as well, such as interviewing, active listening, writing, communication, and working independently (Woolf, 2017); research skills (Yesudhas et al., 2014); and improved information/technology literacy (Buckner & Kim, 2014; Gehring & Eastman, 2008; Levy, 2012; Little, 2010; Oliver, 2008).

Further, student outcomes in HE are showing that IBL results in increased student engagement (Archer-Kuhn, Lee, Finnessey, & Liu, 2020; Caswell & LaBrie, 2017; Healey, 2005; Hudspith & Jenkins, 2001; Justice et al., 2009; Levy, 2012; Little, 2010; Oliver, 2008; Yesudhas et al., 2014) and increased confidence (Gormaly et al., 2009; Little, 2010; Oliver, 2008; Woolf, 2017). As noted by Cooner (2011), "a course design that optimises student engagement and moves away from a purely didactic approach should also encourage learning that has enquiry at its heart" (p. 4).

The following vignette describes a graduate student experience with IBL-HE in a 6-day intensive block-week course. Natalie provides an authentic and raw experience when first engaging with IBL-HE. We chose to use this example so that you can see it is not a simple process for students to take on a new mindset and pursue their own inquiry in a course. As Natalie explains, it can be life changing for some.

Vignette: Doctoral Candidate, Natalie Beltrano

I had the opportunity to participate in Inquiry-Based Learning as Structured Controversy during my second year of my Master of Social Work, block-week, research methods course. In preparation for the course, the instructor provided materials to introduce us to the pedagogy of Structured Controversy IBL. I became quickly overwhelmed in my preparation for the course: How would this work in the classroom? How much work was this going to entail?

Once in the classroom and the goals of the week were reviewed, I was completely *overwhelmed*. It was clear that a high level of engagement was needed; the work would not end at the end of the school day, and we would be required to complete tasks every evening in preparation for the final assessment: a presentation to our peers.

The first task was to identify a research question; I thought I knew how to pose a *good* research question—this process took an entire day! When I attempted to obtain direction from the instructor, I was often given another question. Thankfully my cohort had been together for a year at this time, and I felt comfortable sharing my stress and fears and was relieved to hear that they were feeling the same way: confused and overwhelmed.

Each evening we were expected to search literature related to our question, critically review and synthesize it, and be prepared to present our findings in small groups to debate the strengths and weaknesses. This work was physically and intellectually exhausting, yet I found myself engrossed in the tasks, excited by what I was and was not finding in the literature, and noticeably gaining skills on how to critique literature through the support of my peers and instructor.

In completing the required critical self-reflections, I was challenged to be "more critically self-reflective." This resulted in a high level of emotions, cycling through frustration, excitement, anxiety, and happiness. And just when I thought I felt I was going to give up, the feedback I received from the instructor at midnight inspired me to continue; they were working just as hard, if not harder, than me. The instructor's dedication and commitment to supporting me through the process motivated me to push through the obstacles as I recognized, as much as I was confused and challenged, that I was not alone.

In the end, after the initial nervousness of completing a presentation in front of my peers, I felt this huge sense of accomplishment. In 6 days, I was able to define a detailed research question, search for literature to answer this question, and critically review findings. Through this process, I began developing my skills to critically assess what was and what was not good research. This sparked my interest and curiosity. If this is what it meant to be a researcher, I wanted in.

Engaging in IBL was difficult and frustrating. There were times when I wanted to quit or not fully engage in the process; I felt as if I did not have the energy to continue. Yet the rewards and outcomes as a student were enlightening. My relationships with peers strengthened over the intense week of curriculum. I became self-aware of my responses to what I was reading, learning to refrain from reacting with emotion, to critically evaluate what authors were indicating, and maintaining an open mind. I was inspired to continue researching. When I shared my desire to continue researching with the instructor, they asked (not breaking the pattern), "Why don't you?"

My engagement in IBL led me to my desire to become a researcher; I am proud to say I am now a third-year doctorate student with plans to apply IBL as a pedagogy in my classroom.

What Do Instructors Experience Utilizing IBL?

Research exploring instructor experiences in HE describes diverse impressions of IBL and mostly reflects the constraints of time. In an autoethnographic report of IBL practice, Woolf (2017), a first-time IBL instructor, reported feeling stressed and that utilizing IBL was time intensive, because student projects held such breadth, compounded by the need for instructors to support students through the uncertainty. Others have reported similar demands, such as the need for greater teaching preparation and planning, on top of increased student support and feedback (Archer-Kuhn, Lee, Finnessey, & Liu, 2020; MacKinnon, 2017; Vajoczki et al., 2011). Some have spoken out, suggesting that these additional time demands should be offset by a reduction in traditional classroom hours to account for IBL's involving greater student self-direction (Spronken-Smith et al., 2011). Further recommendations for faculty support when applying IBL include mentorship for new instructors (Woolf, 2017) and an initial structured approach (Archer-Kuhn, Lee, Hewson, & Burns, 2020; Spronken-Smith et al., 2011).

We know that instructor attributes matter when implementing IBL. Successful IBL instructors report embracing a student-centered teaching philosophy in HE, having strong and respectful relationships with students, and spending time on professional reflection (Spronken-Smith et al., 2011). We have also learned that formalized training and institutional support can contribute to an instructor's level of comfort in implementing IBL (Spronken-Smith et al., 2011). Regardless of comfort level, however, even instructors who reported struggling with implementation reported seeing value in the approach for student skill development (Vajoczki et al., 2011; Woolf, 2017).

In many ways, IBL places greater demands on the instructor and could, in part, account for the resistance suggested in some studies. Indeed, philosophical buy-in from instructors is one of the primary limitations noted in the literature, likely due to preference for traditional models that involve imparting knowledge (Spronken-Smith et al., 2011). Faculty report that in addition to taking more time for planning and preparation and individual time with students, IBL requires that instructors provide greater levels of feedback (MacKinnon, 2017; Vajoczki et al., 2011; Woolf, 2017). Since the IBL approach often involves greater self-directed study and fewer direct contact hours between students and instructors, Spronken-Smith et al. (2011) have adapted and reduced the number of classroom hours to account for the additional time in the preparation for and conduct of IBL pedagogy. We have found that open inquiry, in particular, requires a great deal of student independence, with a mindset focused on the creation of new knowledge.

The following vignette comes from a faculty member, Sarah Nutter, at the University of Victoria in British Columbia, Faculty of Counseling Psychology. Sarah's experience utilizing IBL-HE speaks to her desire to teach group dynamics.

Vignette, Faculty Member, Sarah Nutter

I was first introduced to the structured controversy activity in the fall of 2020 when I taught a course that had been previously designed and taught by Beth Archer-Kuhn. This course was part of an embedded certificate program in mental well-being and resilience for undergraduate students in any program on campus. Specifically, the course examined mental health and wellness from an intersectional perspective and was largely informed by the fields of social work and applied psychology. As an early career academic with training in counseling psychology, I was excited to try out a new (to me) active learning activity with my students.

In working through the structured controversy with these students, I was struck by the power of the activity to support a shift from defensive listening to active listening. During the activity, students queried the purpose of the activity and struggled with identifying how it was different from a traditional debate—an activity they were more familiar with. In reading student reflections following the activity, students identified how overcoming the challenge of listening to defend their position allowed them to listen differently to the group members on the other side of the issue. Students noted that listening to understand another perspective rather than defend their own provided the opportunity for perspective taking and recognizing the importance of compromise in exploring solutions to difficult issues. It is also important to note that this activity took place in the context of the COVID-19 pandemic and online learning.

A year following my first experience with structured controversy, I was preparing to teach a course on group dynamics and the social psychology of groups. This course serves to provide upper-year undergraduate students with foundational knowledge to prepare them for graduate training in counseling psychology and group therapy. The structured controversy seemed like the perfect fit with the material and experiential nature of this course. In covering foundational topics related to group dynamics, this course includes material on group goals and process, group communication, leadership, power dynamics, group decision-making, group conflict, as well as the importance of (and barriers to) diversity in group processes. As the structured controversy requires students to work in groups as well as to consider the opposing perspective of another group, it provides the opportunity for students to engage in the development of knowledge and skills related to each of these aspects of the course.

(*Continues*)

(*Continued*)

> I anticipate that students will struggle to transition from a defensive listening to an active listening mindset in similar ways to the students in the undergraduate course on intersectionality and mental wellness. I also anticipate that, upon reflection, students will more clearly be able to identify group-based concepts that are inherent in this activity, due to their exposure to these concepts throughout the course. I am also excited to deliver this activity in person, but do not anticipate any differences in learning experience or learning outcomes of this activity between the in-person and virtual learning environments. One thing I am certain about is that I will continue to use the structured controversy in my teaching for years to come.

Based on the research literature, our own experiences, and detailed interviews with colleagues and students, we believe there are eight fundamental principles of IBL-HE. As much as you might like to see these principles presented in a linear fashion, IBL just doesn't work that way. It is more likely that you will encounter these principles scattered throughout your IBL process. Some of them will become more important during your planning phase, while others are more significant through implementation and/or upon course completion. The order is less important than the principles themselves, which are designed to be actively used, reflected on, and updated as you progress through your IBL experience. Attention to these fundamental principles will guide your construction of IBL-HE learning experiences regardless of your discipline, institution, or students' previous experience with inquiry.

FP 1: The Importance of Fostering a Mindset of Curiosity

As we will discuss in greater detail in chapter 2, modeling and encouraging a mindset of curiosity is key to making IBL-HE more than just a pedagogical tool, a classroom exercise, or a set of skills, but a way of thinking that can result in lifelong and life-wide learning for you and your students. Show them your natural curiosity and model how to become curious when you are not inherently interested in a topic. Let them see your enjoyment of exercising your curious mindset and inquiry skills so that a norm of valuing curiosity becomes the gold standard in your courses, in the classroom and outside of the classroom. Follow the students' curiosity whenever possible, particularly if it relates to the content of the course. If you don't know the answers to a question, let them know, find it, and share it with them later, or better yet, engage them in finding the answer with you. They will thank you for valuing their ideas and taking the time to follow up. This principle is important to remember when introducing students to IBL-HE. They need to hear and see curiosity from the instructor (and peers) and then practice or experience the validation of their curiosity themselves.

FP 2: Being Student Driven

The best way to develop and strengthen students' curiosity involves questions. Through the use of IBL-HE, students are encouraged, supported, and expected to pose their own inquiry questions, which they pursue throughout the course. They are supported by formative feedback from instructor and peers as the inquiry process unfolds. This can be challenging for students who may not be used to following their own interests in a course but rather following the directions of the instructor. In an IBL-HE course students follow their own interests and pursue topics they want to learn more about. In chapter 6, we talk in more detail about how students develop their own inquiry questions with support from instructors and peers. This fundamental principle is important both during your planning and throughout the course. Students having ownership over their choices, with you helping them to reflect on what they have chosen and the outcomes so they can improve their skills and understanding, is a key part of being in a student-driven IBL-HE classroom. You will need to consider how meaningful and constructive instructor and peer feedback can be incorporated into the course (which we will discuss in chapter 9) and how you will also need to consider ways to model for and inspire curiosity in your students.

Critical reflection is key to the student-driven nature of IBL-HE. Critical reflection as a skill brings students to a deeper level of knowing—about self, about others, and about self in relation to others. Students learn to interrogate that which is known and taken for granted to become more independent thinkers. Helping students to develop this skill will enhance their learning in other courses and in other areas of their life. Employers are seeking curious, independent thinkers who bring new ideas and ways of knowing into their work environment. As an instructor who utilizes IBL well, you can help support the needs in society for well-prepared entry-level employees. In chapter 8 we will discuss strategies you can use to encourage critical reflection and questioning.

FP 3: Focusing on Collaboration Not Competition

One of the reasons so many students dislike group work is its perceived competitive nature. Students do not like having their success dependent on the contributions of others, particularly when there is a possibility of social loafing (or a complete takeover) occurring. Students even tend to view testing as a competitive endeavor as they engage in social comparison to determine whether they are succeeding in a course. None of this has anything to do with actual learning. In an IBL course, the learning is not fully dependent (i.e., my learning is based on what we all do) nor is it fully independent (i.e., I alone am responsible for my learning) but is interdependent (i.e., individual learning is enhanced and strengthened by the contribution of others, contributions the individual has the option to utilize or ignore as they see fit). When we emphasize collaboration (even on individual projects) and put the focus on the quality of learning rather than standing in the class, students are much more willing to offer their insights, consider the feedback of others as truly constructive, pose differing views, and engage in making the most of everyone's learning, not just their own. Because the competitive nature of most university students is highly ingrained, you need to make this point up front and remind them of it regularly. It doesn't take long for these same students to embrace the idea that there is more than enough high-quality learning to go around.

FP 4: Balancing Content and Process/Metacognition

Successful IBL-HE comes from a desire to not only have students learn facts but to think critically and creatively about the content and about the process of their own learning (i.e., metacognition). For the instructor, finding a balance between content understanding and metacognition is an important objective in an IBL-HE classroom. The skills students learn and practice while engaging in IBL-HE will serve them well long after they have left our classrooms. Their inquiry skills will allow them to determine what questions need to be asked and how to find the answers, consider multiple perspectives, and communicate their findings—a task worthy of a course in any discipline and certainly vital in modern life. This is an important principle to keep in mind while planning the implementation of IBL-HE in your course. These issues will be discussed in greater detail in chapters 6–9.

FP 5: Scaffolding, Choice, and Growth

There are many ways to include IBL in your practice (activity, course, program) and different levels of structure (structured, guided, open) you can choose from. It is fine to start just outside your comfort zone and grow your practice of IBL from there. Starting slowly is recommended. Remember this is a long-distance event, not a sprint. Some things will go smoothly, and others may not. Remaining reflective and using your own inquiry skills will help you to figure out how to support your students' inquiry learning process. You will begin incorporating this principle during the course planning process. Choosing to start with an activity, for example, and a structured approach can offer students (and yourself) the most support while getting started. This same focus on choices and growth is important for your students as well. Making choices and learning from those that don't work out as hoped increases resilience and ownership of learning.

When you make your choices about the type of IBL-HE that you want to implement (structured, guided, open), you will also need to be mindful of the level of student support that is necessary within each IBL type. Remember, the instructor's role in IBL-HE is a facilitator of student learning. The level of support is highest with structured IBL-HE and decreases progressively as you choose guided or open IBL. Introducing structured IBL-HE then means you are providing a significant amount of student support within a student-led inquiry learning process. This principle requires ongoing check-ins with students about their learning process. The focus on growth is of particular importance and is an important factor in choosing assessment approaches, as you will see in chapter 5.

FP 6: Reflection and Critical Reflection

Reflection is key for success, both for yourself and your students. Make note of what works and do it again. Reflect on why things did not go according to expectations, make some changes, and try again. Learn from your students' reflections on their experience and consult them on ideas you are considering. Be explicit in asking which activities facilitated their learning and which did not, and why. Let them know that you adjust the course based on their feedback. Don't be afraid to share how you are experimenting with your students. As long as students trust that you are there to support them, most will be willing to take intellectual risks with you. Reflection on the student learning process and outcome will steer you in future implementation of IBL-HE.

IBL-HE requires more than simply reflecting on experience and behavior though. It necessitates students and instructors critically reflecting on all aspects of the inquiry journey from the creation of an inquiry question through to the effectiveness of different strategies for disseminating their findings to various audiences. Engaging in critical reflection helps us and our students refine our inquiry questions, identify and confront biases, consider causality, contrast theory with practice, and identify systemic issues, key issues in creating a mindset of critical evaluation and enhancing the likelihood and quality of knowledge transfer (Ash & Clayton, 2009).

Reflecting on your and your students' IBL-HE experience will help you to make the necessary adjustments for the next time you implement this pedagogy. For example, Beth noted that developing good inquiry questions was challenging for students, so she developed a number of activities to support this process, including a checklist and peer and instructor feedback (structured and guided inquiry). Allow them the same freedom for reflection and experimentation whenever possible in their own learning and watch how they bloom as inquiring learners.

FP 7: Embracing the Discomfort of New Learning—Managing Anxiety; Building Trusting Relationships; and Peer, Instructor, and External Support

Implementing IBL-HE will likely raise the anxiety of some, if not all students initially (not to mention your own). They are being asked to trust a process that they very likely have not been exposed to in their educational career. As we know, new experiences can create anxiety. Although the level of student anxiety will vary, a handful of students experiencing a high level of anxiety, or even one or two, can heighten your own anxiety. How the instructor manages their own and their student's anxiety will determine how the students progress. Transparency and modeling are important traits for the instructor. In terms of transparency, let students know what to expect, that this way of learning is new and different and will likely cause some initial anxiety. Modeling confidence in the process and trust in your students' abilities will help to ease their and your own anxiety. Most critically, this principle is important as you begin to introduce IBL-HE and for the first several weeks/sessions of the course. After the first assessment and/or reflection tasks, students' anxiety often decreases significantly.

Communities of learning and mentorship can play a significant role in addressing this issue, as you will see in chapter 12. Relationships matter in IBL-HE. They are indeed a fundamental component of the IBL process. Building and maintaining trust in yourself, between you and your students, between the students themselves, and each student's trust in themselves is worth spending time and energy on. Enlist students as you go to share their experiences with incoming classes. Build community within your classroom for your students and in your professional network so you too can have the support of mentors and collaborators. Consider how professionals, agencies, and organizations in your local community can support student learning.

Interdependent learning and collaboration are key to successful IBL-HE for both students and faculty. The importance of this principle cannot be overstated in the planning phase of the course delivery. How will you facilitate relationship building and network development as a natural component of your course? Strategies discussed in chapters 10, 11, 12, and 13 may help. Support in an IBL-HE course comes in many forms. Modeling inquiry skills, being transparent, and focusing on relationships are supportive components in the IBL process.

Provide students with opportunities to learn independently, then learn with and from others. Arrange activities in your course that allow for independent work that is then shared with peers. Include peer and instructor feedback throughout the IBL-HE process. Support student learning through multiple dissemination processes, for example in small or large groups, and where possible, provide a venue that extends beyond the peers in the course. Thoughtful and intentional planning of activities will allow you to support student learning through the principle of instructor and peer support. Think outside the box when considering how to help students embrace the discomfort of new learning by encouraging them to find support from varied sources: peers, instructors, research literature, and, when possible, community resources.

FP 8: Expecting to Learn From Your Students

Take every opportunity to learn from your students and make your classroom your own IBL project. Use what you are learning to customize the IBL-HE experience for each cohort, to plan for future cohorts, to test out new ideas, and to track your successes as well as your challenges. Remember that if you are doing inquiry well, finding answers will spur the next round of questions. This is exciting because it keeps your IBL-HE practice fresh; you will never be "done" given that as your students grow and change, so will your IBL-HE knowledge and practice. IBL-HE is meant to be dynamic, so each experience brings you new insights, opportunities to try something different, and new questions to explore with your students. This means your course might look a bit different each time you teach it because you have learned from your own experiences and from the students' experiences. We hope that it is apparent that this principle needs to be incorporated from planning through post-course reflection. Whenever possible collect data on your students' IBL-HE experiences and consider writing a SoTL paper or presentation to share what you've learned with others!

Situating IBL in a postsecondary context provides an opportunity to examine its possibilities and implications for applied and nonapplied disciplines. In HE, IBL has been considered from various stakeholder perspectives, including student, instructor, and institutional experiences. Before exploring each stakeholder's perspective, and the benefits of utilizing IBL as a teaching and learning strategy, we need to discuss how IBL-HE is different from other pedagogical practices. Specifically, we want to explore IBL-HE as a mindset.

Summary

Beyond the benefits of IBL as situated in the literature, including the general and specific skills, we find that, employed strategically, IBL offers students greater control and responsibility for their learning, and, in turn, students realize greater pleasure from their HE learning experience. The student-centered approach to learning inspires and enables learners to experience the coconstruction of knowledge. This constructivist learning pedagogy, while not endorsed by all, is best enacted through carefully scaffolded activities that support students in their inquiry process. IBL-HE has a number of underlying principles that provide the student opportunities for independent and collaborative student-led learning. Instructors in the role of facilitator provide transparency about the process, support through trust and relationship building, modeling of skill development, and opportunities for dissemination.

Questions for Reflection

1. Which fundamental principles fit most naturally for your teaching philosophy and approach?
2. How might you envision your students leading their own learning?
3. What kinds of activities might you develop that share the same theoretical orientation as IBL for your courses?

FOSTERING A CURIOSITY-BASED MINDSET AND REIMAGINING THE ROLES OF INSTRUCTOR AND STUDENT IN IBL-HE

Stacey L. MacKinnon and Beth Archer-Kuhn

What to Expect

- Why curiosity as a mindset matters
- How encouraging curiosity as a mindset makes IBL something your students will take with them when they leave your class
- Combining curiosity and inquiry in HE to maximize learning
- Shifting the role of faculty and instructors in IBL-HE

If you are getting started with IBL, chances are you want this experience to be more than just a classroom exercise your students will complete successfully and then forget about on the way out the door. Ideally, you want to create an experience that will allow your students to develop into active learners who take their inquiry skills with them throughout their academic journey and apply them in their personal and professional lives. The first step on the IBL-HE journey: fostering in yourself and your students a curiosity mindset and modeling the "desire to inquire" (FP 1). It all begins with a shift in your perspective on both teaching and learning.

Curiosity as a Mindset: The Desire to Inquire

Deborah Meier, pioneer of the small schools movement, said that "we come out of the womb questioning" (Berger, 2014). Research suggests that between the ages of 2 and 5 years old, children ask on average 40,000 questions (Harris, 2012). By preschool, children are asking their mothers about

300 questions a day, a number that increases to 390 questions per day for 4-year-old girls (Telegraph Staff and Agencies, 2013). Not only does the sheer number of questions increase over the course of this brief time frame, the quality of the questions shifts as well. Once children reach the age of 4, their questions shift from fact-based "Who?" "What?" "Where?" and "When?" to embracing the knowledge garnered from asking "How?" and the infamous "Why?" often repeated over and over until the adult being questioned correctly interprets what the child is asking and answers appropriately (Harris, 2012). In children, curiosity positively correlates with intelligence, as well as superior scholastic and reading ability (Berg & Sternberg, 1985; Nair & Ramnarayan, 2000; Raine et al., 2002).

Unfortunately, though we enter this world naturally inquisitive (Berger, 2014; Slater et al., 1982), we also know that the number of questions children are asking has been consistently decreasing since 1990 (Kim, 2011). Researchers argue that somewhere throughout our academic journey our interest seems to be fading and the number of questions we ask goes down significantly (Berger, 2014; Lang, 2012). In fact, there is a negative relationship between grade level and the number of questions being asked by students (Land & Jarman, 1992). Essentially, the more time students are spending in traditional classrooms the fewer questions they are asking. Often by the time students enter HE, they have suppressed their "desire to inquire," their willingness to exercise their natural curiosity, in favor of simply finding the "right answer" to questions posed by authority figures (Berger, 2014; Minigan, 2017). When they do exercise their curiosity, and question what they are expected to learn in school or why it must be learned in a particular way, they often hear "just do as you're told" or "because this is the right way" (Peterson, 2020; Toshalis, 2015).

As adolescence approaches, many young people redirect their remaining curiosity away from learning and focus instead on exercising it more in their social lives and in risky extracurricular pursuits (Jovanovic & Brdaric, 2012; Jovanović & Gavrilov-Jerković, 2014; Pierce et al., 2005). Even if they have managed to maintain their curiosity about things they are inherently interested in, upon entering HE, many young people still have not learned how to "become curious" about things they must learn but are not naturally interested in, a key component of learning in adult life (Kashdan & Fincham, 2004).

Why Does Curiosity Matter in Adulthood?

Some research shows that in adults, greater curiosity correlates with greater analytic ability, problem-solving skills, and overall intelligence (Berg &

Sternberg, 1985; Nair & Ramnarayan, 2000; Raine et al., 2002). Those who have maintained or reignited their curiosity experience a wide variety of significant lifelong and life-wide benefits. In the work world, these characteristics and skills are highly prized. An IBM poll of 1,500 CEOs identified creativity and curiosity as the most crucial factors for future success, more important than rigor, management discipline, integrity, or even vision (Berger, 2014). Curious people even report more satisfying relationships and marriages thought to be due to their greater attitude of openness and genuine interest in learning about their partner (Barnes et al., 2007; Botwin et al., 1997; Kashdan et al., 2011).

This satisfaction applies more broadly as well. The Gallup organization reported the results of a survey conducted with more than 130,000 people from some 130 nations, a sample designed to represent 96% of the world's population. The poll identified two factors that had the strongest influence on how much enjoyment a person experienced in a given day: "being able to count on someone for help" and "learned something yesterday" (Kashdan, 2009, p. 39). This also supports the idea that curiosity is the entry point to many of life's greatest sources of meaning and satisfaction: our interests, hobbies, and passions (Kashdan & Steger, 2007).

The good news is that if we exercise our curiosity regularly we may even live longer and healthier lives. A 2-year study of more than 1,000 patients suggests that more curiosity is significantly negatively correlated with the likelihood of developing hypertension and diabetes (Richman et al., 2005). These positive findings were echoed by another study of over 2,000 older adults aged 60 to 86 who were followed over 5 years and noted that the more curious they were, the more likely they were to be alive in year 5, even taking into account age, smoking history, and presence of cancer or cardiovascular disease (Swan & Carmelli, 1996). This research strongly suggests that the maintenance and/or reigniting of curiosity is a goal worthy of our focused attention as parents, educators, and administrators.

If we want to give our students the best opportunity to take their inquiry skills out into the world, we need to include the cultivation of curiosity, both natural and developed, as a focus in our IBL-HE classrooms (FP 1). As you can see from Figure 2.1, we believe that maximally effective learning, knowledge transfer, and application involves three components: (a) valuing of a curious mindset or attitude, (b) willingness and opportunity to inquire, and (c) the skills of inquiry itself.

We believe maximum learning and knowledge transfer involves an environment that values and encourages curiosity or the "desire to inquire." In the HE classroom, part of creating this environment is putting your own curiosity on display and explicitly encouraging your students to share their

Figure 2.1. Mindsets and skills for effective IBL-HE learning.

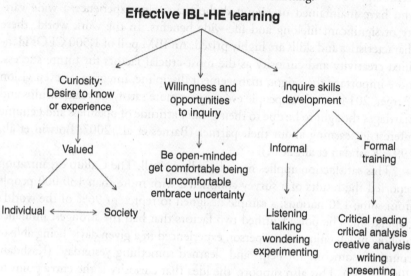

curiosity. When you value their curiosity (and your own), your students will be more likely to value it as well. The opportunity your classroom offers students to focus on embracing curiosity increases their willingness to engage in sustained inquiry. It allows them to embrace the discomfort of new learning as they grapple with uncertainty and engage in inquiry with an open mind, approaching their learning from a critical and creative perspective (Clark et al., 2021; Clark & Seider, 2017; Lamnina & Chase, 2019). If you, as the instructor, demonstrate the value of curiosity and create an environment where students can fully engage it, then the informal and formal inquiry skills they will learn and practice in your classroom have a better chance of becoming a permanent part of their learning repertoire.

Without reigniting and developing the curiosity mindset or "desire to inquire" however, the lessons of IBL may become just another classroom exercise (Stokoe, 2012). We want more for our students! We want to inspire them to take these inquiry skills, to practice them in and out of our classrooms, and to take them and use them for the rest of their lives (Gino, 2018; Kashdan et al., 2020; Ness & Riese, 2015; Schattner, 2020). We want them to take pride in their learning, in their ability to figure things out for themselves, and to work together to build their understanding of complex issues (Kim & Choi, 2019; MacKinnon, 2017; Zammitti et al., 2020). We want them to be able to experience the joy of learning as they once did as small children (Kashdan, 2009; Lindholm, 2018).

This means that we need to elicit, support, and model a curiosity-based learning mindset while we teach and model inquiry skills (Cain, 2019; Maksum & Khory, 2020; Minigan, 2016; Nadelson et al., 2019). You as their guide, explicitly modeling the value of both being naturally curious and becoming curious as needed, enhances the likelihood that students will take their inquiry skills with them when they leave your classroom and use them to enhance their learning in the future. This means that your role as a faculty member or instructor needs to undergo a shift in the direction of being a learning facilitator, sharing your knowledge and experience, and guiding your students in the direction of becoming self-motivated, inquiring learners.

Shifting Roles: Instructor Becomes Facilitator While Student Becomes Learner

As students are encouraged to engage with various resources, support and collaborate with their peers, and work through the struggles of conducting research to answer their inquiry questions (Anstey et al., 2014), instructors are required to become facilitators who support and guide students on their learning journey (Spronken-Smith & Walker, 2010). This allows students to become more responsible for and take ownership of their own learning (FP 2; Love et al., 2015; Yang, 2015). Students and instructors can struggle with this change in dynamic, since it is challenging and goes against the norms wherein the teacher is an authority figure and gatekeeper of new information while the student acts as a more passive "answer sponge." Success in IBL-HE experiences, therefore, requires a significant shift in perspective among these stakeholders (Bolhuis, 2003; Brubaker, 2012; Cuneo et al., 2012).

The good news is that IBL-HE produces a richer learning environment for students and faculty alike, whereby students embrace learning through curiosity and become far more independent and deeply engaged in their learning than through traditional teaching methods (Archer-Kuhn, Lee, Finnessey, & Liu, 2020). The challenge is that these perspective shifts can result in two uncomfortable juxtapositions: (a) for students, enjoying being challenged, while simultaneously questioning their personal competency and inciting fear of failure, often due to delaying numerical assessment in favor of receiving regular formative feedback (Litmanen et al., 2012); and (b) for us instructors who are also enjoying being challenged, but are simultaneously questioning our personal competency and inciting fear of failure, particularly for those who are untenured or in precarious employment situations.

Instructors, like their students, must learn to embrace the discomfort of new learning, given the likelihood of making mistakes, taking wrong turns, and encountering speed bumps along the IBL journey (Boyle & MacKinnon, 2016; Brubaker, 2012; von Renesse & Ecke, 2017). Instructors must use their own inquiry skills and model vulnerability and willingness to problem solve, not only to provide a successful IBL-HE experience for their students, but also to remind students of the joys and challenges of being active learners. Fortunately, IBL classrooms focus on the process of learning as much or more than the final product, leaving little room for procrastination or avoidance for either students or faculty (FP 4).

Shifting From Instructor to Facilitator

When making the shift to IBL-HE in your classroom, you move from the "sage on the stage" or the "knowledge gatekeeper" in the room to being the "learner with the most experience" and "facilitator." Your job becomes less about sharing your content knowledge from a top-down perspective and moves instead to being a guide for students to use as support and as a role model during their learning journey. In many ways, this new role will be uncomfortable as you begin to share some of the power in the classroom with your students (FP7). Students in successful IBL-HE see it this way: "[We] wanted the presence of the facilitator and not to have the dominance of the teacher."

We instructors have to be what we want to see in our students; authentic, excited, fallible, vulnerable learners who are willing to go where the learning takes us. This looks like a classroom that rarely runs smoothly but in which everyone will "figure it out" along the way and will be a stronger learner because of it. In the end, while more power in the IBL-HE classroom is shared than is traditionally the case, the instructor still retains the responsibility for grading and class functioning. The phrase "I have your back" plays an important role in this new relationship between facilitator (you) and learners (students). When the IBL-HE instructor says, "I have your back," it often means, as one instructor put it:

> I take responsibility for doing what I need to do in order to ensure student success in the course. . . . So when I say "I have got your back" to a student, what I mean is, all of those things, but in addition, if you are struggling, I will help. If you are experiencing something that will delay your submission of whatever assignment, I am open to negotiation. . . . So, I tend to clarify that to students by saying, that does not mean that I will make it easy for you, so it is not my job to make it easy for you, but it is my job to ensure that you are building your skills and developing in a way that you can be successful in this environment.

This focus on process and support during the learning journey is key to the expanded role of instructors in an IBL-HE classroom, particularly when approaching students' long-term projects or work across a whole course. Monitoring the process of learners is key to knowing who needs more or less support, what type of support, and when to let them "figure it out" for themselves. This progress in process and inquiry is not observed in grades as it would be in a quiz but, rather, in the regular interactions between the students, between students and the instructor, and often in their written reflections. Having students routinely engage in self-assessment to determine where they feel they need assistance can help the instructor of even large classes maintain progress in student learning over the course of a semester. This also normalizes the need for support in learning and can allow instructors to create "just-in-time" learning opportunities (Enwere et al., 2020; Nuebel et al., 2020; Toriz, 2019), such as workshops, tutorials, or guest speakers to fill in the gaps in students' inquiry skills.

A simple example of this from Stacey's experience is a self-assessment that she conducted approximately 3 weeks into the term at UPEI, whereby she asks students how confident they feel about doing online searches for resources. Typically, one third of her class will indicate they have no idea how to search electronic academic databases while another third will share that they do not know how to search effectively for more mainstream resources using search engines. As a result, Stacey scheduled two separate workshops, an academic search session with our subject librarian and a mainstream search session with herself as lead. Students work along with the workshop facilitators using their own search terms, and by the end of each session everyone knows how to find what they need to move their projects forward. Not everyone will need to attend both, but everyone has the opportunity to do so. It is truly a "teaching-at-the-elbow" or just-in-time teaching moment.

This is one of the key shifts in the instructor's role in IBL-HE. When using an open IBL approach (as opposed to structured or guided), less content preparation is needed in advance of class (e.g., lectures); however, the need to be present with your students in the moment and observe how their learning is unfolding is vital. It is in those moments of teaching at the elbow when students feel heard and valued, when they realize that not knowing is okay, that learning is good, and that sharing that learning experience with others has significant value. Just-in-time teaching is challenging because you don't know what will be needed or when, but it is also exhilarating when a student has a moment of clarity and advances in their understanding and/ or confidence as a learner (FP 2). In essence, a structured inquiry approach requires significantly higher preparation time than even a traditional teaching approach, plus the instructor is "all in" during the class describing instructions and facilitating activities. However, an open-inquiry approach requires little preparation beforehand but requires constant monitoring, feedback, and openness to just-in-time teaching when the students need it. (Further details on this issue of time and preparation are provided in chapter 4.) Which you choose is up to you!

There will, of course, also be moments when you won't know how to help. These moments are important as well, because it is then that the "being human" side of IBL-HE is highlighted. Admitting you don't know, working with the students to figure it out as colearners, or finding someone who can clear the path for all of you to learn models for students that not knowing everything is normal; that you, too, are an active learner; that having a problem isn't as big an issue if you have a problem-solving mindset; and that growth (both in content knowledge and skills) is possible and desirable regardless of your status in the classroom (FP 7).

This idea of valuing "being human" in the classroom lends itself to other possibilities as well. One of the most impactful experiences Stacey had in an IBL-HE classroom was when one of her students became frustrated with his topic choice for his curiosity project. It had lost its appeal early in the term, and the student was becoming resentful of the work being put into something that no longer had intrinsic value. This was a first-time IBL-HE student, so Stacey suggested that the student might want to consider changing the topic. At first he was shocked and insisted that it would be a waste of the time he had already invested. At this point, she shared with him her own academic history, which involved being a part-time and full-time student, trying four diverse majors, and three universities over 9 years, just to finish her bachelor's degree. She told him she took something important from every one of those experiences and brought it into her ultimate passion for psychology, so nothing was "wasted" (plus the credits transferred!). The trick was always to look for connections between where one started and where one was going next. So, the student who was originally studying how high-level university football creates a culture similar to that of a family changed his topic to studying family-owned businesses. Fear of change could have held him back, but hearing about Stacey's journey (longer and more winding than he could ever have imagined) gave him the confidence to take a risk and try something new.

Being human also means the instructor being open to things going wrong and adjusting on the fly (FP 7). You will have times of uncertainty, possibly even make mistakes, and things may not go as planned. One of the most memorable examples of this in Stacey's career occurred when she made an error in a discussion of auditory processing in her first-year introductory psychology class. She had simply reversed two stages of the hearing process and was called on it by a young person in the class. What made such an impact on her students was not only that she graciously handled being told she was in error and fixed the misunderstanding immediately, but that she was open to being corrected, not by an undergraduate student, but by her 5-year-old daughter, who had the day off from kindergarten and was sitting in the front row of her classroom while she taught! Her daughter had sat in on the same topic the year before and remembered that her mom had said something different last time. She had no hesitation in raising her hand politely, pointing out the discrepancy, and asking which was the truth. From that very human moment on, Stacey's students did not hesitate to ask questions or request clarification on anything they were unclear about.

One of our undergraduate students said it best when she shared these thoughts on instructors:

> It's really nice when they like go through and they're talking about their studies and what they're looking into and then it's like this is what went completely, terribly wrong . . . or if they're doing a lecture and they say something or there's something wrong on the slide and they look back and they're like oh well, I messed up. Let's fix it and go on. And it just builds on . . . how human they feel when they're not on that pedestal anymore and they're just like us and trying to figure out their life and stuff like that.

Allowing your students to watch you navigate the speed bumps you encounter as an instructor is also a valuable experience. Every time Stacey incorporates IBL-HE into her classroom, she makes a point of telling her students that their learning experience in that class is actually her own inquiry project (FP 8). She writes weekly learning logs about her experience. She discusses those thoughts with colleagues and the students (often sharing what her colleagues say with the students in her class). She points out where she has made changes over the years in her approach to IBL-HE based on the feedback her students have given her, and she shares with them her concerns about their suggestions or new things she is trying with them—always with the caveat that no matter how it turns out, she "has their back," with support, negotiation, and troubleshooting.

Embracing the discomfort of new learning is indicative of successful IBL-HE. One colleague describes his experiences with sharing his ups and downs with students in this way:

> One of the things that I talked about very openly in this kind of classroom, I have no idea what is going to happen. If certain activities occur, I say "I'm ok with that," but [I add that] it is challenging to not know what is going to happen and I cannot wait to see what you are going to do that I have not seen before or that you are going to say that I have never seen before, so I make it clear that I am open to that. I also have struggled

with some of the areas that I now teach in, and I talk about myself as a "screw-up" in some of the areas that I teach, and I say, "I learned a lot on the way, and these were really important and I've become good at them but I was not always," and I talk about some of the struggles I had. . . . And then I say, each of those things was the best thing I have done in my life but scared the crap out of me at the time.

Having faith in the process of IBL and your own ability to "roll with the punches" in the classroom is an important factor in IBL-HE. As the "most experienced learner" in the room, you as the instructor have to believe you have the capability to "figure it out" as you go, much as you are asking your students to do, and communicate that to them. It isn't about not making mistakes, but modeling how to deal with the situation when you've made one. It is, indeed, a leap of faith every time you walk into an IBL-HE learning environment, as this instructor indicates:

> It is having faith that this approach to learning works. . . . It is having faith that students will see it working and it is to keep that faith continuing, um, continuing, yeah, it is about empowering students to have the confidence to believe in the process. In the quality of the learning?? . . . There is a huge leap of faith for faculty to absolve themselves from being the fountain of knowledge and divesting that knowledge to the students. To me, I suppose it is having faith in the process, having faith in the students.

Trusting yourself, trusting your students, and trusting the process and purpose of IBL will be recurring themes in your IBL-HE practice (FP 7). Rest assured, we will discuss these in detail in chapter 10.

What else should you consider explicitly modeling? Justice et al. (2007) suggest open-mindedness, acceptance, and a critically evaluative mindset. We also believe that putting the focus on the ideas, rather than those sharing them, is a crucial lesson for both professors and students in IBL-HE classrooms to learn. Not taking criticism personally takes practice, and when the instructor in the classroom models the learning rather than the judging mindset (Adams, 2016), students gradually adopt it for themselves. This professor illustrates the ability to critique an idea without critiquing the person who raised it:

> I would add openness . . . an ability to engender acceptance for different views and diversity and abilities, and definitely empowering and I think for all of the people involved a sense that we are equal learners, whether you are a faculty member or a student.

For me it is the openness that a student can ask any question. There are no stupid questions, that everyone's opinions or their questions will be valued. So that is part of it, feeling free to speak their mind and know that they will be listened to, and respected, um yeah. And part of it is also teaching students to be about criticizing the idea, not the person. I think the students need to know about the level of critique that will come through the process. That it is not about them, it is about the ideas. It is part of the research process.

One more shift you will want to consider is your role in and focus on grading. While this topic is discussed in detail in chapter 5, it is never too early to start thinking about how your approach to grading accentuates or impedes your IBL-HE goals. Like all else in the IBL world, this is not an all-or-nothing proposition. For example, Stacey uses a combination of weekly quizzes and The Curiosity Project in her second-year undergraduate class, while in her senior seminars the assessment is done in concert with the students themselves, and the focus is entirely on growth and development as inquirers on the chosen topics over the term, using a portfolio of their weekly thought papers and a final consolidation/reflection paper (e.g., depth and breadth of exploration, critical analysis, improvement in research skills). Beth uses formative and summative feedback from peers and instructors, multiple small and large group presentations, reflective writing, and where possible, other forms of community dissemination.

As long as you remain true to the foundation principles of IBL (chapter 1), including fostering a curiosity-based learning mindset (FP 1), the possibilities for learning in your classroom are vast. Remember, as Stacey told her former student, if you try something and it doesn't work the way you planned, it's okay to do it differently next time. IBL-HE, whether you are the facilitator or the learner, is a dynamic and iterative process. To get started, choose, then evaluate, then make adjustments or choose again, always with an eye on what pieces of value you can bring forward with you in this new attempt. Whatever you do, stay curious!

Summary

In essence, when you pair an active curiosity mindset with opportunities to develop both informal and formal inquiry skills, good learning happens. This good learning then has a greater chance to take root and the likelihood that the students' curiosity and inquiry skills will carry forward in their studies and life more generally increases (FP 1). When people want to ask questions (curiosity), are willing to do so (opportunities), and have the ability to do so effectively (inquiry skills), they can enhance the quality of not only their learning, but the quality of their lives across the board. And it all starts with the shift in your role from formal instructor to curious facilitator and role model. When you show yourself to actively embody a curious mindset and the values of IBL-HE, lay them out explicitly for your students, and create an environment for them to be practiced and strengthened, you have begun the process of developing a community of inquiring learners (FP 7).

Questions for Reflection

1. What might an observer notice about your teaching practices that reveals how you model curiosity?
2. Are there ways in which you are already encouraging students to exercise their curiosity that could be expanded into larger, more substantive IBL project opportunities? What would it take to make that happen?
3. Think of one exercise or project you already have on your syllabus. How could you transform it into an IBL project that encourages students' curiosity? How could you incorporate it further to increase the likelihood that they will transfer that knowledge and skill set to future learning experiences?
4. What is one thing you could do right now to begin your shift from instructor to facilitator and curiosity role model?

PART TWO

HOW DO I START DESIGNING MY IBL-HE PRACTICE?

Now that you are familiar with the fundamental principles of IBL-HE and the importance of supporting the development and growth of a curiosity-based mindset, it's time to start designing your own IBL-HE experiences! Over the next three chapters, you will encounter four key issues you need to decide on in order to incorporate IBL into your higher education classes:

- Should you start from scratch designing something new or adapt an activity, project, or course you already have to IBL (chapter 3)?
- How much IBL are you interested in starting with: Will it be a single activity, a major project, or a complete course? You will also need to decide how structured you want your IBL experience to be: structured, guided, or open (chapter 4).
- What kind of assessment and grading schemes will be used for your IBL students: learning portfolios, reflective research journals, rubrics, contract grading, specifications grading, or ungrading (chapter 5)?

Every new IBL project you design will require you to ask these questions for yourself, and you can make a different choice or combination of choices each time. Remember, it isn't the steps of IBL but the fundamental principles of it that will guide your project design. Let's get started!

3

SHOULD I START FROM SCRATCH OR ADAPT WHAT I ALREADY HAVE?

Stacey L. MacKinnon and Beth Archer-Kuhn

What to Expect

- The option is yours: benefits and challenges
- Focusing on the fundamental principles of IBL-HE

In keeping with the old adage, there is more than one way to cook a goose, and so too are there many ways to implement IBL-HE. Indeed, this is what can make IBL so appealing across disciplines. In this chapter, we will take you through making the decision of where you want to begin: by adapting courses, activities, and assessment tasks you already have, borrowing from others, or starting from scratch. Each of these approaches are acceptable and encouraged. Indeed, if you want to use the materials you have, they can be adjusted to reflect the fundamental principles of IBL-HE. We will share some activities currently being discussed in HE such as signature work and capstone courses to illustrate why IBL-HE can be a good match for these pedagogical activities.

When you are getting started in IBL-HE, one of your first concerns may be whether you need to start from scratch and create something totally new or if you can adapt already existing activities, assignments, or entire courses to include more inquiry. There are benefits and challenges to each of these options, which can help guide your decision-making in these early stages. Let's look at the key issues.

Borrow, Adopt, or Adapt

Nothing says that your IBL journey has to start with reinventing the wheel. Perhaps the least stressful way of beginning your IBL-HE adventure is by adapting activities or projects you already use. Everything doesn't have to become inquiry based all at once; you get to decide how steep a learning curve you are interested in climbing! Every step toward incorporating the fundamental principles of IBL in your classroom is a win for you and your students. Perhaps you start by offering students more choice in terms of their research topics for a major paper/project or include a reflection on not only the course material but their experience of learning in your class (make sure you ask them to discuss the good, the bad, and even the ugly). Teach students how to ask questions so that they take responsibility for instigating and carrying class discussions (we have some ideas in chapter 6 and Appendices C and E you may be interested in). Dedicate time during class sessions to addressing the questions students determine are important or interesting, moving beyond fact to "what if" and other possible angles.

There are many excellent examples in a variety of fields that you can use as inspiration or a stepping-stone to adopt or adapt for your own classrooms. Make sure you read the vignettes throughout this book, provided by award-winning instructors in a variety of fields, including our own areas of psychology and social work, plus English, vertebrate zoology, family science, and business. In addition, take some time to explore the resources included on our website from fields such as biochemistry and molecular biology (Murthy et al., 2014), physics (Simonson, 2019), chemical kinetics (Aumi et al., 2021), the humanities (Feldt & Peterson, 2021), geography (Passon & Schlesinger, 2019), and many more.

Do you want to start smaller with a preparatory IBL activity? When Beth started using IBL-HE it was through one activity in a course. That one experience quickly became an assessment task in future courses. She wanted to help students to further develop critical reflection skills, to reflect more critically on the research literature, and to reflect more on their own and their peers' understandings. Hence, "Structured Controversy" was created. Consider turning your usual lecture or assignment about a hot topic in your field (e.g., the effectiveness of online learning; efforts to ameliorate climate change; improving recycling methods, microplastics, and the ocean biome; the role of young adult fiction in adolescent development; commonalities between Buddhist philosophy and quantum physics; biological bases of mental health; the idea that mathematics is not just formulas or computations or even proofs but ideas; the existence of black holes; sustainable aquatecture; or any discipline-related topic) into a structured controversy (see Appendix A), where the students prepare to learn how to engage in IBL-HE. Remember, you can fill in any gaps in their understanding by paying attention to what they are learning and teaching "at the elbow" or simply asking them questions so content coverage does not have to be a concern. The Academy of

Inquiry Based Learning in the United States offers a great video on what IBL is from the perspective of a math instructor.

QR Code 3.1. IBL from the perspective of a math instructor.

(https://www.youtube.com/watch?v=O5wCqHxzB-w&list= PL7HVaYibt1kkZLK5EULOfJmqUldhrKSm4&index=2)

Honors, Capstone Courses, and Signature Projects

While IBL can be used at any level of higher education and with any size class, it is often easier to start incorporating it into your practice with more experienced learners in upper-year (and presumably smaller) courses. Continuing our theme of adapting what already exists, consider the possibility of including more of the fundamental principles of IBL-HE in your signature projects, undergraduate honors research, and capstone courses. For example, in the University of Calgary's Health Sciences program, Aparicio-Ting et al. (2019) have taken a scaffolded approach by integrating IBL into each year of their undergraduate program, culminating in an independent, student-driven honors thesis in the fourth year (FP 5). While that is too big a step for a beginner, you could easily start out by having your honors students brainstorm their own questions (see chapter 6), keep a reflection journal (see chapter 8), and/or give each other regular feedback on their individual research projects (see chapter 9).

Capstone courses already offer a great deal of flexibility in terms of formats and requirements, and may include research projects, internships, clinical experiences or practicums, e-portfolios, demonstrations or exhibits, performances or recitals, and client- or community-based projects, any of which can have more IBL-HE injected into them (Hauhart & Grahe, 2015; Masiello & Skipper, 2013). If you work at one of the between 75% and 81% of colleges and universities in the United States who offer or require capstone courses (Hauhart & Grahe, 2010; Newton-Calvert & Arthur, 2018), this may be a great starting point for you. Consider this example from Clark

University, where Michelle Bata and Amy Whitney have created IBL opportunities that take place outside the classroom for students in their entrepreneurship minor. This involved constructing a recurrent feedback loop as their students move through academic, cocurricular, and extracurricular experiences using IBL (Bata & Whitney, 2015). "The Graduation Project" at Victoria University also uses an IBL framework for its cross-disciplinary capstone experience with great success (Funston & Lee, 2014).

While honors research and capstone courses can be quite instructor driven and may require more adaptation to convert to IBL, signature work is already more student driven and entails a project, or set of related projects, in which students define questions that they regard as personally significant and answer these questions through their research, immersing themselves in exploration, applying what they learn to real-world situations, and preparing to explain the significance of their work to others.

QR Code 3.2. What does signature work look like?

(https://www.aacu.org/office-of-global-citizenship-for-campus-community-and-careers/integrative-learning)

These signature projects are golden opportunities to reignite students' curiosity (FP 1), have them follow their own interests (FP 2), engage in deep metacognitive reflection on their learning process (FP 4), engage in critical reflection on their issue/topic (FP 5), and build learning communities that go beyond the traditional group learning experience and develop into longer term collegial relationships (FP 7). This can be particularly effective when the individuals working in these courses come from different majors/faculties and can make links across disciplines, thereby enhancing the learning for each person's project.

Starting From Scratch

However, you could choose to start from scratch. As we all know from our experiences with academic writing, sometimes it is better to start over than to continuously tweak what you have already written. Sometimes the narrative or purpose just isn't flowing or has changed since you first began, and as a result you need to begin again. Creating something totally new can be a daunting exercise for your first IBL-HE encounter because it pushes you further outside your comfort zone. While that is ultimately the point of IBL-HE, it doesn't have to happen all at once for you or your students. There is a happy medium between adapting your current practices and starting with a totally blank slate. You can look to others for ideas to bring in your IBL-HE classroom, and by choosing this book you have certainly come to the right place to do that!

While Beth took a somewhat gradual, scaffolded approach to developing her IBL-HE practice, it wasn't long before she had the opportunity to build on her original work with Structured Controversy and use the fundamental principles outlined in chapter 1 and additional activities to develop an entire course utilizing IBL-HE as pedagogy while creating curriculum for a group study program (GSP; study abroad) to the United Kingdom. Taking all of the principles of IBL-HE into account, the planning, implementation, and reflection on this course (see Appendix D for curriculum) proved to be a new and positive experience for students to develop greater awareness and increase engagement in their learning, as GSP students share: "I noticed my awareness changed so much as we would go from different physical locations. My understanding of the situations just broadened how I view things"; and, from another student,

> I also liked the freedom that came with doing something on your own. I was in charge of my learning so this is how I wanted it to be and this is where I was going with it. As opposed to being told what I needed to learn. So that was definitely different, as the others have said.

Critical thinking development increases as students work through the scaffolded activities or assessment tasks, as we see from this GSP student:

> Doing literature reviews, Googling stuff to generate ideas, to start that thinking process for me, talking a lot to my peers. All of those things help to bring it all together. The class presentations, the presenters that came in and when we went into the community, they were a big part of how I applied this to my critical thinking and reflection.

Stacey's initial experience with IBL-HE was one of jumping into open inquiry with both feet, starting totally from scratch and figuring it out as she went. If you wish to start more from scratch you can do so successfully by following the decision-making and in-class practices laid out in the rest of this book. This is certainly how Stacey initially designed The Curiosity

Project (see Appendix B), working from the broad goal of reigniting students' curiosity and desire to inquire (FP 1; see also chapter 2), figuring out how much of her course would be devoted to IBL, determining how much structure she wanted the project to have (open inquiry; see chapter 4), and how she would go about assessing the students' learning (critical learning log portfolios and reflections; incorporating weekly peer feedback; ungrading; see chapters 5, 8, and 9). She tried new ways of getting students to ask questions (see chapter 6), let them choose from a variety of research methods/sources (see chapter 7), and created community both within and outside of the classroom (chapters 10, 11, and 12). When she realized that her second- and third-year undergraduates needed additional support with their inquiry skills, she designed UPEI 1020, Inquiry Studies (see Appendix C), using structured and guided inquiry in order to provide a scaffold into the more open upper-level IBL-HE courses (FP 5).

There is a wonderful freedom to starting with a clean slate, and the excitement it engenders helps to balance the nerves associated with doing something totally new. Starting fresh doesn't preclude learning about the IBL approaches others have taken and adopting what you like from their approaches for your own purposes. Remember, the fundamental principles of IBL-HE are not linked to any one discipline, so look outside your own field for inspiration! This was certainly the case with The Curiosity Project, which was adopted in principle by Marina Silva-Opps in biology, in particular her course on vertebrate zoology. She took Stacey's original Curiosity Project principles and framework and adapted it to her resources, goals, and students' needs. Her focus was on encouraging her science students to be critical consumers of information and improve their interdependent learning and communication skills using a smaller version of The Curiosity Project worth 20% of her students' grades. Silva-Opps shares the following in her course syllabus:

> In this course, we have decided to change things a little bit and give you the chance to be curious and to learn just for the sake of learning! So, what we are proposing here is something very simple that is composed of three steps:
> (1) You will select a topic/question/issue in vertebrate zoology that you are curious about, (2) You will research and learn about the topic/question/issue using all possible sources of information that are accessible to you, (3) You will share what you are learning and how are you learning it with others. . . . Participation during Lab/Class related activities involves: (1) Preparation: the extent of your reading, exploration and curiosity demonstrated by contribution to discussion of your own topic and that of others; (2) Contribution to discussion: the extent to which you volunteered

answers, asked relevant questions, expressed your own opinion and ana-
lyzed contributions of others; (3) Group skills: the extent to which you
allowed others to contribute, avoided class domination, shared ideas with
others, assisted others, provided positive feedback to others and exhibited
tolerance and respect for others; (4) Communication skills: the quality of
your expression, clarity, conciseness, use of appropriate vocabulary, confidence. At the end of the semester, you will produce/create a final product
that could take different forms, including paper, brochure, poster, website
or a video, which will be shared with your classmates.

Silva-Opps is now working on developing a self-assessment tool for her students' Curiosity Projects to further enhance their sense of ownership and
growth. In a quid pro quo sense, Stacey is excited to see how this protocol
may be adapted to her social psychology students' work!

Driving home the flexibility of IBL-HE approaches, The Curiosity
Project was also adapted by English professor and National 3M teaching
fellow Shannon Murray, who used it as part of her already existing English
Research Methods course as a way to allow students to experience the pleasure of doing research while learning the necessary skills, as you can see in
this vignette:

Vignette: Shannon Murray

Some of the best work that's been done in my Research Methods class is
stuff I knew nothing about and would never have assigned in a million
years: gender in the 19th-century school story, subverting the Gothic in
WandaVision, the genres of graffiti, The Song of Ice and Fire, Victorian
soft porn. These topics, all devised by the students themselves, are
fascinating, so much more than the nuts and bolts of the MLA style
sheet. My course, a requirement for all English majors, is structured
as a workshop with peer and instructor consultations, in which novice
researchers discover everything they need to know about doing literary
critical research by following a true passion of their own. So we start with
a simple question: what do you love? From a long list of all the books,
writers, ideas, issues and genres in literary studies that they already know
and adore—their "paracanon," as Elaine Showalter calls it—these young
scholars winnow the list, sometimes painfully, down to one single passion they are happy to spend 4 months on. They work toward a final
focus for their inquiry by answering a few questions: what do you already

---

(*Continues*)

(Continued)

know? Is this something you would gladly spend time on, even if you didn't have to? Is it something you won't run out of questions about, even after the course is over? And can you actually figure out the stuff of research methods while you do it?

By the end of term, through elevator pitches, research panels, proposals, papers, and a final portfolio, students have to demonstrate that they can, in fact, use an appropriate research database, work other people's voices into their own arguments, and cite and quote properly within a stylesheet, but I want those things to feel secondary to the joys of intellectual curiosity and discovery. The real learning goal here is to experience the pleasure of research. This process is not without bumps. Hard though it may be to believe, some English majors don't read much and have trouble thinking of a book or author they actually love, so I open the field to anything that could be taught in any English department anywhere: film, graphic novels, popular culture, stage history, linguistics, television. For example, my student the graffiti artist argued, successfully, for the linguistic underpinnings of his art, and he was off! If you can't honestly find any credible published work on your subject, you just have to widen your search, and so the student obsessed with the very recent WandaVision, about which nothing scholarly had yet been published, explored its generic contexts, grounding her very original arguments in feminist theory and the history of the gothic horror novel. Some of these projects are done when they are done, but some turn into undergraduate conference papers, honours theses, and in at least one case, a PhD (that was the Victorian porn project, by the way). For me, there are three joys here. The students do some amazing work, often more than is merely required, because they already love the topic. (I tell them that if they are bored by the course material, they have only themselves to blame, since they chose it!) The second joy is the constant surprise and delight through the course, as students excitedly share things they just found out and as they learn from and support each other. One student last term bounded into my office when she discovered that THERE ARE SO MANY BOOKS ABOUT THIS SUBJECT IN THE LIBRARY! And for me, I also have the joy of learning new things: and I don't have to spend my days lecturing on where the commas go in Works Cited lists.

Even before the COVID pandemic hit, Charlene VanLeeuwen was working on adapting The Curiosity Project for use in the online components of her courses in family science, kinesiology, and nursing.

Vignette: Charlene VanLeeuwen

A few years ago, well before the pandemic, I was teaching one of my favorite courses . . . a third year current issues course exploring children's health and development. Teaching this course never gets old because the students and I cocreate it each time it is offered by selecting topics that they are keenly interested in learning about. This most recent time we were facing some scheduling challenges and we decided to go with a hybrid or blended delivery format. The in-person class time was reserved for Socratic seminars related to our readings and guest lectures from professionals and service providers in the community. The online component presented the perfect opportunity to try out an idea that had been sitting on the back burner for some time . . . a version of the Curiosity Projects that I learned about from one of my colleagues in Psychology, Stacey MacKinnon. The Family Science and Kinesiology students in this course used much of the structure for a Curiosity Project to develop a conference style poster on a topic related to children's health and development. Use of posters is well-documented in higher education literature as an effective teaching and learning strategy. What was less clear was whether moving to digital forms of presentation and interaction about the research students were conducting to develop their poster was effective in promoting student learning and communication.

Starting in the first week of the course, students worked toward the creation/development of a digital poster which synthesized the research literature on a topic of their choice. We started by dividing the class into groups of five. While we had a few in-person discussions, most of the activities for this inquiry project were done asynchronously online. Here, each group worked independently, starting with an invitation for each student to choose their own topic to research. Each member of the group was part of a blog style discussion forum, set up within the university's learning management system. Throughout the semester students worked collaboratively in developing their individual plans to gather and synthesize research on their chosen topic. For example, early on they helped each other brainstorm keywords and phrases to use when searching journal databases for relevant literature on their topic.

Each week or two they wrote a short blog post in response to a prompt that helped them outline their progress and what they learned about their topic that week. As students in each small group read each other's posts they were encouraged to share ideas, constructive feedback or thought-provoking questions with their classmates which would help

(*Continues*)

(*Continued*)

them gather and synthesize relevant information from peer-reviewed or highly reputable sources of grey literature. While they were required to respond to at least two of their classmates, I noticed that they frequently responded to all four members in their group. I monitored but did not directly intervene with the blogs and encouraged the students in each group to support each other online and during the face-to-face class meetings. Where appropriate, I occasionally sent a private message to a student rather than reply within the blog. These messages might have been a suggestion for a keyword to help refine their literature search, a link to recently published relevant literature, a reminder, or some words of encouragement. Each group's blog discussions were private to the group and were not seen by the other groups. Students used their blogs to share their ideas and work toward their individual poster in tandem with other group members.

Students were provided with some poster design templates to work with, and once they saw what was involved, their creative minds built on this. They ended up creating their posters in a variety of ways, and these were eventually posted as PDF files into purpose-built websites. We used this site for sharing posters with classmates and a broader audience within the department during a 2-day asynchronous poster session. During the digital poster session, students and invited guests (other faculty in the department) shared comments, feedback and questions with the creators of the posters. Everyone checked in a few times during the poster session to view posters, leave comments, questions or compliments and then later post replies to comments about their poster.

Students were marked for their blogging and separately for their posters. If I were to do this again, I would likely incorporate an ungrading approach and have the students propose their mark for the project. Combining blogs with group discussion toward the development of research-based posters enabled students with a variety of different disciplinary backgrounds, prior knowledge, and interests to work effectively together. The design worked well in encouraging students to explore a topic and to do their own research. Students used the members of their online blogging group as sounding boards. In addition, although they worked very closely in these groups, students were not concerned their individual grade could be influenced by the comments or questions posed by classmates.

During the pandemic I modified this assignment for a fully online course. In this case the students were second year nursing students in a human development course. Some of the modifications were the option to work together [with] one or two other students (those working with partners were distributed into blogging groups with other classmates), opening up to allow a broader range of assignment deliverables—from a website to a photo essay or a digital resource/brochure that could be used for patient education, and the introduction of a synchronous presentation of their projects using breakout rooms in Zoom.

As you can see, this one "started from scratch" IBL framework, built on the fundamental principles we discussed in chapter 1, is still going strong in psychology, and the nondisciplinary "First Year Inquiry Studies" course has been adapted for biology, English, family science, kinesiology, and nursing. It has also been used in women's studies and environmental science.

Other disciplines have also developed significant IBL practices, including social justice in social work (Archer-Kuhn, 2020), process-oriented, guided inquiry learning (POGIL) in physics (Simonson, 2019), inquiry-based mathematics education (Laursen & Rasmussen, 2019), case-based learning in medicine (McLean, 2016), and integrating history and IBL to develop science students' understanding of invention, innovation, and commercialization processes in business entrepreneurship (Pittaway, 2009). These approaches are also not limited to the fields that inspired them but can be adapted to fit in many different disciplines.

Even if you start fresh by designing something totally new, that is only the beginning of your IBL experience! This is key to the practice of IBL-HE, if you are doing it right, is that it is never done because your students' IBL should also always be your IBL project. Over time, and with experience and feedback from your learners, you should be making adjustments, trying new approaches, experimenting, reflecting, and trying again, always keeping in mind what your students need from the experience.

Summary

The choice is yours: Will you adapt something you already use, build off existing IBL-HE models, or go rogue and start completely from scratch? The good news is that there is no wrong answer. In the end, what matters is that you bear in mind the fundamental principles of IBL-HE and that you immerse yourself in the IBL-HE experience along with your students so you can edit, adjust, refine, and expand the learning that is happening in your classroom.

Questions for Reflection

1. What pieces of your current teaching practice could you quickly and easily adapt to an IBL approach?

2. How much time do you have to devote to your first IBL-HE project? Starting from scratch and/or tackling large IBL-HE projects takes more planning (e.g., Stacey was on sabbatical when she designed The Curiosity Project). If you've got the time, use it for a larger project, but if not start smaller. Remember, IBL is a marathon, not a sprint!

3. How concerned are you about your ability to engage your students in IBL-HE? There is nothing wrong with starting small and building from there. There is also nothing wrong about jumping into the deep end as long as you are willing to learn how to swim as you go. Consider starting with what feels just outside your comfort zone.

4. Read Appendices A, B, C, and D. Are there ideas there that spark your interest and that you could use as inspiration for your own IBL-project? Remember, just because the examples in this book may come from a specific discipline does not mean you can't adapt them (or parts of them) for your own field of study!

4

HOW MUCH IBL AND HOW MUCH STRUCTURE SHOULD I INCLUDE WHEN GETTING STARTED?

Beth Archer-Kuhn

What to Expect

- Choosing IBL as an assignment versus an assessment, versus a major project, versus a course, versus a program
- Types of IBL-HE: structured, guided, open

In this chapter we will take you through the variety of ways in which IBL-HE can be used, including as an activity in a course, as an assessment task, as a major project, and as an entire course. We will also briefly discuss how IBL-HE is being implemented as an entire program in some HE institutions (e.g., McMaster University, Hamilton, Ontario). Next, we will share the three ways in which IBL can be implemented in HE—namely via structured, guided, and open inquiry. Each of these types of IBL can be implemented within activities, assignments, and courses and will depend on your purpose and comfort level in implementing each type. We illustrate through description, examples, and appendices how each of these types can look in your classroom. We also discuss how you can scaffold these IBL structures within a course or program to build students' skills and confidence in engaging in IBL.

IBL-HE brings a new context to teaching and learning in many disciplines. Instructors are facilitators of the learning process; power is shared; and students develop greater independence, ownership, and agency in their learning. As a bonus, IBL synergizes naturally with the principles of social justice and equality, which is why it is so surprising to find limited studies of IBL published within social work education.

One of the beautiful parts of IBL is how this pedagogical method can be infused into higher education, including professional schools such as nursing, teaching, law, and social work teaching, learning, and practice. IBL can be applied to coursework and field education to support students during their degree program and as a step toward lifelong learning. The benefits students gain reflect the critical skills needed for professional practice, for example, increased critical thinking, problem-solving, technology literacy, and improved interpersonal skills. Here is one YouTube video I use when discussing the many benefits of IBL with students, so they know why this pedagogy is being used and how it can support and improve their learning.

QR Code 4.1. VIDEO: The Benefits of Inquiry-Based Learning.

(https://www.youtube.com/watch?v=2ylmVT5lkck)

However, you can choose any of the many resources available on the internet.

We'd like to begin with a discussion of some of the decisions you will have to make when choosing IBL-HE as pedagogy. First you will need to consider how you want to use it: as an activity, an assessment task, a course, or a program. Then we will move to the various types of IBL: structured, guided, and open.

How Do I Use IBL in HE: Activity, Assessment Task, Course, or Program?

Deciding on how you want to use IBL-HE will likely depend on your comfort level. How comfortable are you with change? How comfortable are you with the unknown? How comfortable are you in partnering with students in their learning? It is important for you to acknowledge your level of willingness to share power in your course because successful IBL-HE demands that you do so. Maybe you have read about the many benefits of IBL and the increasing evidence on increased student outcomes and that intrigues you to see for yourself. Perhaps you want to see more engagement from students in their learning. Whatever your motivation, starting slow would be our recommendation. Starting slow means choosing an activity or an assessment task, something you already do in your course. Then, apply the principles of IBL (chapter 1) and make the adjustments necessary to align the assignment or assessment task with the IBL-HE principles. After you have implemented IBL-HE through an activity or assessment task, once or multiple times, you may then be ready to design an entire course using IBL-HE. You will recall from chapter 3 that faculty member Shannon Murray did just that in the department of English with "Graffiti, WandaVision, and Porn: A Curiosity-Based English Research Methods Course."

You may recall that Shannon chose to use IBL-HE for an entire course; all assessment tasks were designed with IBL pedagogy. Now that you have considered how you will implement IBL-HE, you are ready to start. To get you started, we want to talk a bit about the value of scaffolding.

IBL can be incorporated into single classroom activities (Archer-Kuhn, 2013), larger projects (MacKinnon, 2017), an entire course (Simonson, 2019), or as a guiding principle for full curriculum design (Plowright & Watkins, 2004; Weaver, 1989). Scaffolding is important for each way it is utilized: scaffold steps in an activity, and scaffold assessment tasks in a course (FP 5). Entry into IBL-HE can be scaffolded by progressing through level of instructor versus student control (structured to guided to open IBL) over longer or shorter time frames. Lastly, the flexibility of this pedagogy makes it ideal to be applied across a range of contexts in HE, including fieldwork (Yesudhas et al., 2014); undergraduate and graduate courses (Aditomo et al., 2013); and throughout many disciplines, such as science and math (Laursen et al., 2014; Simonson, 2019), psychology (MacKinnon, 2017), social work (Archer-Kuhn, Lee, Finnessey, & Liu, 2020), and the arts/humanities (Levy, 2012). The flexibility and complexity of IBL is what we intend to share with you throughout the various chapters in this book.

In the example that follows, we illustrate how IBL-HE can be introduced as an activity or assessment task and can then move to an entire course. Regardless of how you start, the principles of IBL-HE are the same. With time and experience, you too will know how much support your students need from you and at what point you can move to guided or even open inquiry.

Scaffolding the Learning Process (FP 5)

Here we share our mixed-methods study of how we have engaged social work students successfully in their learning using IBL-HE across seven cohorts, seven social work courses within the classroom. The GSP aspect of this study is discussed in chapter 11 and Appendix D. For full details of the study, see Archer-Kuhn, Lee, Finnessey, and Liu (2020). We examined the student experience of IBL in undergraduate, graduate, and doctoral education when it is introduced in a structured way, then supported students with guided and open inquiry for the remainder of the courses.

Beth developed her understanding and utilization of IBL over the past 10 years, through trial and error, starting slowly with an activity and moving to an assessment task and eventually to an entire course (see Hudspith & Jenkins, 2001). For some, IBL has multiple forms of delivery and support: structured, guided, or open inquiry (Spronken-Smith & Walker, 2010). Thought of on a spectrum, types of IBL reflect varied levels of instructor support and student independence. In structured inquiry, the instructor offers greater support through increased structure. For example, students explore a topic that is chosen by the instructor, whereas in open inquiry, students choose their own topic for inquiry, make all decisions about their learning process, and receive minimal guidance from the instructor (Spronken-Smith & Walker, 2010). Based on findings from our study, we agree with prior study in higher education that reveals students' initial need for more structure and guidance (Yesudhas et al., 2014), while we also move through guided and open inquiry.

What We Did

Following the recommendation of several authors, Beth began to construct an IBL course. Yesudhas et al. (2014) suggest that students be introduced to IBL prior to beginning their experience, while Friesen and Scott (2013) identify three key strategies of IBL that lead to deep learning, including scaffolding; formative assessment; and powerful, critical, and essential questions. Dunleavy and Milton's (2009) three criteria for increasing student engagement in the learning environment include (a) learning from and with each other and people in their community; (b) connecting with experts and expertise; and (c) having opportunities for dialogue and conversation. Together these criteria and strategies made up the IBL course. For example, to accommodate the prior knowledge component, Beth created an online module that students viewed prior to the beginning of the course, along with some readings. Together these provide an opportunity to gain a basic understanding of IBL.

She then integrated strategies within each of the seven courses, including scaffolding of assessment tasks and formative feedback to support the inquiry process, such as the development of powerful, critical, and essential questions, known as the central question (Hudspith & Jenkins,

2001) utilizing a structured controversy (Archer-Kuhn, 2013), videos, brainstorming, and a checklist for the development of an inquiry question (Roy et al., 2003) to take in the lessons from Friesen and Scott (2013). Finally, Beth provided access to multiple sources of information, including many peer consultations and field trips into the community for varied types of knowledge. In this way, students from all seven cohorts received not only information and education about IBL and the process of developing inquiry questions to pursue, but they also enacted their own teacher-supported, student-directed learning. Further, Justice et al. (2002) propose a five-stage pedagogical process: (a) engaging with a topic through a review of the literature, (b) developing questions, (c) gathering and analyzing data, (d) synthesizing and communicating the new knowledge, and (e) evaluating the output. Our IBL process, tied to each of the seven courses, also incorporated these strategies. Hudspith and Jenkins (2001) add that IBL is artful and creative, allowing students to develop critical thinking skills. We also observed creativity in the student learning journey with IBL. Regardless of how it is defined, the purpose of inquiry as a pedagogical tool is to help students develop the necessary skills to enable them to explore and find answers to their central question (Hudspith & Jenkins, 2001). The focus of the IBL instructor is to support each student in the learning journey.

You may be wondering how you might make the decision about which type of IBL to choose for your course: Do I start slow with IBL through the use of an activity, structured or guided, or do I go all in with an open-inquiry approach? Learning what the literature tells us (chapter 1) and what we have observed about the student and faculty experience with IBL-HE, we believe, will help to inform how you think about this pedagogical approach, the ways it might fit within your course, and how you and your students might respond to this way of teaching and learning. After all, thinking critically about the research literature is an important component of IBL-HE. Next we describe the various types of IBL-HE for you to consider.

Types of IBL

We subscribe to three types of IBL noted by Spronken-Smith and Walker (2010): structured, guided, and open. Each can be used in different ways—for example, as an activity or assessment task, as the design of the course, and for an entire program. An instructor can also combine the different approaches of IBL, for example using structured and guided together in a course. In Table 4.1, you can consider how the types of IBL are similar and different.

TABLE 4.1
Comparing Structured, Guided, and Open IBL

	Structured Inquiry	Guided Inquiry	Open Inquiry
Topic choice	Instructor or student	Student	Student
Instructor preparation	High level	High to medium level	Low level
Decision on question development	Student	Student	Student
Support for question development	High level	Medium level	Low level
Monitoring during implementation	High level	High level	High level
Instructor support re: research strategies	High level	Medium level	Low level
Peer support	High level	High level	High level
Dissemination opportunities	High level	High level	High level

Structured Inquiry

In structured inquiry, the students investigate a teacher-presented question through a prescribed procedure and receive explicit step-by-step guidelines at each stage, leading to a predetermined outcome, similar to following a recipe. This is similar to the ways in which most traditional science labs unfold. Given the social nature of experiential learning practices (Frey & Shadle, 2019; Seaman & Rheingold, 2013), one way to provide a structured inquiry experience is by offering the Structured Controversy assignment (see Archer-Kuhn, 2013). Beth engages students in Structured Controversy, as either an activity in the class or as an assessment task, depending on our purpose, to prepare students for the remainder of the course that utilizes IBL as pedagogy.

Structured Controversy is used as an active learning activity (details are in Appendix A). Students work together in one of two teams. The structure of the activity looks something like this: Through research, students explore a theme that has been determined by the instructor, develop a central inquiry question related to their theme, and present or argue information they have gained from their research. The arguments put forward are one team's positioning against their opposing team's arguments. Central to this activity is the requirement to understand the opposing arguments, both the intent and the content, which means that listening with an open mind is fundamental. This active and deep learning activity goes beyond the achievement of learning outcomes from traditional group presentations, since students learn to listen to the opposing team's position, become familiar with disputed positions on issues, and gain starting points for inquiry (Hudspith & Jenkins, 2001). At the end of the activity, students debrief the experience as a large group and then write an individual reflection on their experience as it relates to their learning and their role on the team (how they contributed).

The following is an example of the instructions that students receive prior to engaging in a structured controversy. You will notice in this example that students are provided the "theme" to explore. This is consistent with a structured inquiry. Beth typically uses a topic that most if not all students will have some knowledge of and will be mindful of how others view this topic as well. You can use anything related to your discipline and, ideally, specific to the course. She uses a full 3-hour class for this activity. In a 90-minute class, students complete the activity over two classes. Doing it over one class period is preferable as students are "in the moment" when they engage in the work of a structured controversy. Outlining the time frame is important so that students know the limits of their tasks. The fast-paced activity helps them to focus quickly as a group and get down to work.

Remember, structured inquiry requires the highest level of support from the instructor of the three types of inquiry. This cannot be overstated as it may be their first experience with this new (to them) pedagogy. Providing instructions ahead of time, reviewing expectations as a large group, and setting out a timeline in class all help to support the students to complete the activity successfully. You are walking them through the steps of the activity in multiple ways to support their learning process. The last piece is the debrief, which allows students to discuss their learning process in relation to the activity. Depending on the topics chosen and the students' life experiences, there may be times when the debrief is required to support the emotional labor students have committed.

Students are provided instructions about Structured Controversy (Figure 4.1) to help prepare them for the activity. In sum, when introducing Structured Controversy in a course, Beth first shares the instructions with the students to help prepare them, then reviews it as a large group to ensure clarity of expectations. Finally, a table is used to support students with the timeline of the activity (Table 4.2).

Finally, a rubric can be helpful to students in providing transparency in the grading process. The following example of a rubric can be used for this purpose (Table 4.3).

Figure 4.1. Structured Controversy instructions.

Divide into two groups/teams.

Each group will argue a position on a particular issue with a vulnerable population: homelessness. Using a YouTube clip and a brief case scenario, one group will take on the positions presented by the Homeless Coalition and the other group will take on the position of the community leaders. Pay particular attention to the time limits in each section of this activity. The course instructor will be the timekeeper.

Each side/team is provided time to research their position, requiring a few in each group to have access to a laptop. With your team, spend 15–30 minutes planning your arguments. You will then spend 45 minutes researching your agreed-on arguments. You will have 15 minutes to regroup and discuss your findings and provide your team members your research. At the end of the hour and a half, each team will be ready to present. The instructor can be used for consultation by both teams.

Team 1 chooses a spokesperson and has 10 minutes to make their argument. Team 2 listens intently to and documents team 1's argument. Team 2 then has 10 minutes to make their argument, with team 1 noting team 2's positions. The teams then have 10 minutes to meet separately to discuss the opposing team's arguments and research data. At the end of that time, team 1 has 5 minutes to reflect through a spokesperson what they heard team 2's position to be. Team 2 must be satisfied that team 1 has heard them correctly, both in content and intent. Once team 2 is satisfied, they reflect for team 1 in 5 minutes what they heard team 1 argue. Once team 1 is satisfied, each team has 5 minutes to gather for their final arguments. Team 1 then argues, in 3 minutes or less, their final position, and team 2 then does the same.

The final argument is to take into account both your own team's position and, at a minimum, an acknowledgement of the other team's position. The idea is that each team wants to convince the other that their position is correct. The trick is to do so in a manner that is clear, concise, supported by research, and convincing. You can choose to be demanding or collaborative, using a social action or asset-building approach. The value of your strategy is discussed at the end of the activity as a large group. Each team then takes 10 minutes to submit the role each student contributed to the structured controversy to consider the distribution of the workload when assigning the student grades. The rubric can be used to help you understand how you will be assessed.

TABLE 4.2
Timeline Sample of Structured Controversy

What	Time (minutes)	Content
Preparation	10	Teams gather to review arguments and decide on presentation format (who/how many presenters).
SC presentation	14	Each team has 7 minutes to present. Team 1 presents, and team 2 takes notes; when team 2 presents, team 1 takes notes.

What	Time (minutes)	Content
Team reflection on opposing team argument	10	Teams regroup and decide: What did you hear? Who will present what you heard from the other team?
Opposing argument reflection (intent and content)	10	Each team has 5 minutes to present what each heard from the opposing team.
Team final argument (small group)	6	Teams agree on final arguments (both own team position and a minimum acknowledgment of other team's position) and on who will present.
Final argument	6	Each team has 3 minutes to present final argument.
Debrief	8	Large group discussion on process. Each group submits the role each student contributed to the argument.
Peer feedback	15	Large group: How did you like or dislike your role?

In a professional discipline such as social work, Structured Controversy can not only prepare students for IBL, but also has the added benefit of challenging their critical thinking by bringing research to bear on their central question (Hudspith & Jenkins, 2001). Social work is arguably unlike any other profession in the greater degree of importance placed on values and principles (e.g., commitment to social justice, to individual well-being, to vulnerable and oppressed people) and on the influence of changing social or individual values that guide professional practice (Chechak, 2015). Accordingly, students develop heightened awareness through IBL of the influence one's values have on day-to-day decisions and actions. Structured Controversy can be implemented easily during in-person classes and in an online format, using breakout rooms.

The following vignette describes a graduate student's experience as a research assistant supporting an IBL-HE research project. This student was an observer and also a videographer in a class where Structured Controversy was implemented. The following is their understanding of this pedagogical tool with attention to the differences they observed to traditional teaching.

TABLE 4.3
Structured Controversy Rubric

Domain/Criteria	Specific Criteria Present	Specific Criteria Missing	Comments
Delivery/Clarity	• Concepts are clearly presented • Appropriate contributions among group facilitators • Coordination between team members, with seamless, flowing teamwork • Presentation was well structured/organized/planned	• Concepts are not clearly presented • Inequitable contributions among group facilitators • Poor coordination between team members, without seamless, flowing teamwork • Presentation disorganized or not well structured or not well planned	___ out of 3 pts
Engagement of Participants	• Each participant engaged in group planning • Each participant identified and researched one of the following factors related to their topic: historical, social, cultural, political or economic	• No evidence that each participant engaged in group planning • No evidence that each participant identified and researched one of the following factors related to their topic: historical, social, cultural, political or economic	___ out of 3 pts
Content	• Group thesis and issue introduced • Demographics, literature search and statistics presented • Relationship between need and social justice clearly articulated and argued • Implications to community identified	• Group thesis and issue unclear • Demographics, literature search and statistics missing • Relationship between need and social justice not clearly articulated and argued • Implications to community not identified	___ out of 3 pts
Timing of presentation	• Presentation arguments were made within the allotted time periods for each section of the structured controversy	• Arguments ran over the time limits allotted for some or all of the sections of the structured controversy	___ out of 1 pt

Vignette: Graduate Student, Lavender Xin Huang

When I was a research assistant asked to observe and record what was happening at the structured controversy classroom the first time, I had thought the structured controversy was another debate, but when I followed through and watched again what I had recorded of the process of the structured controversy, I was totally attracted and amazed by the structure, the format, and the feedback from Beth and the class.

Difference to Debate

The aim of a debate is to convince the opposition that your organized argument or content of ideas is right; you can only have one winner. But, as my observation continued, I noticed that the team members would cooperate and sum up their different views from the evidence-based investigation and research, and then listen carefully to the perspectives/views of the opposition to acknowledge that they were hearing correctly about the opposing team's perspectives. The aim of the structured controversy is to find the common ground from the identified differences, thus forming such a win-win situation and/or solution. And the following four questions used for a student debrief will continue to highlight the benefits of the structured controversy.

1. What role did you play in the activity?
2. How do you like or dislike your role?
3. What was the learning for you from the activity?
4. What theoretical lens would you apply to the activity and why?

During the debrief and the feedback from the class, some students felt uncomfortable about their role after they heard the opinions from the opposing team. Later, they said they would like to shift their roles by combining the theoretical lens from both sides to form a new win-win.

Difference to Unstructured Group Discussion

During the pandemic and/or after the pandemic, online teaching and learning will be a new norm to all levels of education and how our students could be learning effectively, making pedagogue transformation imperative. Why? When some of my classes of the MSW program had to move online, most of my classmates, including myself, complained

(*Continues*)

(*Continued*)

that the classroom delivery quality and efficiency were totally dropped. Even though some discussion groups were initiated into the online teaching, still, there was no preparation, either the discussion was just superficial, or the involvement was limited to a few students. Also, the timeline was a big issue: either too long so we were chatting about something else because we had not prepared to discuss the depth with evidence-based research with a higher education standard; or too short for us (most of the time), because there was not a group leader for the discussion group to manage time restrictions while some classmates talked too much or too broad or totally straying from the discussion topic. At first, it was novel for us involving the online discussion, but little by little, the numbers (let alone the quality) of the engagement and the involvement decreased.

But structured controversy was designed in a way that encouraged appropriate contributions among group facilitators and each participant. Within the allotted time limit, team members were coordinated and engaged with seamless, flowing teamwork, and each participant identified and researched the related historical, social, cultural, political or economic factors to their topic in depth and in a well-organized way. And I highly recommended it to all the online teachers in higher education.

Guided Inquiry

A guided IBL approach offers more flexibility than a structured IBL approach, yet still offers some structure. Specifically, carefully crafted scaffolded inquiry activities are used to support students in constructing their own knowledge (Simonson, 2019). Guided IBL, for example, can be utilized to support students in their development of an inquiry question. However, before they can create an inquiry question, students must first choose a topic or theme to explore.

To support students in their decisions about their topic to explore (area of interest), Beth has used this guided approach in higher education courses for several purposes, including (a) students choosing their area of interest by reviewing three related peer-reviewed articles; (b) instructors providing a template in which students can share information with peers about what they discovered in their research (Table 4.4); and (c) instructors facilitating a process of peer and instructor feedback to guide and support students in developing their inquiry question.

This third step can be facilitated using YouTube videos on how to create good inquiry questions (chapter 6); a checklist based on research literature

TABLE 4.4
Area of Interest Form

Full APA Reference	Type of Study	Research Question	Methodology	Theoretical Framework	Summary	Key Findings

Figure 4.2. Refining and assessing your inquiry question.

Things to consider	Yes	No	Suggestions from a colleague	How will you use suggestions?
Does it interest you?				
Is it open to research?				
Do you already know the answer?				
Are there multiple answers?				
Is there a clear focus?				
Is the question reasonable?				
Have you avoided questions with a premise?				
Have all the terms been defined?				
Is there room for new questions once the information is gathered?				
Does having the right answer matter to you?				

Adapted from Roy et al. (2003).

(see Roy et al., 2003; Figure 4.2); and small group activities allowing students to share their areas of interest and research findings with peers, and to both give and receive formative peer feedback. Through a guided/scaffolded process, students gain support in developing their information literacy, a critical component in facilitating HE student learning in IBL (Yesudhas et al., 2014). Importantly, students need to be encouraged to explore their area of interest and take ownership of their learning.

Use of inquiry tools such as the Right Question Institute's QFT (Rothstein & Santana, 2011) and Reading With Purpose (RWP) have also proven effective in providing a guided inquiry experience in our classrooms (see chapter 6 for details). Another excellent resource on guided inquiry is Simonson's (2019) POGIL. Similar to structured inquiry, guided inquiry can be utilized easily during face-to-face classes or in an online format with breakout rooms.

Open Inquiry

The third type of IBL is open inquiry. Open inquiry requires the most independence from students and can be more challenging when a traditional teacher-led approach to teaching and learning has been the historical norm. We have observed a significant amount of anxiety and stress for students when the instructor begins with an open-inquiry process. Students may require more support than is offered through an open-inquiry approach in order to begin to shift their understanding of IBL and ownership of their learning, if for example, they have no experience with IBL. An open-inquiry approach places the student in the driver's seat without the same level of support as a structured or guided approach. Students choose their inquiry question and pursue their inquiry independently throughout the course. In open inquiry, the instructor's role is utilized for consultation purposes. However, the tools used in the guided approach are forgone or used only by choice. An open-inquiry format is easily adapted in an online format or face-to-face. In an online format, instructor and peer consultation can be as a large group, in smaller groups accessing breakout rooms, or in written discussion forums on a classroom management system.

The decision as to which type of IBL approach to take will depend on your purpose and comfort level. Although we can imagine someone new to IBL experiencing a successful open-inquiry course (which is how Stacey's The Curiosity Project started), we recommend starting with a structured or guided approach that can be built on into a future open-inquiry course. We have learned that both students and instructors new to IBL find the new way of learning and the unknown a bit challenging initially. A structured or guided approach to IBL can help to ease both the instructor and the students into a shift in mindset, one that sees students taking greater responsibility for their learning.

Summary

Preparing to implement IBL-HE requires you to make a number of decisions about the level (assignments, assessment tasks, course, program) and type of IBL-HE (structured, guided, open). Knowing yourself and your comfort level with uncertainty and your desire to share power with students in the classroom will all determine how you begin. All decisions you make will include alignment with the IBL-HE principles. No matter your discipline, IBL-HE principles remain consistent. We recommend starting slow, with an activity or assessment task, and tailoring it to your course. Offer structured IBL-HE to begin to ensure your students feel supported with this new pedagogy, and then grow and expand as your confidence and comfort level increase.

Your decision to implement IBL-HE is just the beginning of the many decisions you will make to implement a successful inquiry course for students. Choosing the type of IBL-HE will determine the level of support and guidance offered to students. Although the more structure and guidance that you offer will mean more planning ahead and work for you, your students may find it easier to engage with this pedagogy with your additional support. The more students engage, the more likely they will experience the many benefits offered through the use of IBL-HE.

Questions for Reflection

1. Which assignment in your course might be open to allowing the most student choice? How can you adapt it to allow students more freedom?
2. In what ways might you incorporate peer and instructor formative feedback into that assignment?
3. How will you incorporate student feedback about their experience with IBL-HE into your decision to make further adjustments?
4. Which of these three types of IBL-HE make the most sense for your course?
5. How might you approach explaining the use of IBL with your students?
6. What do you hope to achieve through the implementation of structured, guided, or open inquiry?

5

WHAT ARE MY OPTIONS FOR ASSESSING LEARNING IN IBL-HE?

Stacey L. MacKinnon

What to Expect

- What we know about grading, feedback, and assessment in HE
- Goals of the IBL project and the purpose of the assessment
- Levels and types of assessment

In this chapter we describe why assessment is one of the biggest concerns voiced by both students and instructors who are considering incorporating IBL-HE in their classrooms. We will discuss the impact of numeric/letter-grade assessment on learning, how to get students to read, and how to use formative and summative feedback. We will address the evaluation of both process and outcome and the question of who can and should be involved in the assessment process. Finally, we share several alternative approaches to traditional assessments, including learning portfolios (Scott, 2010); specifications grading (Nilson, 2015); contract grading (Hiller & Hietapelto, 2001); and ungrading (Blum & Kohn, 2020).

One of the first questions we are asked about IBL-HE is inevitably, "How do you assess IBL?" Professors are concerned about workload, giving effective feedback, and student evaluations of teaching, while students worry about getting good grades. In our experience, there are many approaches to assessment in IBL that can address these concerns and make assessment a more positive and effective piece of the learning puzzle.

Most HE institutions require professors to submit letter or number grades at the end of a course. Unfortunately, research by Kohn (2006) suggests that grading has three very predictable effects: (a) decreasing interest in learning, (b) a student preference for easy tasks on which they can achieve high grades, and (c) shallow levels of thinking. Butler (1988) also determined that students who only get grades, or even grades with feedback, see failure or poor performance as a reflection of who they are as people (i.e., "I am a loser"). Regardless of whether they succeeded or failed, students who got lower grades tended to avoid potential failure situations, even at the expense of enhanced learning. Blum and Kohn (2020) observe that students view the feedback that accompanies a numerical or letter grade as simply justification for the mark, not as encouragement or guidance to expand their learning. Taking it one step further, Blum and Kohn (2020) suggest that

> if there is feedback without a grade, then students can see the feedback for its own sake and act on it. . . . When you get rid of grades, revision is no longer a reward, and it's no longer a punishment; it's just what you do in order to improve and learn more. (pp. 96–98)

When students receive formative feedback, they are more engaged in their own learning and view the work, not themselves, as a success or failure. Even when failure happens, they are more likely to view it as something that can be corrected, rather than a fixed assessment of their own abilities. This is very similar to Dweck's (2008) mindset theory, wherein feedback alone promotes a growth mindset, while the introduction of grades promotes a fixed mindset, potentially leading to a sense of learned helplessness, whereby the student comes to believe that because they have been unable to succeed in the past, there is no point in trying anymore (Apple et al., 2018). This research suggests that finding ways to postpone assigning grades as long as possible (given that most of us cannot get rid of them completely), while providing regular rich, learning-focused feedback, should be a key focus in instructors' assessment choices.

It is important to note that, as with IBL more generally, there is no one-size-fits-all approach in assessing learning via IBL. There is nothing wrong with finding the starting point just outside your comfort zone and then moving incrementally toward more open, student-centered forms of assessment. Remember, IBL is a process of inquiry in and of itself; therefore, trying new things, reflecting on their success, and trying again is an important part of the learning process for all of us. We ourselves, the authors, and as teachers and researchers, have moved over time from highly structured assessment using detailed rubrics and driven solely by the professor to a version of "ungrading" (formative assessment) in which peers provide the feedback primarily and students themselves suggest the final grade for the project. The approach you take will depend on your own ability to embrace the discomfort of new learning and your goals for the students and their skill development.

The first question to ask yourself in designing or choosing an assessment approach is "What is the focus of my assessment?" For example, if your focus is strictly on information retention and recall, you can use traditional testing (e.g., multiple choice, short answer, essays) to determine the extent to which your students have learned. Even here, however, there are opportunities to take the focus off the grade by offering opportunities for "second-chance" quizzes. This means that the first quiz is a litmus test the student can use to determine which topics or types of questions they are experiencing as difficult. Many of us have done this in the past with cumulative final exams. Making it so that the original grade is formative and not summative (i.e., the higher mark is retained) can take some of the pressure off students so that they focus on learning rather than performance.

That having been said, you are reading this book because you are interested in IBL, so it is likely that your focus is broader and more complex than simple information storage and retrieval. Due to the inherent emphases on reflection, critical analysis, and growth as a learner in IBL projects, many instructors incorporate high-impact teaching practices such as developing a learning portfolio into their courses (Capaldi, 2015; Kori, 2021; Richards, 2015; Scott, 2010). We prefer the flexibility of Zubrizarreta's (2004) definition of a learning portfolio:

> A flexible, evidence-based tool that engages students in a process of continuous reflection and collaborative analysis of learning. . . . The portfolio captures the scope, richness, and relevance of students' learning. . . . [It] focuses on purposefully and collaboratively selected reflections and evidence for both improvement and assessment of students' learning. (p. 16)

Portfolios have been found to enhance student learning in general (Arter & Spandel, 1992; Burch, 1997; Cambridge, 2001; Campbell et al., 2000; Gordon, 1994; Seldin, 1993, 1997; Wright et al., 1999) and in IBL more specifically (Chaudhuri, 2017; Hanusch, 2020; Hofhues, 2019; Kyza et al., 2002; Smits et al., 2005). These portfolios, whether on paper or electronic, provide a basis for an ongoing formative, as well as an end-of-term summative, assessment of information learning and reflective growth. They can be shared with the professor, teaching assistants, and even the learner's peers, enabling them, over the term, to receive feedback from multiple sources and perspectives. IBL portfolios can contain formal and informal written pieces, visuals, videos, audio files, or any other approach to recording ongoing learning individually or in combination; the only limit is your imagination.

Once you've decided whether you are going to use traditional testing, portfolios, or some combination of both, the next question is, "How are you going to deal with grades?" Letters? Numbers? Regular? Sporadic? End of term? Every piece of work in the portfolio? Selected pieces? The portfolio as a whole? Professor assessment or student self-assessment? Fortunately, there are several different approaches that can help you clarify these decisions for yourself and your students.

Specifications Grading

The first of these is specifications grading (Nilson, 2015; see also Blackstone & Oldmixon, 2019; Carlisle, 2020; Martin, 2019; Quintana & Quintana, 2020). Specifications grading is essentially a pass/fail grading of assignments and assessments that is assessed on a continuum. In essence, with specifications grading, students decide at the beginning of the term what grade they want to achieve in the course and then complete the modules and assignment/ assessment bundles that the instructor has determined correspond to that grade, receiving feedback and revising until they have achieved proficiency at that grade level. The instructor organizes the content of the course into these distinct modules, each with their own associated learning outcomes. Each module, and each bundle of assignments and assessments within that module, correspond to a particular grade. Bundles that require more work, more challenging work, or both, earn students higher grades. For example, in order to get a "C" grade in the class, the student may have to "pass" five quizzes and five written assignments; however, to get a "B," the student may need to "pass" all of those, plus two extra of each. Alternatively, assignment or assessment bundles can be based on the level of learning students require, for example using Bloom's (1956; Krathwohl, 2002) taxonomy. That is, a "C" grade may require achieving mastery at Bloom's taxonomy's level of understanding (i.e., remembering facts), while a "B" grade may necessitate understanding the content at the higher level of application (i.e., remembering and applying factual knowledge). An "A" student would need to achieve all of this (mastery of understanding and application), plus demonstrate an ability to evaluate the material critically.

The benefit to specifications grading is that it's an all-or-nothing approach: A student who shows mastery of the learning level receives full credit (i.e., if you master all the material at the level of understanding and applying factual knowledge specified for a grade of "B" you will receive credit for a grade of "B"); incomplete or unsatisfactory work that does not meet the mastery criteria for the grade level does not receive credit. This means students cannot skip the directions or pass the course based on receiving partial credit for slapdash, last-minute work. By enabling students to choose the bundle they want to complete based on the final grade they want to earn, you are allowing them to factor in their motivation for taking the course (i.e., is it a requirement or elective?); the time they have available to devote to the course (i.e., based on course load and work schedules); grade point "needs" (e.g., to retain scholarships); and their commitment to learning in your class. It also increases the students' motivation to revisit material they did not master and encourages them to think critically about what they did and did not learn at each step. As the instructor, your hard work at the front end of and during the course is rewarded with a much-reduced grading workload at the end of term (Mirsky, 2018). The challenge to this approach is that, just like any rubric, you must describe exactly what features in the work you want and will look for. This may include content, organization, work habits, and levels of cognitive understanding. This can be very time-consuming at the front end of a course, but this investment pays off with the clarity provided to students, supporting their working toward achieving these specifications. But unlike traditional rubrics, there is no need to describe multiple levels of mastery (pass/fail is absolute), or debate whether an assignment merits a "B" or "B-." Students have simply either met the assignment expectations or they have not.

Specifications grading has been shown to be very effective in helping students and instructors focus on meeting course learning goals, particularly in the shift from in-class to online learning during the 2019 COVID pandemic (Quintana & Quintana, 2020; Wasniewski et al., 2021). It has also been shown to increase students' thought processing, willingness to take intellectual risks, and ability to communicate their ideas effectively through writing, even in math courses (Prasad, 2020). It also appears to significantly improve students' writing quality and influence in end-of-course assessments (Mirsky, 2018), their strongly positive opinions of their learning. Specifications grading appears to increase students' self-regulation (e.g., choosing the grade they are willing to work for), mastery learning (i.e., you either master the material at the level specified by the grade chosen and get credit for that grade or you do not), and instructor transparency in that it is clear what is needed for each grade level (Pope et al., 2020). Mastery is not subjective.

Specifications grading can be a good starting point for those entering IBL for the first time, since it involves some of the approaches you are used to using, such as rubrics, and allows you "dip your toe" into mastery approaches to learning as opposed to partial credit approaches. It may also be suitable for courses that are focused more on content mastery, since it can easily include traditional testing as part of the assignment/assessment bundles. However, despite allowing students choice over their investment and subsequent grades, specifications grading is still very instructor driven, the antithesis of true IBL. One step closer to becoming more student focused may be to consider using contract grading.

Contract Grading

Contract grading is a broader version of specifications grading and gives students more control over the learning. As with specifications grading, there is an expectation of mastery over content or skills. However, while specifications grading focuses on basing grades on depth of learning (e.g., showing mastery at higher levels of Bloom's taxonomy leads to higher grades), contract grading is based primarily on the quantity of work the student will complete (e.g., completing more assignments leads to higher grades).

For example, Litterio (2018) shares this example of a possible contract grading structure:

> To contract for a final grade of an A, students will have **no more than three absences**, complete six assignments, participate in all class criteria sessions, and complete all self-reflection exercises due with each final draft.
>
> To contract for a final grade of a B, students will have **no more than four absences** and will complete **five assignments, participate in some in class criteria sessions, and complete half of self-reflection exercises due with each final draft**.
>
> To contract for a final grade of a C, students will have **no more than five absences** and will complete **four assignments, participate in some class criteria sessions, and complete 1–2 self-reflection exercises due with each final draft**. (p. 4, bold in original)

While traditional contract grading still has the instructor in charge of developing the criteria for success (Elbow, 1997; Potts, 2010), newer versions of contract grading encourage having the students as a class involved directly in determining the success or completion criteria for each assignment (Litterio, 2018). Unlike specifications grading, there are no bundles of assignments in contract grading. Instead, students are given the full menu of assignments to choose from to decide which they would like to complete.

Research by Litterio (2018) shows that students value having input into the assignment/assessment process; specifically, they appreciate having a say in generating criteria, establishing clear expectations, and being able to participate in their own learning more autonomously. That being said, there are benefits and challenges to this approach as well (Hiller & Hietapelto, 2001; Lindemann & Harbke, 2011). While contract grading, like specifications grading, eliminates much grading anxiety, since the student knows exactly what grade their completed work will earn them from the beginning of the course and may be able to meet their individual student needs better, all too often the quantity of work becomes the focal criteria for contract grading. It is also very difficult to use contract grading to evaluate the quality of diverse types of projects within a class, resulting in criteria that are often too ambiguous to be useful.

Thinking back to the goals of IBL in HE and the negative impact of grades/marks on meaningful student learning, many of us have chosen an even more student-focused approach to assessment: *ungrading* (Blum & Kohn, 2020; Guberman, 2021; Newton et al., 2020). Contrary to how this sounds, there can still be a numerical or letter grade assigned at the end of term; however, that grade/mark is based primarily on a student's own self-assessment of their portfolio of work, a self-awareness skill that is essential to develop in the work world and in life more generally. This portfolio could include more than just content-based written contributions, for example a self-assessment of their participation in group or class discussions, the quality of feedback they have given others to enhance others' and their own learning, evidence of how they incorporated feedback they received on their work, evidence of "big-picture" understanding of the course content, their ability to think critically and creatively about the material, and so on.

Again, students are receiving meaningful feedback all term (see chapter 9), often with a midterm reflective self-assessment exercise to guide them toward maximal learning of both content and skills. The end-of-term self-assessment then requires them to reflect on the entire term, noting evidence, through examples in their portfolio, of their growth and development. At the end of this detailed self-assessment, the student then proposes the grade they believe they have earned based on the evidence available. The instructor then reviews the assessment (in conversation with the student if possible; in written format if not), and the evidence determines if the grade is an accurate reflection of the learning demonstrated. If it is, the mark is maintained. If it is not, the instructor has the flexibility to adjust it, providing the student with a rationale for doing so. Stommel (2020) suggests that most students' self-assessments of their work are accurate, with the small exception being those who (primarily women) "offer no good reason other than modesty for giving themselves the A- rather than an A" (pp. 35–36).

As an approach, ungrading is highly reflective of the goals of IBL in HE, including information retention and understanding, and application, critique, creativity, reflection, and metacognition (FP 4). This approach focuses on the quality, as opposed to quantity, of work; encourages honest assessment and accountability through the use of the portfolio as evidence; and allows students the freedom to grow and develop over the course of a term. Ungrading in particular offers the flexibility of being used for a single assignment, larger project, full course, or even an entire program.

Summary

How you choose to assess your students' learning in an IBL-HE classroom is entirely up to you, based on your goals for student learning and your willingness to embrace the discomfort of new learning. If you are just starting out with IBL-HE, challenge yourself to move a step outside your comfort zone, and include your students in the assessment discussion. If you have some experience or are feeling adventurous, go ahead and try moving further toward ungrading. The key to finding success in IBL-HE assessment is to treat the IBL assignment or course as your own curiosity project—trying things out, figuring out what works and what doesn't, and always reflecting on the "why" to refine the "how." In this way, you can also model for your students how to recover when things don't work out, and the importance of critical reflection. If you trust them and create an environment focused on learning rather than grades, meaningful learning will happen for both you and your students!

Questions for Reflection

1. Take a moment to consider your current assessment practices. How do they reflect the goals and outcomes of IBL? How could they be adjusted to be more encompassing of procedure as well as product?
2. When you look at some of these possibilities for alternative assessments, what is the next logical step to branch out from your current assessments?
3. How could you include meaningful peer feedback to enhance interdependent learning and ease your own workload?

PART THREE

HOW DO I GET MY STUDENTS STARTED WITH IBL-HE?

A t this point, you are already thinking about the four key decisions you need to make to kickstart IBL-HE in your own classroom. You are already deciding on

- whether to start from scratch or adapt something you already have
- how much IBL-HE to use (assignment, major project, full course)
- what kind of IBL-HE you want to offer your students (structured, guided, or open)
- your assessment options

The next questions are often "How do I get my students started with IBL-HE? What am I going to get them to do? How can I help them learn and practice the skills they need for effective inquiry?" In this section of the book, we will discuss the four key skills students (and instructors) need to develop for successful inquiry:

- owning their own learning and asking good questions (chapter 6)
- choosing and evaluating research methods/approaches (chapter 7)
- reflecting on content and process (chapter 8)
- giving and receiving feedback (chapter 9)

Let's start with the primary goal of inquiry: asking questions!

6

HOW DO I ENCOURAGE MY STUDENTS TO ASK GOOD QUESTIONS?

Stacey L. MacKinnon and Beth Archer-Kuhn

What to Expect

- Students' experiences with asking questions
- The Question Formulation Technique (QFT)
- Reading with Purpose (RWP)
- Guided inquiry to develop good inquiry questions

We all have waited with eager anticipation after asking "Do you have any questions?" and received only stony silence in return. Because of this, getting students to engage and ask questions is a key concern of faculty who are getting started in IBL-HE. In this chapter we discuss several approaches you can use to get students started and help them learn to refine, expand, and prioritize their questions. In particular, we will focus on the use of three techniques, which are not domain specific, that can be used in the IBL-HE classroom: the Question Formulation Technique (QFT; Rothstein & Santana, 2011), the Reading With Purpose approach (RWP; Stacey), and guided inquiry to develop good inquiry questions (Beth). We will also touch on the importance of creating a "question-friendly" environment in your classroom.

Why Is It Important to Learn to Ask Good Questions?

In 2016, the World Economic Forum (WEF) asked employers to indicate the top 10 skills they believed would be needed by 2020. According to the WEF's "Future of Jobs" report (Gleason, 2018), by order of priority, these skills included complex problem-solving, critical thinking, creativity, people management, coordinating with others, emotional intelligence, judgment and decision-making, service orientation, negotiation, and cognitive flexibility. In 2020, the European Commission (EC) hosted a blog post indicating the 10 most useful competencies for learning in the 21st century.

QR Code 6.1. 10 most useful competencies for learning in the 21st century.

(https://eur-lex.europa.eu/legal-content/EN/TXT/PDF/?
uri=CELEX:52018SC0014&from=EN)

The WEF and the EC, along with the National Association of Colleges and Employers (NACE), all agreed on five key areas: solving complex problems, critical thinking, coordinating with others, leadership, and communication. The ability and willingness to ask questions underpins each of these competencies and more. But our students often aren't asking questions—why and what can we do about it?

Students' Experiences With Asking Questions

No matter how effective we are as teachers or how well written the textbook is, it isn't possible that every student in our classes understood everything they read, heard, or saw, but yet they most often will not, or cannot, ask questions. As we have discussed in other chapters, many higher education students have lost the desire for or willingness to engage in inquiry because our traditional education programs use the banking method defined by Freire to instill knowledge and remove the need for students to question, thereby weakening their questioning skills. In addition, they are afraid to look "stupid," ask a "dumb question," or be the "only one" who doesn't understand despite research on pluralistic ignorance (Miller & McFarland, 1991), which suggests that in these situations often many others in the room are also unclear but afraid to acknowledge this out loud. In IBL-HE we want to shift the mindset from students at best asking questions about information that is already located in the syllabus (assignment due dates, number of pages required) to students asking questions about content and process, about topics of interest to them, things they feel passion for and want to learn more about.

In addition, thanks to the advent of the internet, our students need the skills to be able to sort through the quagmire of information available at their fingertips, to question it, to deconstruct it to determine its veracity and usefulness, to put it together in new ways. Sadly, employers indicate that the ability to ask questions, gather information, and solve problems are three of the key characteristics they are looking for in future employees, but which recent graduates are lacking (Coplin, 2012; Rancourt & Archer-Kuhn, 2019).

QR Code 6.2. National Association of Colleges and Employers.

(www.naceweb.org)

If society's success depends on well-thought-out innovation, creativity, problem-solving, and lifelong and life-wide learning in everyone from ditch diggers to research scientists (Berger, 2014), then we have to create an environment in which students can learn to question, explore possible answers, see the big picture, and try things without constantly being afraid of being "wrong" (Adams, 2016). To do that, students need to feel invested in their learning, believe they have the support to learn the appropriate skills, and come to understand that persistence and resilience in learning are essential life skills. That is where IBL-HE comes in!

But how do we overcome students' reticence about asking questions and strengthen their inquiry skills? The good news is that with a few simple tools, our students can be asking thought-provoking, critical questions that can expand their own learning and that of their classmates. Let's begin with the QFT.

Question Formulation Technique

The QFT was originally developed by Rothstein and Santana (2011) to help parents in a dropout prevention program who were not participating in their children's education because they didn't know what questions to ask the teachers. Using a social justice framework (more on that in chapter 15) based on the principles of micro democracy, the QFT is now being used by 300,000 educators around the world, from first graders learning about biomes to doctoral students learning how to ask better, more transformative research questions (Rothstein & Santana, 2011). Their impressive selection of resources are available for free download.

QR Code 6.3. Resources from The Right Question Institute.

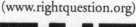

(www.rightquestion.org)

The QFT process is surprisingly simple and can be done individually or in small groups. Once you have a question focus (usually just the topic you are interested in exploring), you begin to produce your questions according to four simple rules:

1. Ask as many questions as you can.
2. Do not stop to discuss, judge, or answer any of your questions.
3. Record each question exactly as stated.
4. Change any statements into questions.

In small groups, you want to ensure that each person takes a turn suggesting a question, so it can be helpful to give everyone in the group their own writing utensil (or typeface color if you are using a collaborative document online) and have them write and share their questions orally, in turn. Stacey's undergraduate students really enjoy working with colorful markers and easel paper taped to the wall (they call it "going back to kindergarten," which ironically is a time when we engaged in inquiry more freely!). This process allows everyone in the group the opportunity to contribute and avoids having louder voices drown out those that are quieter or more reserved (FP 3).

Once students have created an extensive list of questions, their next job is to categorize those questions as being either closed (answerable with a single word) or open (requiring a longer explanation). Students are then encouraged to change questions from one type to the other to uncover hidden assumptions and expand their inquiry.

The next step is to prioritize the questions based on the goal, understand their own rationale for those choices, and create an action plan for investigating the answers (which is the focus of chapter 7). The final step is to reflect (a common theme in this book!), not only on the content of the questions but on the process of questioning itself. Consider whether there may be other perspectives that could result in different questions, how the prioritization of questions might change if the goal of the exercise was to create a "how-to" manual for the general public versus writing an academic research paper, think about who participated most/least, and how the group could encourage people to make space for others.

Remember, not all questions created during the initial QFT need to be addressed, and others may certainly emerge over time, but going through this simple process will jump-start any inquiry project, even those about which little is known of the topic. In addition, the QFT can be used several times during the course of an inquiry project to direct, deepen, and broaden students' thinking. Don't be surprised if your students are initially uncomfortable or looking to you to see if their questions are "right." Many of them have been taught that the evaluation of others is what matters, and it takes time and practice to let go of that idea and trust your own judgment.

Reading With Purpose

Building off the principles of the QRT, Stacey has developed a process she calls RWP to assist students in getting the most out of their reading using inquiry. Again, this is a simple set of steps that can help students read material more deeply, critically analyze what they are reading, and see directions where the research should go next.

The first step in IBR involves the student writing out questions that come to mind as they are reading rather than waiting until they have finished the selection. As they read, previous questions they posed may (and likely will) be answered, so they can check them off on their list. At the end of their reading, they have a list of unanswered questions they can categorize and prioritize for a variety of purposes:

- clarification questions they should approach the instructor with in class or office hours
- critique questions or observations about assumptions that can be used for a debate, thought paper, or a position paper
- possibilities or "what-if" questions that can spur research projects

And of course all of these questions can be brought to class and used as fodder for in-class discussions! An interesting addition to RWP can involve having students compare their lists, looking for perspective differences, assumptions, and other issues that can impact what questions are asked.

Stacey and Beth have used this RWP approach very successfully in both third- and fourth-year undergraduate courses, where students use their IBR to come up with a question to write about in a weekly thought paper and bring their list to class for small group discussion. It has been so successful, in fact, that Stacey's class actually asked to be allowed to do their 75-minute in-class small group discussions on a day when she was unable to attend because they felt prepared to do it on their own! She is continuing to research RWP's effectiveness with undergraduate students, particularly when having to read online, so stay tuned for an update.

Both of these approaches (QFT and RWP) require little in the way of planning or supervision by the instructor and can be used by individuals or groups. If you prefer a bit more structured, hands-on approach, however, Beth's structured controversy activity may resonate with you.

Using Guided Inquiry to Develop Good Inquiry Questions

Beth wanted to shift the mindset from students asking questions about information that is already located in the syllabus (assignment due dates, number of pages required) to students asking questions about a topic of interest to them, something they feel passion for and want to learn more about (FP 1). She structures each class to use about half the time to cover substantive course content and the other half for activities to support students in their inquiry. Here are some strategies that Beth has found helpful for students in developing their inquiry questions.

Beth focuses on encouraging students to get more comfortable being curious about a subject or topic that is of interest to them and is also related to the course. In each of her courses, whether a GSP, block-week, 6-week, or full-semester course, students practice asking questions (FP 1) and learning about what constitutes "good" inquiry questions. Also, as a homework activity and before class begins, students choose an area of interest and explore it in the literature (FP 2). Using a guided-inquiry approach, students learn to explore their inquiry question (FP 3).

When developing inquiry questions, Beth tends to use resources on YouTube because they are visual and usually brief and present specific steps to the inquiry process that allow students to understand the process in stages. First, she wants students to begin asking questions—really just getting comfortable being curious about a subject or topic that is of interest to them and also related to the course. Two processes happen at about the same time. In class, students practice asking questions and learning about what constitutes "good" inquiry questions. Following is a description of learning how to ask inquiry questions and then the homework assignment.

Learning How to Ask Questions

Using a guided-inquiry approach, students learn to explore their inquiry question. Beth begins with a discussion during which students can only ask questions (FP 1).

QR Code 6.4. VIDEO: Good Inquiry Questions.

(https://www.youtube.com/watch?v=p0-D0VID7D0)

Next, staying together as a large group, they look at a visual borrowed from the internet. In keeping with the structured controversy activity, she locates an image of what might appear to represent, for example, homelessness. Students ask questions about what interests them or what they are curious about from the image. This brainstorming session usually results in questions, going from simple to complex as students learn from each other. Here is another resource that can be used as a quick reminder of the process.

QR Code 6.5. VIDEO: Steps of Inquiry-Based Learning.

(https://www.youtube.com/watch?v=SLjVOlnUoXU)

The next step is to discuss different types of questions. What makes a good inquiry question? This brief video demonstrates level 1, 2, and 3 questions.

QR Code 6.6. VIDEO: "Instant Inquiry. Level 1, 2, 3 Questions."

(https://www.youtube.com/watch?v=7j6BM002ksk)

Students quickly begin to see, while searching for answers to their question, that the inquiry process is complex and requires a question that will involve complexity (FP 3). For example, students see that using Google is not going to be a sufficient means of answering their inquiry question. They may start at level 1 questions (name, define, list) and move to level 3 questions (evaluate, judge, predict, forecast, claim) that require students to think critically, use multiple resources, and draw their own conclusions. This video also provides examples of the three levels of questions so that the students can understand what is expected of them when creating an inquiry question.

Exploring an Area of Interest (Homework Assignment)

Prior to the class on learning to ask good inquiry questions, students are given a homework assignment wherein they are to research three peer-reviewed journal articles related to their area of interest (FP 2), summarize each article, and come to class prepared to share with their small group of peers what they learned about each article. They bring to class with them a completed "Area of Interest" form highlighting each article (Table 4.4).

This simple activity immediately begins to develop information technology skills. Students then use the information they discover in their articles to draft an initial inquiry question. Beth has developed a checklist (FP 7) to support students in their assessment of their own inquiry question prior to their sharing it with colleagues (Figure 4.2).

This activity not only supports students in their inquiry question development, but it also presents them with an opportunity to begin to analyze and describe the information they have found (FP 2). At this stage, students are using critical questioning and anticipating findings (FP 6). Their approach to research is tailored to their central-question selection. Critical questions are directed toward the evaluation of evidence. Anticipated findings focus on evidence, and students can begin to analyze critically the anticipated and unanticipated findings (FP 6).

Now that they have found three articles related to their topic and have a better understanding of the type of questions that are required for inquiry questions (video, checklist), they are provided time in class to create their own inquiry question. Then they have a chance to try it out with their small group of peers (FP 7). Students take turns sharing what they found about their topic (Area of Interest form) and what they have drafted as their inquiry question. Students also make their completed Area of Interest form available for peers to review while they are discussing it (hard copy if in-person learning or electronic if online learning). When they are finished sharing what they learned and posing their draft inquiry question, their peers provide feedback (FP 7). They use the inquiry question assessment checklist (Figure 4.2) to provide written feedback, and they discuss possible ways in which the student might improve their inquiry question. Once all group members have had a chance to share and receive feedback, Beth will have a large group discussion about the experience of giving and receiving feedback. It is an opportunity for peers to learn how their feedback was helpful to group members' learning (FP 4, FP 7). This is important, since there will be many more opportunities for peer feedback throughout the inquiry process.

As a final step, students submit a one-page document outlining their inquiry question and a summary of their inquiry journey process for assessment by the instructor. Here, I provide both summative and formative feedback, and the assignment is used as one of the assessment tasks in the course (FP 6, FP 7).

Beth and Stacey agree that addressing what makes "good" questions should not be taken lightly. You can't practice what you don't know, and given that so many of our students come from learning environments relatively devoid of questioning, we cannot make assumptions about their inquiry skills level. Even graduate students who have not had previous IBL-HE experience can find it challenging to learn to ask good inquiry questions, as you can see in this student quote:

"The first task was to identify a research question; I thought I knew how to pose a good research question—this process took an entire day!" (Natalie, third-year PhD student).

Summary

These are by no means the only ways to get students working on their questioning skills, but they are three very straightforward ways to achieve that goal. Aside from these approaches to asking questions, it is important to remember that the environment in which the questioning is happening is extremely important. Many of our students have had their questions ignored, ridiculed, or shut down by peers, parents, and teachers, leaving them uncomfortable putting their ideas out into the arena. Others come from backgrounds where asking questions was not only discouraged ("children should be seen and not heard") but was actually dangerous. We, as instructors, have to meet our students where they are and help them build their confidence as much as their skills in asking questions. This is where the collaborative nature of IBL-HE can play an enormous role in moving students forward as learners. This is why a focus on process and growth is essential for IBL-HE to succeed. In chapter 10, we will discuss one more of the key components to a successful IBL-HE classroom, namely trust.

Questions for Reflection

1. What is your history with students asking questions in your classroom? What do you do to open them up to asking questions? What have you done that might have inhibited questioning?
2. Think about how you ask questions in your own learning. What approaches do you use to figure out what questions there are to ask? Could these be refined and shared with your students?

3. What is the inquiry skill level of your students generally? What areas do they need to strengthen in order to be able to be effective inquirers? How can you help them reach that goal?

4. Which students in your classes tend to be least likely to ask questions? Why might that be? How could you make space for them to be able to participate more often?

7

HOW DO MY STUDENTS AND I CHOOSE RESEARCH METHODS IN IBL-HE?

Beth Archer-Kuhn

What to Expect

- Pursuing inquiry questions
- Deciding which sources to use
- Challenges and benefits of moving beyond peer-reviewed journal articles
- Collecting data in IBL-HE projects

Due to its focus on critical analysis and reflection, IBL-HE offers an excellent opportunity to not only refine students' ability to engage with scholarly material but also to explore beyond the traditional academic sources. In this chapter we discuss how to decide what resources you are interested in introducing to your learners, how to encourage critical reflection on sources, and the challenges and benefits of moving beyond peer-reviewed journal articles. The decision of whether to include active collection and analysis of data for their IBL-HE projects is one to consider as well. It is a wonderful addition to any learning experience, but it requires an additional layer of planning on the part of the instructor. We will discuss the issues to consider and ways in which we have been successful in including data collection in IBL-HE.

As we discussed in chapters 1 and 2, the instructor's role in IBL-HE is different from that of a traditional classroom. With IBL-HE, your role is one of facilitator, allowing students to become more responsible for and take ownership of their own learning (Love et al., 2015; Yang, 2015). This extends not only to the questions students ask but also to the methods and resources they choose to try and answer their questions.

Pursuing Inquiry Questions

Once students have an initial inquiry question, how they access information that may help to answer that question or may lead to further questions can take a number of forms. You may have designed the course so that students have guests coming into the class or students are going into the community to learn from "experts" in the field. You might be on a group study program where you are moving from various countries and community organizations that provide students a wealth of information to support their inquiry question. You can also remain in your classroom. All of these and more are possibilities. It's up to you to design what you want your students to have access to.

Deciding Which Sources to Use

At a minimum, students can have access to you as the instructor, a host of peers in their course, resources through your university library, and the World Wide Web through internet searches. Your role is to assist students in pursuing the area of interest they defined through their inquiry question. Two of the most common questions IBL-HE instructors hear from students are "How many resources do we need to have?" and "What kinds of resources can I use?" In IBL-HE, these are questions that students will need to address for themselves, critically evaluating each choice and understanding the limits each poses on their understanding. This is not a small task, and to a generation raised on algorithmic searches it can be a significant learning curve.

The easiest place to start, of course, is by accessing resources on campus, such as a campus librarian who can help students appreciate the many knowledge keepers who can assist them on their inquiry journey. For example, the librarian can model for students some key strategies to widen, narrow, or strengthen their searches. The librarian can illustrate the various search engines, key terms, peer-reviewed articles, texts, and government documents that can support a student in finding critical information to inform their inquiry question. Inviting the librarian into your classroom or scheduling an appointment with the library during class time are two ways that you can introduce the students to the librarian for a tutorial about researching sources. Once you have done this, here is one way that Beth supports students using a guided inquiry approach.

Exploring an Area of Interest (Homework Assignment)

Prior to a class on learning to ask good inquiry questions (see chapter 6), students research three peer-reviewed journal articles related to their area of interest, summarize each article, and come to class prepared to share with their small group of peers what they learned about each article. They also bring to class with them a completed Area of Interest form highlighting each article (Table 4.4).

This simple activity immediately begins to develop information technology skills. Students then use the information that they have discovered in their articles to draft an initial inquiry question. Beth has developed a checklist to support students in their assessment of their own inquiry question prior to their sharing it with their peers (Figure 4.2).

This activity supports students in their question development, and gives them an opportunity to start analyzing and describing the information they have found. At this stage, students are using critical questioning and anticipating findings. Critical questions are directed toward the evaluation of evidence. Anticipated findings focus on evidence, and students can begin to analyze critically the anticipated and unanticipated findings.

Once they find three articles related to their topic and have a better understanding of the type of questions that are required for inquiry questions (video, checklist), Beth gives them time in class to create their own inquiry question. Then they have a chance to try it out with their small group of peers. Students take turns sharing what they found about their topic (Area of Interest form) and what they have drafted as their inquiry question. Students also make their completed Area of Interest form available for peers to review while they are discussing it (hard copy if in-person learning or electronic if online learning).

When students are finished sharing what they learned and posing their draft inquiry question, their peers provide feedback. They use the inquiry question checklist (Figure 4.2) to provide written feedback, and they discuss possible ways in which the student might improve their inquiry question. Once all group members have had a chance to share and receive feedback, Beth usually has a large group discussion about the experience of giving and receiving feedback. It is an opportunity for peers to learn how their feedback was helpful to group members' learning. This is important, since there will be many more opportunities for peer feedback throughout the inquiry process.

As a final step, students submit a one-page document outlining their inquiry question and a summary of their inquiry journey process for assessment by the instructor. Here Beth provides both summative and formative feedback, and the assignment is used as one of the assessment tasks in the course.

Gathering Data to Explore Inquiry Questions

During the remainder of the course students focus on finding answers to their inquiry question. As a homework assignment, they are to find another set of three peer-reviewed journal articles, quantitative studies that can provide information toward their inquiry question. Students use the same table template (Area of Interest) as in their prior step (developing an inquiry question) to provide a summary of each article. This information is shared with members of their small group. As before, each group member verbally shares what they have learned from the articles and how this new information has informed their inquiry question. At this stage, it is not uncommon for students to adjust their inquiry question based on what they have learned from peers, the instructor, and from the literature.

By now students are beginning to take ownership of their learning and are gaining confidence. To further these developments and to provide a broader scope for peer feedback, students convey their findings in a 10-minute presentation to the full class. As a large audience, students provide verbal and written feedback for their peers. The entire process is repeated for a third time a couple of weeks later, when the homework assignment is to find three peer-reviewed journal articles on qualitative studies that can provide information toward their inquiry questions. Students learn that they discover varied knowledge from the different types of research designs. Sometimes a few students tweak their inquiry questions at this stage.

Students may not have developed an understanding of the quality of a research report at this point. One resource that Beth has developed to support students when assessing the quality of the study reported in the peer-review article is a checklist—one for qualitative studies and one for quantitative studies. The checklist doesn't determine the quality as much as highlight for the student what they should be looking for within the article and what is missing. In this way, they can begin to critically assess the research literature when determining the value of the article in relation to their topic. The checklist in Figure 7.1 is used when researching quantitative articles.

Importantly, students gain an understanding of the differences between quantitative and qualitative research and studies. The checklist in Figure 7.2 is one that Beth uses to support students in their assessment of qualitative articles.

Figure 7.1. Quantitative article quality assessment checklist.

Section of Article and Criteria	Yes	No
Introduction		
Is the rationale for conducting this study stated?		
Is the purpose of the study stated?		
Is there a comprehensive and balanced review of the literature?		
Method		
Are the techniques used in the sample selection process specified?		
Is the time frame for sampling stated?		
If there are other unique features of the sample, are they mentioned?		
Is the type of study design specified?		
Is the time frame to complete the study mentioned?		
Do you specify where and how data were collected?		
Did you mention the ethical considerations of data collection, including whether REB approval was obtained or why it was not necessary?		
Are all outcome measures used in the study specified and referenced as appropriate?		
Do you comment on the reliability and/or validity of the outcome measures?		
Is the intervention described in sufficient detail to permit replication, or are citations provided to primary sources fully describing the intervention?		
Results		
Are all statistics used to analyze the data mentioned?		
Do all inferential tests include levels of significance and/or effect sizes or proportion of variance accounted for (if appropriate)?		
Are the results discussed within the context of the study's purpose?		
Do you use literature to discuss the results?		
If applications to theory are described, are they genuinely relevant and appropriate?		
Are the study's limitations mentioned appropriately?		
Is the discussion appropriately targeted to stakeholder groups?		
Do you clearly tie the discussion to the applications to practice?		

Figure 7.2. Qualitative article quality assessment checklist.

Section of Article and Criteria	Yes	No
Introduction		
Is the rationale for conducting this study stated?		
Is the purpose of the study stated?		
Is there a comprehensive and balanced review of the literature?		
Method		
Are the techniques used in the sample selection process specified?		
Is the time frame for sampling stated?		
If there are other unique features of the sample, are they mentioned?		
Is the type of study design specified?		
Is the time frame to complete the study mentioned?		
Do you specify where and how data were collected?		
Did you mention the ethical considerations of data collection, including whether REB approval was obtained or why it was not necessary?		
Does the researcher situate themselves in the study?		
Are the research methods described in sufficient detail for the reader to understand how the project proceeded?		
Results		
Does the analysis fit the methodology?		
Is triangulation of data used to understand the findings?		
Are the findings discussed within the context of the study's purpose?		
Do you use literature to discuss the findings?		
If applications to theory are described, are they genuinely relevant and appropriate?		
Are the study's limitations mentioned appropriately?		
Is the discussion appropriately targeted to stakeholder groups?		
Do you clearly link the discussion to the applications to practice?		

Challenges and Benefits of Moving Beyond Peer-Reviewed Journal Articles

Variability in sources helps students to better understand what is understood and taken for granted as knowledge and who can be a knowledge keeper. Whenever possible, consider opening your students up to using (and critically reflecting on) documentaries, TED talks, websites, interviews, newspapers, blogs, and other forms of media outside the realm. These are sources they will face in their everyday lives, and now is a wonderful time to practice determining what is reliable and what is less so. In addition, moving outside the peer-review realm can show alternative perspectives not reflected by academic work, which can be unpacked and considered. Making contacts within the community can also provide valuable insight and support in learning for students. Dare greatly when making these contacts; one of Stacey's students contacted a *New York Times* best-selling author via email, which ended up with the two engaging in an enlightening hour-long conversation by telephone! For support in critically evaluating nonacademic resources, check out the Global Critical Citizen Foundation's "The Ultimate Cheat Sheet for Critical Thinking" (see Appendix E).

If you are considering engaging in a GSP (see Appendix D) or a course provided in the community as Beth has done, the course content may be delivered by various people at the host universities and local communities. In the case of social work, for example, community-based trauma models; child welfare, mental health, or disabilities practices; or a reflective practice framework may be covered by international academics or their community-based practice partners. In the case of a community course, local community partners may deliver important content specific to that region. IBL provides the flexibility to incorporate course content based on the delivery model and allows for a variety of sources to be assessed by students and critically reflected on as a potential viable source for their inquiry.

Collecting Data in IBL-HE Projects

We love it when students can design surveys/interviews/experiments and collect data during their IBL-HE projects! However, this is one place where the discipline you are working in may impact the decisions you can make on data collection. The greatest challenges seem to occur in collecting data from human and/or animal participants. Whether to collect data during IBL-HE projects depends in large part on the ethics guidelines and timelines at your institution. At most universities, students wishing to conduct research surveys, interviews, or experiments with live participants for a course are required to apply to a departmental ethics review committee, if not to the university-level research ethics board. In a single semester course where ideas are being generated by students during the course of their reading exploration, there simply may not be time to go through the ethics approval process, thereby making it impossible for the student to collect the data. If there is some sort of expedited process in place for class projects, then the experience of collecting data can be invaluable and very validating, particularly for undergraduate students. Just make sure you check the regulations at your institution before committing to a data-collection project.

Summary

So many sources are available to support students in their inquiry process. Providing some structure and guidance may be helpful for your students to know which sources to use. Regardless of what type of research methodology your students use for data collection, what matters most is their ability to engage in critical analysis of not only the material itself but the reliability and validity of the source. Much can be learned from nonacademic resources such as documentaries, websites, blogs, and videos; however, just as we encourage critical analysis of academic research, so too do we have to remind our students how to use nonacademic sources judiciously. In addition, while collecting raw data is a wonderful way to expose students to the process of research, it is not always feasible from an ethics or time perspective to do so. When it is, enjoy it, but when it is not, discuss with your students how they would go about doing so and what they think they might find. You never know when an IBL-HE project will blossom into an honors thesis, signature work, or graduate project.

Questions for Reflection

1. What do your students already know about how to analyze or critique sources? How can you help them fill in the gaps?
2. Who do you know that might be able to offer an informed discussion to support student inquiry?
3. What human resources at your institution might support student knowledge of inquiry? For example, does your faculty have a designated librarian?

8

I KNOW REFLECTION IS IMPORTANT, BUT WHAT DO I ASK STUDENTS TO REFLECT ON?

Beth Archer-Kuhn and Stacey L. MacKinnon

What to Expect

- How we understand reflection
- Critical reflection and IBL-HE
- Activities to encourage reflection

Reflection and *critical reflection* (CR) are watchwords for 21st-century learning, but what do we mean when we talk about reflection? Why does reflection matter, and how do we incorporate it in all disciplines? How does reflection link to our learning goals and assessment plans for our students? What kinds of reflection have the most impact on student development? This chapter discusses the key considerations for introducing meaningful CR in your IBL-HE classroom and how to inspire students to engage in it on a regular basis.

Through historical educational scholars we have come to understand that we do not necessarily learn from experience but rather from reflecting on experience (FP 6; Dewey, 1916/1980) and that reflection in action helps us to incorporate new understandings as we reflect on our behavior and experience in the moment (Schön, 1983). Regardless of conceptual understandings, some researchers maintain ongoing theoretical inconsistency (Fook et al., 2016a; Moon, 1999; Thompson & Pascal, 2012), leaving the literature portraying various understandings.

IBL-HE requires more than simply reflecting on experience and behavior. It behooves students and instructors to critically reflect on all aspects of the inquiry journey from the creation of an inquiry question (How and why did they decide to pursue that inquiry? What resources supported their decision? How credible are the resources? How did life experience and cultural and societal influences inform their decision?) through to dissemination of their findings (Who is my audience? What is the most effective way of ensuring their attention to what I have to share?).

CR is understood by some as having a focus on social change and power structures; for example, Brookfield (2016) discusses CR as a revealing or uncovering of power and hegemony. Fook et al. (2016b) support Brookfield's notion of CR and also advance the discussion that CR can lead to change and meaning making. In many ways, IBL holds true to both of these definitions in so much as students learn to uncover power structures, including gaining power while they lead their own learning process, and at the same time, students in all disciplines begin to make meaning of what they have learned, what they understand as knowledge, and how they come to appreciate knowledge creation.

Both of us (Beth and Stacey) support the notion that IBL-HE has transformational learning properties (Mezirow, 1990; see chapter 17) and that through the use of skills such as CR students' understanding of self and their beliefs shift and change. Although CR can be used across disciplines, outside of Schön (1983), the literature about CR in STEM (science, technology, engineering, and mathematics) has received little attention (see Otfinowski & Silva-Opps, 2015 for an exception). Additionally, Fook, Psoinos, and Sartori (2016) explored the use of reflection in higher education and found little research across disciplines that is focused on how instructors can help students apply CR in their courses. Further, students' perspectives on reflection have been ignored with the exception of a recent study by Arend et al. (2021) who explored students' understandings of CR across varied disciplines. Their findings reveal tensions around how to explain CR given the varied understandings, methods of use, and meanings across disciplines, yet both instructors and students in the study said they value the process of learning that comes through CR.

When you choose to utilize IBL-HE as pedagogy, you are inviting a focus on students' experience of their learning or metacognition (FP4 and FP6). Although some studies have encouraged CR through teaching practices (Kaplan et al., 2013), it has not been the student experience of learning that has been the focus, but rather the teaching practice (Fook et al., 2016a). IBL-HE revolves around the student experience, and students learning to use their voice to share their learning experiences. This chapter discusses the key considerations for introducing meaningful CR in your IBL-HE classroom and how to inspire students to engage in it on a regular basis.

CR and IBL-HE

CR is a key response to becoming aware that we are experiencing conflicting thoughts, feelings and actions. Questioning the integrity of our assumptions and beliefs based on prior experience is a powerful engine for transformational learning at both the personal and societal levels (Mezirow, 2000). Taylor (2009) points out that in addition to immediate personal experience, course content targeted to exploring held values can both instigate and facilitate change. For example, in his Curiosity Project, a student of Stacey's who had been a competitive figure skater and coach explored for his IBL-HE project the topic "how not to be a lousy sports parent" (a value-laden concept for certain). Through CR on his own experiences as a skater, coach, and judge, and on the competitive figure skating environment more broadly, he not only changed his own views toward his role as a coach to his young skaters, but also developed a handbook for parents on how to avoid falling into the trap of becoming a negative influence in their child's sports life.

While personal experience alone can be enough to spark CR, you as the instructor can also "trigger" reflection by providing intense experiential activities in your classroom. Beth does a wonderful job of this in her social work courses, particularly those in which she takes her students out into the community to be immersed in the issues (Archer-Kuhn, Lee, Finnessey & Liu, 2020; Archer-Kuhn, Wiedeman, & Chalifoux, 2020). This transformation is personified by a student from an immersive group experience in Ireland:

> We visited Queens University Belfast where they were holding a conference on intergenerational trauma and the risk, resilience, and impact on children, families, and communities due to The Troubles in Northern Ireland that lasted from approximately 1968–1998. We later heard from service users from the WAVE Trauma Center . . . about their experiences of trauma during The Troubles and the impact on their lives, as well as the impact on the lives of other intergenerational family members. These were just a glimpse into the stops made on this Group Study Program that contributed to my learning; the discussions with locals, other service providers, service users, students, and others all had a part to play as well in my inquiry-based learning journey. (Archer-Kuhn, Wiedeman, & Chalifoux, 2020, p. 112)

Whenever possible, CR should include a written format, which will strengthen the process by requiring learners to be explicit in their understandings, observations, and linkages. It also provides a record or artifact of the learner's thoughts at a moment in time, which the student can return to at a later date for further reflection and consideration. Students can write weekly learning logs or thought papers (MacKinnon, 2017), reflective journals (Otfinowski & Silva-Opps, 2015), or create online blog posts (Boyer et al., 2006; Ziegler et al., 2006). Making these writings and discussions available to others (e.g., peers, teaching assistants, instructors) moves the learner one step closer to the third core element of transformative learning: dialogue.

It is important to remember that transformation does not occur in a vacuum. CR is at its most powerful when it is used to engage in meaningful dialogue, and IBL-HE offers many opportunities for in-depth discussion between peers and with the instructor. This could involve written feedback on each other's reflections, face-to-face discussions, or small and large group interactions. For example, throughout the development of an inquiry question, Beth structures class time to include small group sharing of each students' learning progress, oral and written peer feedback on each student's progress (see chapter 4 checklists), and large group presentations to encourage CR and support on a larger scale to scaffold peer feedback for the students.

Encouraging students to interact with stakeholders who are directly impacted by the concepts the learners are exploring can be very effective in uncovering the underlying issues that derail attempts to make positive change. For example, in Stacey's "First Year Inquiry Studies" course at UPEI (UPEI, 2021; see Appendix C), students are working on IBL-HE projects focused on Indigenous issues, particularly the final report of the Truth and Reconciliation Commission on residential schools.

QR Code 8.1. National Centre for Truth and Reconciliation reports.

(https://nctr.ca/records/reports/)

After students engage in their own personal reflection and gather information from academic resources, their instructors have them prepare for and engage in conversation with Elders from the local Indigenous community. For many, this is their first experience in discussions with those who have been impacted directly by the decisions made by government and society, residential school survivors themselves. Reading about and reflecting on their learner stories in written form is a good starting point for learning, but it is the dialogue with survivors, the humans behind the stories, that makes the stories real and brings what some see as historical acts into the present context.

Activities to Encourage Reflection

There are endless activities that can be used to support students in developing CR skills. At the Center for Teaching Excellence at the University of Waterloo in Canada, there are a number of example activities you can use to support the development of CR in your IBL-HE course.

QR Code 8.2. Guidelines for integrating reflections into your course.

(https://uwaterloo.ca/centre-for-teaching-excellence/teaching-resources/teaching-tips/planning-courses-and-assignments/course-design/critical-reflection)

As a guide, they suggest you consider the following: create curiosity, make it continual, connect it, give it context, consider class size, mode the reflective process, break down the assignment, encourage multiple perspectives, provide a safe environment, assess it, and provide clear grading criteria. We hope you can easily connect how these guidelines for CR are congruent with the principles of IBL-HE and all that we have been discussing so far in these chapters.

The Taylor Institute for Teaching and Learning at the University of Calgary has an online module about CR you can consider that comes complete with videos, worksheets, templates, reflective questions, and additional resources.

QR Code 8.3. Critical reflection learning module.

(https://taylorinstitute.ucalgary.ca/resources/
module/critical-reflection)

We suspect you can find updated and ongoing resources to support the development of CR skills in your own institutions as well. Making the connection with CR and IBL-HE, Stacey and Beth provide examples of activities that they find useful to support the development of CR skills.

As you can see in more detail in Appendix B, reflection on both content and the learning process are core components of the IBL-HE experience in Stacey's Curiosity Project classes. It all begins with the weekly learning logs or thought papers. The purpose of these learning logs/thought papers is to enable students to

- spread out their learning over time, allowing for the kind of breadth and depth of thinking that is one of the keys to success in university and the work world
- develop their ability to critique resources
- develop their ability to express their ideas clearly in writing as they "think on paper"
- give students time to think about/analyze what they are learning, rather than just summarizing other people's thoughts
- reflect on their past ideas, creating a bigger picture/context for their topic
- find links between weekly course work, other classes, other students' projects, and their chosen topic

Students are instructed to write until they have nothing more to say and they feel that they have given their very best thinking. Written in the first person, the language of learning logs is very much of the "writing to learn" variety

(Fry & Villagomez, 2012), a conversation with oneself and one's readers in which ideas are explored, considered, reconsidered, dissected, and put together into a meaningful whole. In the event that they change their mind, begin to disagree with something they've written about earlier, or experience an "aha" moment, students are strongly encouraged, in an approach similar to freewriting (Li, 2007), to continue writing instead of editing or deleting their previous thoughts. The metacognitive process of watching one's own thinking unfold is a vital component of The Curiosity Project, whereby we celebrate students' efforts to follow their thinking where it takes them without pretending it was the destination they had in mind all along (FP 4 and FP 6).

Small Group Discussions

Every Friday the students meet face-to-face during their usual 50-minute class time to talk with each other and their senior undergraduate learning facilitators in small groups (five to six students) about what they are learning and how they are learning it. The purpose of the in-class discussions is to enable students to

- get spontaneous feedback from both peers and experienced learning facilitators
- improve their ability to think on their feet, reflect on, and question, helpfully and respectfully, others people's ideas or interpretations
- learn more about other topics and find links among the group's projects
- give and receive from others constructive suggestions, guidance, and resources

Online feedback on the weekly learning logs of their peers again serves many of these same purposes but allows for the time to reflect more deeply and give more considered feedback to others. They also can take their time in reflecting on the feedback they themselves have received in written format.

For their final submission/presentation, students need to reflect on all they have learned over the semester and distill from it the key points they feel the general public (or target audience) needs to know. Students should not include everything they've learned all semester in their final submission; their choice of what to include is an essential part of the process. Then they consider the best way to share this information with their target audience so that the audience will be maximally receptive and willing to consider the students' positions on their topics.

In concert with the final submission, students are asked to submit a detailed final reflection about their experience in The Curiosity Project. Its purpose is twofold: (a) to reflect on how far they have come in their learning about their chosen topic and how much there remains to learn, viewing that as a positive, not a personal failure in learning; and (b) to reflect on their learning process over the semester and what they have learned about how they learned (metacognition). This final reflective write-up includes the students' justification for the approach they chose to take for their final submission, both in terms of content included and mode of delivery; conclusions they feel they can (or cannot) now draw about their topic; any initial ideas that they found not to be valid; and questions that remain unanswered and new questions that formed. Equally importantly, it also addresses skills they acquired or honed in their exploration of their topic; challenges they faced, overcame, and/or wish they had tried to overcome over the course of the semester; lessons they learned about themselves as students and people; and what they are proud of themselves for and what they regret from their experience in the class.

You will find that Beth and Stacey use activities that have similar components, purposes, and outcomes. For example, Beth uses blog posts for courses offered with shorter duration (3-week GSP), whereas full-term (13-week) courses provide more time within the course itself for additional types of reflective activities. For this reason, we will not repeat all of that which was previously outlined but rather will highlight a few additional reflective exercises.

Reflecting on Credible Sources

One activity that was shared in chapter 7 was the checklists used when supporting students to pursue their inquiry (see Figures 7.1 and 7.2). Students choose three peer-reviewed journal articles that they believe will advance their inquiry in some way. They summarize each article and provide the written summary to each member of their small group. Each student spends about 5 minutes describing the content of each article, its relationship to their inquiry question, why they chose the source, and why they believe it is a good source or not. Group members can then ask questions for clarity and provide critical feedback.

This activity can have multiple purposes and goes beyond helping students choose their research methods, because inherent in the activity are (at least) two CR components. The first is for students to review peer-reviewed articles related to their inquiry question and critically reflect on the rigor reported in the article or source. The checklist for quantitative articles provides a number of areas that the student must assess to determine if they want to include the contents of this article in their project or dismiss it and move on to another source. The second CR component involves giving peer feedback. In small groups, students share their "findings" from each of the three articles. Using the checklist, peers provide critical verbal and written feedback about their peers' chosen article in relation to their inquiry question. The small group verbal dialogue and written CR comments support students to further reflect on the sources they have chosen in relation to their inquiry question.

A second activity that encouraged CR are large group presentations. Once students have had a chance to search for their sources, share their findings with their peers, and receive critical feedback, the next step is a large class presentation. Each student has 10 minutes to share their learnings to date, critically reflecting on their sources, and presenting formative feedback they have received from peers and instructor and how what they have learned will propel them into their next level of inquiry. After each presentation there are 5 minutes allotted for students to engage the class in dialogue about their next steps. These 15-minute presentations are completed twice in a course. The final presentation incorporates all learnings from their inquiry.

A final activity that encourages CR is the final assessment task. Following the final presentations, each student submits a critical analysis of their learning process and receives both formative and summative feedback from the instructor. There are many purposes and outcomes for this activity that are noted in the section on Stacey's activities.

Summary

Reflection is a critical component of the IBL-HE course because it is so important in supporting student learning on their inquiry journey. Gaining an understanding of how reflection is understood and utilized within your discipline can help to inform you about the ways in which you might implement it within your IBL-HE course. It cannot be overstated the extent to which CR skills are required in so many careers and expected by employers. Developing CR skills through the use of IBL-HE will position your students beyond your course to their next courses and into their future employment. Searching websites within your own university or others for resources within your discipline can make the transition easier for you to incorporate critically reflective activities for your course.

Questions for Reflection

1. How does your discipline conceptualize CR?
2. Consider one assessment task you currently use and reflect on the ways in which you might be able to adapt it to include CR.
3. Who do you know within your HE institution who you might be able to engage in a discussion about potential CR activities for your discipline?

9

WHAT KIND OF FEEDBACK DO STUDENTS NEED FROM ME AND EACH OTHER?

Stacey L. MacKinnon and Beth Archer-Kuhn

What to Expect

- Formative and/or summative feedback
- Formal and/or informal feedback
- Process- and/or product-oriented feedback
- Immediate and/or delayed feedback
- Instructor and students and/or peer feedback
- Scaffolded (teacher-supported) and/or independently performed feedback
- Receiving and using feedback

Giving and receiving feedback is an issue we all struggle with. What kind of feedback is useful? How does the feedback link to our learning objectives and assessment approaches? What constitutes good feedback? How effective is peer feedback? How can we help our students (and ourselves) take constructive feedback more positively? In this chapter, we will discuss these issues and more that will help you to engage in more meaningful feedback with your students and have them engage actively with giving feedback to each other.

Feedback on progress is incredibly important in IBL-HE, particularly if you are avoiding giving numerical grades until the end of the project/course or if you have students engaging in self-assessment. While students have received feedback throughout their educational career, it is highly likely that most of it was summative (i.e., given at the end of a project in order to justify a grade) rather than formative (i.e., given throughout the learning process with the goal of improvement), and that once they saw their numerical grade they may have ignored the written comments. To that end, we have to take the time to show our students not only how to give constructive feedback but teach them how to use the feedback they are given in order to improve their learning. Trumbull and Lash (2013) suggest that there are a variety of considerations in deciding what types of feedback to use, and for the purposes of IBL-HE, we are going to focus on feedback that is

- formative and/or summative
- informal and/or formal
- process and/or product oriented
- immediate and/or delayed
- from the instructor and student(s) and/or peers
- scaffolded (teacher supported) and/or independently performed

Formative and/or Summative Feedback

There are two types of feedback most often used in HE classrooms: summative and formative. Summative feedback is a judgment, an evaluation of a completed piece of work, and it is often a justification for a numerical mark. Formative feedback is developmental in nature. It highlights the strengths and weaknesses in the learning and allows for the opportunity to improve on it over the course of time or multiple assignments by supporting specific student needs as they emerge (Theall & Franklin, 2010). While HE institutions require that students receive summative feedback for transcripts (usually in the form of a numerical grade, though letter grades and pass/fail options also exist), it is formative feedback that helps guide students toward deeper and broader learning. Formative feedback can bolster students' abilities to take ownership of their learning when they understand that the goal is to improve learning, not just earning marks (Trumbull & Lash, 2013).

Formal and/or Informal Feedback

IBL-HE provides a unique opportunity to give students both formal and informal feedback over the course of their learning experience. The ideas of "teaching at the elbow" or "just-in-time teaching" are informal, in-the-moment, responsive forms of feedback and instruction intended to promote growth and development in our learners. The responses students receive from peers during discussions of their projects can also provide wonderful informal feedback to learners from a different perspective. This kind of spontaneous feedback allows students to think on their feet and to improve their ability to give and receive feedback that helps expand others' learning. In these informal encounters, students also learn how others express themselves and ask questions in ways that differ from their approach, taking ideas that can improve their own skills. Informal feedback opportunities tend to be orally shared and allow for exploration of possibilities and connections in the moment, where the focus isn't on "Is this right?" but on "Is this possible?" Making time in the classroom for students to share their learning with you and/or each other in an informal, conversational way is an easy approach to building interdependent learning relationships. While informal feedback is often given orally and therefore easily forgotten, the act of learners taking 5 minutes at the end of a discussion to make notes on the feedback received goes a long way toward the information being used at a later date.

Formal feedback also has an important place in IBL-HE. While the value of more spontaneous, informal feedback is clear, formal feedback has the benefit of being more considered both at the immediate time and possibly at a future time. Students and instructors have the time and space to think more deeply about the project, look for links between ideas, and critically analyze the information. Formal feedback is often challenging since simply agreeing with the writer or saying "that's interesting" will not suffice, and to be effective it should question assumptions being made, encourage deeper and/or broader thinking, and offer useful resources. Ironically, many of those giving feedback, including instructors, focus more on spelling, grammar, and sentence structure, which, while important, does not improve the level of thinking students are engaged in. Giving formal feedback takes time, training, and practice, and when the goal is to increase and expand learning, the more attention students and instructors give to the process, the more each learner benefits. Another positive of this approach lies in the fact that the written format of most formal feedback serves as a concrete record of the ups and downs of a given project and gives learners the opportunity to reflect on their progress over time, which also benefits metacognition. Formative feedback is constructive and instructive; it lets the student know the strengths and areas for improvement and also informs them what changes need to be made and how.

Process- and/or Product-Oriented Feedback

You may recall that one of the fundamental principles of IBL-HE we laid out in chapter 1 was the need to balance content and process in planning inquiry projects. This holds true when we are considering feedback. There is a balance to be found between the growth orientation that allows for improvement over time and the day-to-day feedback on the final product. Both have a place, but the importance of one over the other may well shift from the beginning to the end of an inquiry project. In the beginning, the focus is mainly on process, how the student is thinking and writing about their ideas, their ability and willingness to be critical of what they are learning, and the extent to which they are using the feedback they are receiving effectively. Over time and as their sense of self-efficacy with the process grows, feedback can begin to focus more on the product, pinning down key ideas, focusing on the finer points of writing and communication, and determining what the ultimate product will be and why.

Immediate and/or Delayed Feedback

If you want feedback to have the maximum chance of being effective, it is important to give it to the learner as soon as possible. This is particularly important with formative feedback, which you are expecting to be used to enhance and improve the next step in the learning process. As you heard from the doctoral student in chapter 1, written feedback is most helpful to student motivation in their inquiry journey. While you may be tempted to utilize close feedback options such as checkbox rubrics in order to save time (or to make IBL-HE possible in large classes), students often find this impersonal approach uninspiring, and it definitely does not teach them the vital skill of giving feedback. Instead, save the checkbox evaluations for things like spelling, grammar, sentence structure, and ensuring all the pieces of the puzzle are in place and focus instead on giving feedback on the ideas the student is exploring. This is where sharing the feedback responsibilities with your students can help to supply a steady stream of feedback for every learner, teaching them an important life skill and without burning out the instructor. Also remember that while immediate feedback is best, there is nothing wrong with adding to it after the fact. Often after a delay, new thoughts emerge, new resources are found, and all these should be shared with the learner. You can even change your mind on the feedback you originally gave if, after further consideration, you think there may be another way of looking at the situation. Modeling these feedback-giving behaviors shows students the dynamic nature of learning and encourages them to see their inquiries as open to new ideas and change. It also demonstrates FP 7, "being OK sitting in discomfort," and shows students how a little discomfort can be a positive thing.

Instructor and Student(s) and/or Peer Feedback

While we value the feedback loop between instructors and students, we firmly believe that peer feedback should occur throughout the inquiry process, from the initial stages of developing inquiry questions through the working phase of finding resources to answer the inquiry question, to the final class presentation or dissemination stage. Stacey has found that focusing on monitoring the feedback students are giving each other and stepping in only when more is needed (or she has a really great resource to share) is a far more effective use of instructor time and energy than the traditional approach of all or even most of the feedback coming from the instructor. Students need you to teach skills, let them practice, monitor their progress, and step in only when necessary to support their self-efficacy and ownership of their learning process.

In our experience, it is best for students to be assigned groups in the first class of a course. The number of small groups is determined by the class size, and we try to keep groups to no more than five students per group. It's important to recognize that for many of our students, working in groups can be challenging. Group work is often not their preferred method for completing assignments because in the past they have had to rely on peers for joint efforts in all aspects of the assignment, from planning to presentation, and feel they lose control over the level of effort and the possible implications on the grade they receive.

Group work in IBL differs from traditional group work in that each student's inquiry-question project is an individual project, and each student is responsible for the work they do and the grade they receive. Peers in the group provide critical feedback verbally and in writing to help each other improve their work. The feedback is formative, not summative. In IBL-HE, a student's peers act in the role of consultant, offering praise, sharing helpful resources, and providing a critical lens when providing feedback. When students find resources they share that information with peers. This critical and constructive feedback provides students with guidance as they move forward with their inquiry. Peers also become a mini cheering section when the group's students run into speed bumps in their thinking or are presenting various stages of their inquiry process to the larger class. This built-in support system is helpful when students are struggling, are uncertain, or simply need to bounce ideas and thoughts off of their group members to gain confidence in the decisions the student is making.

To support work in small groups, Beth provides her students with a resource called the Tao of Groupwork (University of New South Wales, Sydney, n.d.) that aids in opening communication within the small groups as to how they want to work together. This is particularly important given that, in our experience, students are wary of giving each other in-depth feedback because they are concerned about hurting the other's feelings. When a group comes together and decides that the feedback is about improving the work, not criticizing the worker, the social pressures can reverse and focus on giving the best constructive critical feedback possible to help ensure the others' success. Remember, working together in groups, giving and receiving feedback, is not only an important skill in academia but one that learners carry forward into the work world and their personal lives, which we will talk about more in chapter 17 when we discuss lifelong and life-wide learning.

Scaffolded (Teacher-Supported) and/or Independently Performed Feedback

As you have already likely determined, we are big fans of scaffolding learning whenever possible. This also holds true for the issue of feedback. Whether you are scaffolding across experience levels (e.g., lots of support for first-year students, minimal support for fourth-years) or within a project (e.g., lots of support early on, gradually relinquishing that support over the course of the term), there is no need to rush to students taking full responsibility for giving feedback immediately (FP 5). For example, Stacey spends time at the beginning of each IBL-HE course teaching students how to give useful feedback, models what good feedback looks like, then lets them practice their feedback skills and monitors the feedback they give their peers, stepping in only when necessary. This scaffolded approach allows the students to build their skills and self-efficacy, ameliorate their fear of offending others by giving critical yet constructive feedback, while simultaneously allowing them to support their peers' learning in a meaningful way. The ultimate goal is, of course, that they are giving high-quality feedback independently, but the road to this independence is smoother when it is built one brick at a time.

You may already be familiar with Emily Wray's RISE approach to giving and receiving feedback.

QR Code 9.1. RISE approach to feedback: Reflect, inquire, suggest, elevate.

(http://www.risemodel.com)

This is a favorite of Stacey's. Based on Bloom's taxonomy for higher-order thinking, this approach encourages students to (a) reflect, (b) inquire through analysis, (c) suggest ideas for improvement, and (d) elevate each other's work. It can be used by instructors and peers or as a self-evaluation tool. It helps students overcome their concerns about offending others by offering them a common understanding of what the feedback is for and how it was derived, and it gives sample language to use in explaining their ideas to others (see Appendix E).

Good feedback in IBL-HE includes lots of opportunity for formative feedback, both formal and informal, process and product oriented at different times in the inquiry process, as immediate as possible with the option to be updated or changed as needed, modeled by the instructor, then provided by students as much as possible with monitoring in a scaffolded manner that supports the development of skills and confidence. Summative feedback is also important and can include more normative feedback along with it. What we have not talked about yet is a taken-for-granted assumption that may not be so straightforward: Do our students know how to receive feedback and use it to improve their learning?

Receiving and Using Feedback

A challenge even greater than giving good feedback is how we receive and use feedback we ourselves are given. This is particularly the case for students who are used to receiving primarily summative feedback where there is little or no expectation they will demonstrate its use. Just as students have to be taught and have modeled for them how to give feedback, we have to ensure that they are prepared to use the formative feedback that is so key to IBL-HE (Heen & Stone, 2014; Stone et al., 2010). One great resource for this is Stone and Heen's (2015) book *Thanks for the Feedback: The Science and Art of Receiving Feedback Well Even When It's Off-Base, Unfair, Poorly Delivered, and Frankly, You're Not in the Mood*. Stacey picked it up precisely because of the title and has kept it in rotation in her students' reading list because of the value of understanding the three triggers Stone and Heen identify as being key to receiving feedback: truth triggers, relationship triggers, and identity triggers. Beth spends time incorporating how feedback is considered in the final assessment task.

Our students (and we ourselves) deal with these three issues whenever we are faced with receiving feedback. The extent to which we can move past them will determine how we will respond to feedback from those who are trying to help us develop and improve our work. In brief, truth triggers occur when the feedback that is given is somehow off, unhelpful, or untrue. It can also encompass "cheerleader" feedback, or feedback that is designed solely to say "good job" even when the job isn't good. When a learner receives this kind of feedback, they feel indignant, wronged, and exasperated. This is especially true for students who make an extra effort to give useful feedback and resent when others do not put the same effort forward. Often these truth triggers arise in the early stages of the feedback cycle when students are just learning how to express their ideas and critiques. Avoiding truth triggers requires that instructors ensure that students know how to give good feedback and are monitoring the feedback that is being given to ensure everyone gets useful information.

Relationship triggers are cued by the person giving the feedback. While students are used to receiving feedback from authority figures, they are not usually well versed in receiving it from peers in a noncompetitive manner. In these cases, students can have negative reactions based on what they believe about the giver or how they feel treated by that person. In essence, the learner's focus shifts from the feedback itself to the audacity of the person delivering it. This is the "What do they know!" experience and is one of the key reasons why building positive, trusting relationship environments is so important to the success of IBL-HE FP 7.

Lastly, identity triggers are all about the individual and how they see themselves. In the face of critical feedback they often feel overwhelmed, threatened, or ashamed. This is particularly poignant when it happens to a student who has had great academic success in areas that require the ability to memorize large amounts of information verbatim. Their view of themselves as an excellent learner can be shaken when they enter an IBL-HE classroom and discover that their ability to remember and recall details is not enough for success. Ensuring that students are reminded that the feedback is about improving everyone's work, not criticizing who they are as a learner, is key to working through these identity triggers. Being transparent with students about these potential issues and feelings is very important in normalizing FP 7 and sets up the expectation that we are all working on embracing the discomfort of new learning, stepping outside of our comfort zones to expand our learning. This kind of transparency early in the project will go a long way to ameliorating the severity of these identity triggers.

Summary

Giving and receiving feedback are skills that everyone needs for effective learning in an IBL-HE classroom. Being transparent about the challenges and teaching, modeling, and practicing these feedback skills benefits not only the immediate IBL projects but encourages students to use those skills in their wider experience. Take the time to consider your feedback goals, trust your students to support each other's learning, and listen to the feedback they give you about their experiences and you will create an atmosphere that welcomes constructive, critical, and collaborative feedback (FP 3).

Questions for Reflection

1. What kinds of feedback do you usually give your students? Have they used it successfully in the past? If not, why?

2. What has been your experience with peer feedback in the past? What do you think you could do to improve the feedback students give each other?

3. How can you create a positive feedback experience for your students without it becoming a burden on your time, particularly in larger classes?

PART FOUR

HOW DO I BUILD THE SUPPORTIVE RELATIONSHIPS THAT ALLOW IBL-HE TO THRIVE?

Now that you have a sense of the nuts and bolts of getting your students started on the skills of IBL-HE (e.g., asking questions, choosing research methods, reflecting, and giving/receiving feedback), we can turn our attention to laying the groundwork for and maintaining the supportive relationships that allow IBL-HE to thrive. There are a variety of relationships that enhance IBL-HE learning experiences:

- trusting relationships between instructor and students as well as between the students themselves in the classroom (chapter 10)
- relationships with the larger community (chapter 11)
- mentors and communities of practice (chapter 12)
- institutional support (chapter 13)

Let's start with the most immediate relationship, that which develops and grows between instructors and students in IBL-HE classrooms!

PART FOUR

HOW DO I BUILD THE SUPPORTIVE RELATIONSHIPS THAT ALLOW ISL-HE TO THRIVE?

10

HOW DO I CREATE A TRUSTING CLASSROOM ENVIRONMENT THAT SUPPORTS INTERDEPENDENT LEARNING?

Stacey L. MacKinnon and Beth Archer-Kuhn

What to Expect

- Why does trust matter?
- How is trust defined in HE, particularly in classrooms employing intellectual risk-taking such as IBL?
- How do you build and maintain trust in IBL-HE classrooms?

This chapter addresses the importance of developing trust among instructors and students in IBL-HE and helping instructors understand how to develop and maintain trust in IBL-HE classrooms. We base this discussion on both our day-to-day work and our qualitative constructivist-grounded theory study of trust within IBL-HE environments, where we examined the experiences of instructors and students through four focus groups and nine individual interviews (Archer-Kuhn & MacKinnon, 2020). This project engaged experienced instructors, learners, and authors of IBL-HE from Canada, the United States, New Zealand, and Ireland and identified three themes: (a) creating an environment of negotiated mutuality; (b) emerging relationship/community building; and (c) internalizing and applying a mindset shift.

Why Does Trust Matter in IBL?

As students in IBL-HE engage with a variety of new and familiar resources, support and collaborate with their classmates, and figure out how to conduct research to answer their inquiry question, their instructors become facilitators who support and guide students on their learning journey (Anstey et al., 2014; Spronken-Smith & Walker, 2010). This allows students to become more responsible for and take ownership of their own learning (Love et al., 2015; Yang, 2015). This change in dynamic can be difficult for both instructors and students as it goes against the norms wherein the teacher is an authority figure and gatekeeper of new information and the student is an empty pitcher waiting to be filled (Bolhuis, 2003; Brubaker, 2012; Cuneo et al., 2012). Making these shifts in role can result in the confusing juxtaposition of enjoying being challenged while simultaneously questioning one's own competency and inciting fear of failure, often due to delaying numerical assessment in favor of receiving regular formative feedback (Litmanen et al., 2012).

In addition, IBL-HE classrooms focus on the process of learning as much or more than the final product, meaning that, for both instructor and student, procrastination or avoidance is not an option. As a result, IBL-HE can initially increase anxiety for both students and instructors who must learn to "be okay sitting with discomfort" given the likelihood of making mistakes, taking wrong turns, and encountering "speed bumps" that will need to be addressed along the IBL journey (Boyle & MacKinnon, 2016; Brubaker, 2012; von Renesse & Ecke, 2017). Building and maintaining trusting relationships in IBL-HE classrooms is the bedrock of ameliorating much of this anxiety, forming a solid foundation for moving outside our comfort zones and taking intellectual risks.

How Is Trust Defined in HE?

A great deal has been theorized about the importance of trust in HE classrooms generally (Burke, 2015; Curzon-Hobson, 2002; D'Olimpio, 2018; Haynes, 2018; MacFarlane, 2009). Previous research in HE indicates that mutual trust between students, professors, and communities, and trust in the pedagogy itself, is an important antecedent to success (Archer-Kuhn, 2013; Archer-Kuhn, Lee, Finnessey, & Liu, 2020; Boyle & MacKinnon, 2016; Curzon-Hobson, 2002; Goguen et al., 2010; MacFarlane, 2009; MacKinnon, 2017; Wright et al., 2009).

Whereas trust is widely accepted to be a key component of the learning process in general (Henschke, 2013; MacFarlane, 2009), the unique constellation of circumstances presented by the university experience make the quick and meaningful development of trust a necessary but challenging condition for taking intellectual risks. These unique circumstances include short semesters (4 months to 1 week), larger classes (30–100-plus students), high stakes and an outcome focus in which students and instructors feel the pressure for goal achievement in the service of career development (Boyle & MacKinnon, 2016; Shin & Jung, 2014), as well as unrealistic expectations and negative stereotypes of what learning in HE will/should be (e.g., Bunce et al., 2017; MacKinnon, 2017). To further complicate matters, scholars have identified a variety of trusting relationships as necessary antecedents to successfully facilitate IBL in HE, including mutual trust between the students (particularly when group work is involved), students and/instructors, instructors and administration, and trust in the pedagogy itself (Cook & Borkovitz, 2017; Cooper et al., 2017; Cuneo et al., 2012; Harvie et al., 2017; Justice et al., 2009; Love et al., 2015; Yang, 2015). ·

Surprisingly, while most agree that trust is a vital piece of success in IBL-HE classrooms, few have studied how trust is developed and maintained when instructors and students are attempting to step outside their comfort zones (Aditomo et al., 2013; Friesen & Scott, 2013; Ghosh et al., 2001; Risley & Petroff, 2014). In-depth qualitative research examining the lived experience of trusting in IBL-HE environments is virtually nonexistent (see Boyle & MacKinnon, 2016, for an exception). Indeed, our recent rapid systematic review of trust in IBL-HE showed that research on how trust works in HE classrooms incorporating IBL is virtually nonexistent (Beltrano et al., 2021).

Building and Maintaining Trust in IBL-HE

To begin to fill in this gap, we conducted an in-depth, qualitative study involving focus groups and individual interviews with experienced instructors, learners, and authors of IBL-HE from Canada, the United States, New Zealand, and Ireland (Archer-Kuhn & MacKinnon, 2020). We wanted to know (a) what trust means in an IBL-HE classroom and (b) how those involved create and maintain it. Figure 10.1 shows our full model of trust development in IBL-HE, which we will break down into its component parts for discussion.

The success of IBL-HE starts with you, the instructor. You are the first link in the chain that leads toward transformational learning for your students. It stands to reason then, that it is you who gets the process of building trust started. You then work with your students to develop trust between

Figure 10.1. Pedagogical model of trust in IBL-HE.

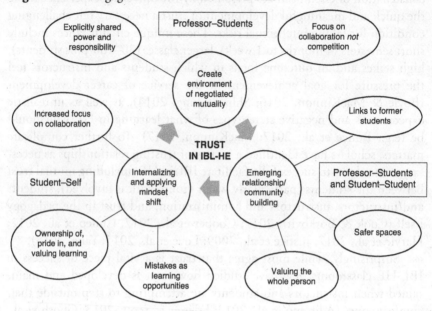

them and you as well as among themselves, with the ultimate goal being they develop sufficient trust in themselves to be able to translate their IBL-HE experience into enhanced learning moving forward. This process unfolds within three phases: (a) creating an environment of negotiated mutuality; (b) emerging relationship/community building; and (c) internalizing and applying a mindset shift.

Phase 1: Negotiated Mutuality and Willingness to Risk

The first step in building trusting relationships in the IBL-HE classroom is creating an environment of negotiated mutuality and modeling the willingness to engage in the type of intellectual risk-taking that you hope to see in your students. IBL-HE requires everyone involved to move out of their comfort zone, take intellectual risks, and be willing to be vulnerable in the learning process.

Willingness to be Vulnerable

For students, the risks of IBL include sharing their ideas with classmates while fearing they appear uninformed, not learning sufficiently, not getting the grades they need to move forward, and having to learn to act on formative feedback rather than relying on numerical assessments to guide their learning and often their feelings of self-esteem (Boyle & MacKinnon, 2016). For this risk-taking to be successful, students must allow themselves to experience vulnerability, allowing their thoughts to emerge only partially developed so they can be refined and enhanced. Students have to learn to shift their focus from their own vulnerability and fear of losing face to putting the quality of the work and learning first. Instructors can help facilitate this vulnerability by modeling for students what it looks like and what its benefits are. When students see their instructors as vulnerable, risk-taking learners, they are more likely to take new chances themselves.

Sharing Power and Responsibility

For instructors, the first risk we face is the sharing of power within our classroom. We have to be willing to step off our stage, relinquish our position as "all-knowing knowledge transmitter," and be open to being questioned. We have to deliberately make space for our students to take ownership and responsibility for their learning and that of their classmates. Moreover, we have to embrace the discomfort of new learning in our own practice, questioning and reflecting on our own learning processes and thinking critically about how learning is unfolding in our IBL-HE classrooms in real time. It is incumbent upon us to be open about the need for (and fear of) taking risks and demonstrate that there are plans in place to ameliorate these risks, provided everyone in the class buys in and gives their best effort.

The good news is that with practice, knowledge gained from learning more about IBL-HE, and developing trust in your own ability to deal with challenges as they unfold in the classroom, this process can become exciting (though still uncomfortable!) and sustain your enthusiasm for teaching over time. After all, every semester brings a new cohort of students to figure out, inspire, model for, and engage with in inquiry!

Student Buy-In

The second risk faced by instructors of IBL-HE is the lack of certainty concerning student buy-in. Unlike lectures or other top-down approaches, where disengagement is irritating but not disastrous, in IBL-HE if even a small group of your students do not fully engage in the process, the learning experience can be negative for all. We, as the instructors, are risking the learning of all students and indeed our own professional evaluations when engaging in IBL-HE. Fortunately, there are ways to increase student buy-in in IBL-HE that are related to trust.

Be explicit so you can learn from your students. How do we begin to counter these risks? One effective approach is very simple: You can let new students know that you are learning from observing their learning process using IBL-HE (FP 8) and that nothing you try will negatively impact them. Be explicit that while things may not always go according to a preset plan in the classroom, they can count on coming out of the term having learned what they need. Reassure them that because IBL-HE is a dynamic process, backup plans can be used as needed—but that both IBL-HE and the backup plans rely on them giving themselves over to the learning process and being willing to try new things. Be sure to ask your students to anonymously let you know if they are concerned they are not learning what they need to or are concerned about their grade; then you can address these issues directly in class either by acknowledging that there is indeed a gap and filling it in or by reassuring them that the material they are concerned about will be forthcoming as the term unfolds. When students learn that they can be upfront with you about their fears and concerns and you will respond promptly and directly to those concerns, they know that you "have their back." In our experience, by the middle of term, students are usually more than happy to talk with us directly about their concerns and make suggestions for dealing with any emerging issues. You can also offer to go over their contribution to the IBL-HE learning process with them one-on-one to help identify where they may be feeling challenged and support them in finding ways to strengthen their contribution.

One of the beauties of IBL-HE is that it allows you to share the power and responsibility for learning with your students. The question is, how much of the power in your classroom do you need to share with your students? Our research findings suggest that while students do want to have a significant say in how their learning unfolds, they are not interested in having full control over the classroom. In truth, they don't believe that power can or should be evenly shared in an IBL-HE classroom. The reality is that whenever one person has the final say on how grades are distributed, there is a power differential. Lessening that power differential is the goal, and making space for appropriate transfer of responsibility and ownership of learning is key to phase 1 of building trust in IBL-HE classrooms (see Figure 10.2).

As you can see from Figure 10.2, shared power also means shared responsibility. This is what we mean by negotiated mutuality. With the sharing of power from instructor to students, there also needs to be a shifting of responsibility for learning from instructor to students. In IBL-HE, instructors have to trust students to fully engage in their own learning process, often in ways they never have before. Students take on the responsibility to fully engage, reflect, figure things out, and ask for assistance rather than relying

Figure 10.2. Phase 1: Negotiated mutuality and trust in IBL-HE.

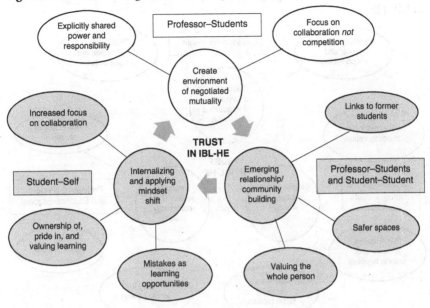

on being told exactly what to do by an authority figure at each step on the journey. Mutuality also means that instructors have to stand back and give their students the space to figure things out, even when they don't work out as expected, and trust that students will find their way with less interference from authority. This doesn't mean you refrain from jumping in if they are drowning, but rather that you become directly involved as a last resort rather than their first call. If they know you believe in them to figure it out, they will work hard to do so.

Collaboration not competition. When you create an environment of collaboration rather than competition, this process goes even more smoothly. Students who feel they do not have to compete for top of the class focus less on social comparison and more on temporal comparison (i.e., their own growth). They will also be more likely to support each other and work together to solve problems if they share the responsibility for enhancing one another's learning (FP 3). We call this "interdependent" learning because students are graded independently but the expectation is that every student will help facilitate their peers' learning by giving quality feedback and support. In this sense, everyone can have a high-quality learning experience.

When the mutual negotiation of power and development of a collaborative learning atmosphere have been explicitly explained and reinforced, basic IBL-HE learning can begin. This leads us into phase 2

Figure 10.3. Phase 2: Emerging relationships and community building for trust in IBL-HE.

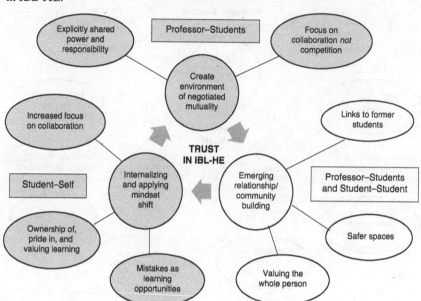

of the trust-building process: emerging relationships and community building (see Figure 10.3).

Phase 2: Emerging Relationships and Community Building

Once you have laid this foundation for trust and the process of IBL-HE learning has begun, trust can be reinforced by focusing on the emerging relationships and building a community of learners. As you can see from Figure 10.3, there are several components to this phase of trust building and maintenance.

Making the Most of Time

The first component is time. Simply said, it takes time to develop trust, and time is something that is in short supply in a HE classroom. Yet, time is a key component because it helps to keep our expectations in check regarding how easy it is to form a trusting relationship. Trust cannot be rushed and requires patience to develop. Start early and work to make the most of the time you do have with your students. For example, Stacey makes a point of teaching first-year students so she can introduce them, even if only in small ways given the size of the class, to the mindsets and skills of inquiry. The good news is that once the relationships are established, students agree that trust is more easily and quickly established in the next IBL-HE course, as this student shared, "because we all knew each other it was easier to be vulnerable," and indeed knowing their peers made all the difference, as noted by this student: "The real trust came and the risk taking came from being in it with my peers." Ideally you want to take the time to have your students working with inquiry skills in small groups, but if, like Stacey, you have very large classes (e.g., 150-plus students), that does not always work logistically in lecture theatres. With her experiences over the past 2 years, however, Stacey believes incorporating mindsets and skills of IBL-HE in her large classes is easier when she is teaching online simply because she can have students work more practically in breakout rooms, track their conversations in the Google Docs they share with her, and encourage one-on-one (or one-on-group) interactions with her that are not always possible in face-to-face situations when the next class is coming into the room. Getting creative to enhance the time you have to build trust is key to success in IBL-HE, not only in the short term but also in terms of getting students to seek out more IBL-HE opportunities in future classes.

Word of Mouth

The second component of this phase helps to alleviate some of the time pressure we experience in HE. Many of us jump-start the emergence of relationship and community building in an IBL-HE classroom by linking current students to those who have successfully completed the course in the past. Some instructors incorporate senior undergraduate learning facilitators into our IBL-HE classrooms, typically former students who have engaged in IBL courses previously and can support current students in their inquiry journey. Some are paid teaching assistants, and others may do it for course credit; however, all 140-plus students that Stacey has engaged over the past 10 years have volunteered their time to help others have a positive IBL-HE experience. This is very impactful on student buy-in, because as one student put it,

> the experiences past students have had with it can really be a great indicator of what's gonna come. . . . I had facilitators that were as wonderful as R was and kinda helped encourage so much discussion and openness. . . . Having somebody else who successfully did it made me feel so much more comfortable to be able to go and do it.

Although Beth has not used learning facilitators given her typical smaller class sizes (less than 40), she has found that students who engage in her courses using IBL are eager to share their knowledge of IBL with others, either through engaging in research projects, which includes recruitment of student participants, presentations at conferences, or participating in writing manuscripts.

The reality is that students tend to trust experienced peers more than they do an unknown professor. The real impact comes when former students not only extoll the virtues of IBL-HE but also speak frankly about the challenges they faced during the IBL process. When former students share the experience and approach they used to navigate IBL, current students have a better understanding of the reality of learning, potential ways to ameliorate these challenges, and the confidence to know that if you just keep working at it you will make it through to the other side.

If you don't have the potential for experienced undergraduate learning facilitators, there are other options as well. One term when Stacey's health prevented her from being in the classroom to introduce The Curiosity Project to the newest group of students, one of her previous IBL learners offered to fill in. Amazingly, that term the students in The Curiosity Project exhibited significantly more buy-in in the early stages of the course than Stacey had previously observed. When the students were queried at the end of term why this was, they shared that having a former student volunteer their time to introduce the project, coupled with the fact that the instructor trusted that student to do so, indicated to them that this was a project worth taking seriously from day 1. This same student created a video version of their talk to introduce new students to those who came before them and share advice. It is still very successful in inspiring students to take the risk of trusting in both Stacey and the process of IBL-HE. You can view both versions of the video on our website (projects.upei.ca/curiosityandinquiry) or click on the QR codes.

QR Code 10.1. Video: Curious About Curiosity.

https://youtu.be/VzN3nUH06hA

QR Code 10.2. Video: Curiosity and Inquiry.

https://youtu.be/VzN3nUH06hA

For those who may not have the option of learning facilitators, Beth has found engaging students as research assistants another way to increase students' knowledge of IBL while supporting IBL practice for students and instructors. For example, she has engaged students as research assistants to create resources for the project that can be used by students and instructors. To date, students have helped to develop an IBL module that students view prior to taking a course with IBL, an instructor guide for getting started with IBL, videos of the specific instruction of IBL (Beth teaching IBL) for instructors to observe the IBL process in action, and presentation slides that can be used during lunch-and-learn sessions or workshops to introduce instructors new to IBL and provide them with the resources they need to begin using IBL in their courses, and can be found throughout her project website (https://live-ucalgary.ucalgary.ca/node/339351; sessions 1–3).

QR Code 10.3. Video: An introduction to IBL resources.

https://www.youtube.com/watch?v=Cs0_TTm8eXM

QR Code 10.4. Video: The practical side of IBL.

https://www.youtube.com/watch?v=yrgKBJWKBzQ

QR Code 10.5. Video: Supporting students through IBL.

https://www.youtube.com/watch?v=1V5eoP62lpU

Creating Safer Spaces

The third component of successful relationship and community building is creating safer spaces. Students and instructors agreed that a safe space is one in which they are not judged; however, we decided to use the more realistic term *safer spaces*. In this, we were guided by the observations of one of our student participants who noted that, particularly for groups traditionally discriminated against based on race, religion, sexual orientation, and gender expression, "We don't believe a safe space is achievable. [We] think safer spaces can be achieved but an ultimate safe space [we] don't think is achievable."

Peer Support

Peer support for both faculty and students is one way to facilitate a safer space and encourage a sense of community in IBL. Students noted that the key for them was "the ability to be honest and the ability to trust the honesty of other people in the room" and "professors encouraging exploration."

As with power in the IBL-HE classroom, both faculty and students discussed responsibility for safe spaces as shared and mutual. When creating a respectful environment, a faculty member indicated that "openness, an ability to engender acceptance for different views and diversity and abilities . . . a sense that we are all learners, whether you are a faculty member or a student" is the primary characteristic of a safer space.

Safer spaces are also an outcome of the collaborative (as opposed to competitive) relationships with peers that phase 1 emphasized (FP 3). To our student participants, this meant

> we were more willing to be vulnerable with one another and risk being wrong because we weren't competing with one another to be the top of the class because we were being graded on our process not just on getting it right.

Students agreed that their sense of community and safety is enhanced in the IBL environment when peers are engaged in their learning process: "Trust in your peers, they're gonna hold your hand while you're jumping down that scary rabbit hole." They recognize that community building in an IBL-HE environment requires "mutual agreement to be curious together and to explore together and also to . . . take risks together." More specifically, students indicated that they had to learn to get

> comfortable being around other people that also may have different perspectives but are willing to sort of navigate the issues with you. As you inquire and draw conclusions you have to trust that if you don't have the same conclusions as they do, they still sort of see where you're coming from.

How important is this development of safer spaces? One student proudly stated that "the confidence to say something rose up because this person made you feel that no matter what you said, would be received with such kindness." Students also noticed that the safe spaces provided "a richness to be gained by having students come together from multiple places to like share in that kind of discovery process," "instilled a lot of motivation in me . . . the aspect of um how active I had to be in my learning kind of motivated me," and "it is a matter of discovering my own curiosity."

Valuing the Whole Person

Part of creating safer spaces in IBL-HE classrooms is the valuing of the whole person. One participant described this as a place where "you can be OK to be yourself and make mistakes, and say things that you might be embarrassed about what [discussion] we are having in another kind of space." The instructors agreed on the importance of "taking the time to get to know the whole people that your students are and creating an environment where they can also learn about the whole person that I am." This kind of mutuality and appreciation of the whole person we each bring to the classroom opens the door to the kind of intellectual risk-taking we encourage in IBL-HE.

When collaboration is the focus, power and responsibility are mutually negotiated and shared, and relationship and community building emerges, transformational learning can happen (Archer-Kuhn & MacKinnon, 2020; Damianakis et al., 2019). In our study, IBL-HE instructors marveled at "watching them actually quickly move into understanding what inquiry-based learning is about and seeing transformational change in them, not just in their trust but in their confidence about what they can do." Most student participants agreed: "I found it enhanced my learning quality so much because I was able to create these key relationships in my classes that allowed me to learn and open my eyes in so many different perspectives." When trust is mutual, collaboration is emphasized, and community spaces are safer places to explore and present oneself as a whole person, the impact can be felt in the depth of student learning: "I'm comfortable in this space . . . I really felt like I had the safety of my group around me, I was able to kind of push myself deeper into it and really challenge some of my own preconceived notions."

By the end of phase 2, we have put the groundwork in place for professors to create an environment where they can trust their students, the students can trust them, and the students can trust each other. Transformation has begun!

Phase 3 is the ultimate goal in IBL-HE classrooms: students learning to trust themselves and seeking out more IBL-type learning opportunities.

Phase 3: Internalizing and Applying the Mindset Shift

Just as the trust-building process started with you trusting in yourself as an IBL-HE instructor, the cycle ends with the hope that our students will further develop their trust in the process and, more importantly, in their own curiosity mindset (FP 1) and inquiry skills (see Figure 10.4). Phase 3 focuses on the student internalizing and choosing to apply their IBL-HE learning, seeking out opportunities to learn in this way, and when those opportunities are unavailable, creating them for themselves.

Mistakes Are Learning Opportunities

This often begins with students' beginning to trust that mistakes really are learning opportunities and not judgments of character or intelligence. They are more likely to explore what went wrong and try again rather than take

Figure 10.4. Phase 3: Internalizing and applying the mindset shift for trust in IBL-HE.

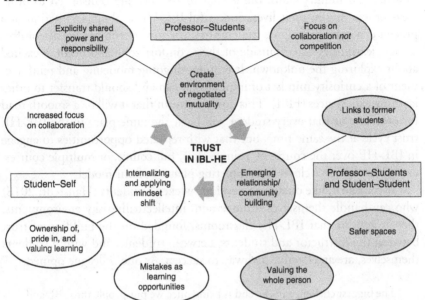

it personally or blame others. They become more likely to own their role in any mistakes. They are also more likely to support the successful learning of their peers by sharing what they know works with other students both in and outside of the original IBL-HE classroom. As one student put it:

> I found I would have a responsibility in my other classes if somebody wasn't comfortable or has never done IBL before that I would kind of feel the need to say like oh well look, we're gonna be talking about things like this. It's like I try to give them a bit of background of my own experiences. . . . Having knowledge of somebody else's experience kind of may help them.

This desire to engage with the learning of others as a result of a successful IBL-HE experience was echoed by another student who indicated that

> everybody's got their own projects but essentially here while you're in charge of your projects, you're also learning about 5, 6, 7, however many people are in your group, all of those other projects in probably fairly reasonable levels of depths and . . . maybe you know, setbacks that someone's had. Oh, you know "I ran into this problem so, you know, I'm telling you guys this so you guys can avoid this kind of setback in your own project," so there can be a lot of peer learning.

Once phase 3 has begun and students are trusting in their own curiosity mindset and inquiry skills, the lessons of IBL-HE are transferred to other areas of learning in their lives. Successful IBL-HE is about facilitation of a process in a space that allows students to learn how to embrace the discomfort of new learning, to step outside of their comfort zone and become excited about exploring the unknown. It requires ongoing modeling and reinforcement of a curiosity mindset of inquiry that can and should transfer to other learning experiences (FP 1). This does not mean that it will be a smooth road for everyone or that every student will be at the same place in the IBL-HE trust cycle at the same time, but that with repeated opportunities to engage in IBL-HE over the course of a single class, full course, or multiple courses, everyone will move closer to completing phase 3 of our model.

If your goal, like ours, is to develop "wicked" students (Hanstedt, 2018) who can handle themselves in uncertain, intellectually risky environments, then it appears that IBL-HE classrooms, founded on the building of trust between the instructor and students, between students, and within students themselves, are an effective pathway to success. As one colleague opined:

> The biggest challenge in the end is being once we put people into IBL and [they are] transformed now, we're having [other] faculty complain that the students are far too disruptive, they ask questions, they're interested in the subject matter, they don't want to just listen to what's being told to them.

What better "problem" for a HE instructor to have? And when the rewards are potentially this high, the risk is definitely worth it for both you and your students!

Summary

Building and maintaining trust at a variety of levels will allow you and your students to take the kinds of intellectual risks inherent in IBL and high-quality learning. It starts with you, the faculty member, and grows into your classroom and hopefully beyond. It takes time, but more importantly it takes consistency and openness to allow trust to flourish. Taking the time to reflect and model the kinds of trusting behaviors you want to see in your students, admitting your own humanity when things do not go as planned in the classroom, coming back from your mistakes with grace, and always putting the learning process ahead of the product will move you toward the kind of trusting relationships that will have students seek out your courses in the future and use the mindsets and skills they have developed moving forward as they transfer their knowledge and experience.

Questions for Reflection

1. As an instructor, how do you show your students that you trust them to know what it is they need to learn?

2. How can you increase your knowledge and support so you can better trust yourself to be in the moment in your IBL classroom?

3. What signs do you see that your students trust you? Each other? Themselves? How can you foster those trusting behaviors on a daily basis?

4. How can reflection on past group work experiences play a role in supporting both yourself and your students in building trust? How can you use reflection during your class to address trust challenges as they emerge?

II

HOW CAN I INCORPORATE THE COMMUNITY IN MY IBL-HE PRACTICE?

Beth Archer-Kuhn

What to Expect

- IBL on GSP
- Integrating an international model with IBL
- IBL on campus

A student's project may be created within a classroom, yet the answers to the inquiry question can be sought and discovered both inside and outside the classroom and through multiple sources. In this chapter we consider how we can help students move beyond the tradition of seeking information solely from peer-reviewed journal articles to a broader understanding of what knowledge is and how knowledge created from various sources can support students' deep learning. We will share some of the ways in which, through IBL-HE, we have facilitated the creation of a village of local contexts; academic and community-based collaborators; peers; diverse modes of learning; and instructor-supported access to enhanced resources and guided strategies for students to engage in their learning journeys.

Pedagogy such as IBL requires students to engage with their world through curiosity, since IBL represents a question-driven search for understanding. "What do I want to know?" and "How can I go about finding answers to my questions?" are foundational to IBL. A student's project may be created within a classroom. Yet the answers to the inquiry question are sought and discovered both inside and outside the classroom and through multiple sources. In this chapter we consider two examples of how students can move beyond the tradition of seeking information solely from peer-reviewed journal articles to a broader understanding of what knowledge is and how knowledge created from various sources can support students' deep learning. We will share some of the ways in which, through IBL-HE, we have facilitated the creation of a village of local contexts; academic and community-based collaborators; peers; diverse modes of learning; and instructor-supported access to enhanced resources and guided strategies for students to engage in their learning journeys.

In social work education, students learn that relationship is the cornerstone of the profession. Change happens through relationship. Through our work with IBL, we have considered relationships of change, relationships understood as that between teaching and research, knowledge and practice, student and teacher, and university and community. McKinney (2014) identifies one such relationship, teaching and research, whereby the focus of IBL should be placed on engaging students in a culture of learning, and active engagement should be done through peer learning groups. McKinney (2014) submits that there are four ways for students to be involved in research: authoring, producing, pursuing, and identifying. It is here that we begin our discussion of how to engage with a village.

As a newly tenure-track academic, Beth was designing a course for a GSP, supporting 13 students in the United Kingdom for 15 days. It seemed the perfect venue for which to design a course with IBL as the teaching and learning strategy (Appendix D). It was time to try out the teaching/research relationship. During the course design and given the destination, she also integrated the Zubaroglu and Popescu (2015) model for international social work education. Here is Beth's reflection on this experience.

Implementing IBL on a Group Study Program

Friesen and Scott (2013) identified three key IBL strategies leading to deep learning: scaffolding; formative assessment; and powerful, critical, and essential questions. These strategies were incorporated into the course design for our GSP. As an example, I developed an online module for this project to introduce IBL and its benefits, along with some prereadings to allow students an opportunity to gain a basic-level understanding prior to our departure. Additionally, the scaffolding of assessment tasks and formative feedback was integrated into the course design. I used "Structured Controversy" (Archer-Kuhn, 2013) as a springboard to support students in their developing powerful, critical, and essential questions, also known as the central question or inquiry question (Hudspith & Jenkins, 2001). Formative feedback came in multiple ways, including replies to peer blog posts. Activities implemented with IBL can be used online or face-to-face.

Our 15-day GSP course began with our attending an international qualitative methods research conference in Glasgow. As a result, students were able to explore their substantive area of interest in relation to their inquiry question, while also appreciating the linkages between research questions and the research process. At this and other venues, students had multiple people (presenters and nonpresenters) with whom to interact on their inquiry question and from whom to receive formative feedback. Further, research and relevant published materials were shared during conference presentations. The remaining stops for our GSP included universities in Edinburgh, Leeds, London, and Belfast and covered a wide array of topics related to child welfare and trauma. In addition to sessions with academics, we visited local social service agencies and engaged with service users, service providers, and others in each of our destination communities—what Dunleavy and Milton (2009) call connecting with experts and expertise. Students had numerous learning opportunities, such as lectures, skill days, research seminars, visits to community agencies, and cultural tours. Each day brought multiple sources through which to explore their inquiry question, creating a village within which each student could pursue their learning.

Our GSP course included readings and the following four assessment tasks: (a) facilitation of a structured controversy (25%); (b) development of an inquiry question (15%); (c) reflective writings through three blog posts (25%) and two responses to colleagues' blog posts (10%); and (d) construction of an analysis paper (25%). Colleagues and the instructor provided formative feedback on assessment tasks, such as the Structured Controversy, development of an inquiry question, and reflective blog posts. The instructor provided summative feedback on all assessment tasks.

Peer Feedback

A critical component of IBL is peer feedback. Students need regular opportunities to test their ideas and receive constructive feedback. Although it may feel a bit awkward at first if peer feedback is unfamiliar to them, students learn quickly to appreciate the praise, ideas, and suggestions from peers that help steer their inquiry processes and contribute to their confidence. Peer feedback, then, is built into all aspects of the inquiry process, starting with developing individual inquiry questions and continuing through the blog posts. Beth created feedback forms to formalize peer feedback and to provide some structure as students became comfortable with the process (see chapters 4 and 7 and Appendix E). Additionally, we scheduled debriefing time at the end of each day, which students used for many purposes, including providing feedback to their colleagues about their learnings.

Integration of IBL and the International Model

The international social work education model (Zubaroglu & Popescu, 2015) was implemented in three phases: preparation, knowledge building, and experiential learning. Scaffolding of IBL in the GSP course—via those preparation, knowledge building, and experiential learning phases illustrated—is not intended to suggest a linear nature to learning. For example, knowledge building continues to occur through experiential learning. During the course it looked like this: preparation (email, orientation day, prereadings, online module, research, Structured Controversy); knowledge building (developing inquiry question, blog posts, reply blog posts, activities including people and places); experiential learning (course presentation, interactions with people and places, reflection paper, conference participation and presentation, manuscript, research). Each of the activities honored IBL insofar as being student-led self-directed learning (FP 2), collaborating with peers and instructors (FP 3), and comprising multiple sources of information to help students articulate and challenge assumptions, while knowledge building also imbedded instructor support through scaffolding (FP 5; see chapters 1–5). The following illustrates the integration of IBL with each phase of the international model.

Preparation Phase

According to O'Mahony (2014), study-abroad learning experiences can only be realized when pedagogical practices receive attention. To help prepare students for the GSP, a number of activities occurred prior to their departure for the United Kingdom. Students were introduced to IBL through an online module and readings. They participated in orientation meetings (in person and online), including discussion of activities, accommodations, the course syllabus, and expectations as set out by the given university's international office. For more challenging or complex questions between the students and instructor, email and telephone calls were arranged. Students were informed during the orientation meeting about an opportunity to participate in the instructors' research project after completion of the course, should they choose to do so as an additional way to learn about research.

After we arrived at our first destination and settled into our accommodation, students participated in a structured controversy based on a general theme of poverty and homelessness. This provided them an opportunity to debate a familiar, current, and meaningful social issue. In two large groups, students developed a thesis, then researched and presented compelling arguments through a critical assessment of the literature on their team's topic. The instructor can see how a number of skills are required and are being further developed: teamwork, negotiation, critical thinking, and research. This assessment activity enabled students to gain information, explore alternative perspectives, and prepare for developing their inquiry question (Archer-Kuhn, 2013).

Knowledge-Building Phase

Friesen and Scott (2013) indicate that inquiry questions are powerful and critical if they are important to the discipline, connect students to practice, reflect the outcomes of the course, and ask students to discern among options. Further, they suggest that inquiry questions are essential if they uncover the fundamentals of the subject (Friesen & Scott, 2013). On our second day of the GSP, students were asked to develop inquiry questions that were powerful, critical, and essential; these inquiry questions could be changed and developed throughout the course. To support students in developing their inquiry question, we reviewed a number of specific YouTube videos that could be accessed easily with WiFi. These videos help students begin to "think in questions'" and also understand the various levels of questions—for example, surface-level questions versus deep-level questions—that make up good inquiry questions (see chapter 6). Their inquiry questions were to represent something important that they wanted to learn during the course. Providing students with choice over their inquiry questions aligns with the principles of IBL and is also motivating to students in pursuing their inquiry.

As we arrived in new countries (England, Scotland, Ireland) and met with our hosts, the students engaged in dialogue through introductory sessions, which included information about the given country's history; social, economic, and political structure; social problems; and effects of globalization. For example, a half day at Toynbee Hall chronicled social welfare from the origins of community development and settlement houses; from case work to clinical work; and from a social welfare safety net to a neoliberal era. Students were able to make links of influence to our Canadian social welfare system and took the opportunity through their blog posts and peer-reply posts to connect these active learning sessions to their inquiry question.

Students were also introduced to new models of practice in the United Kingdom, during which further knowledge-building opportunities occurred. For example, teachings about the involvement of service users were expanded beyond the Canadian context to planning and service delivery, education of postsecondary students, and policy development. In this knowledge-building phase, students had the opportunity to learn from and with each other, in addition to connecting with experts and the expertise (Dunleavy & Milton, 2009). By engaging with multiple sources of information, students considered the ways in which their self-directed questions were leading them to more exploration, and to refining and further exploring their inquiry questions. An example of knowledge building occurred during a walk to the hotel, following a day of sessions at one of our host universities. Stopping at an outdoor café for discussion and a beverage, students reflected on their daily learnings, which led to an extensive dialogue about epistemology and theory as the students began to integrate their knowledge into interrelated conceptual systems. They explored answers to their inquiry questions long after the "lesson" of the day had ended and moved, through peer interactions and discussions, beyond surface learning into deeper conceptual discussions. This experience highlights that the classroom is but one learning environment and maybe not always the optimal one. Walking through communities provided a natural experiential environment for conversation and learning through being in context, critical reflection, and dialogue with peers.

Experiential Learning

This phase entails applied knowledge, contextualization and reflection, and knowledge sharing and dissemination. Throughout the GSP, students were able to apply the knowledge they gained from community organization providers and service users to their inquiry question. To assist with contextualization and reflection, the students had daily debriefings and peer feedback for knowledge application, skills building, and reflection that enhanced their self-directed learning and search for understanding. Here, all three findings from Dunleavy and Milton (2009) are clear. Students not only connected with experts and expertise, but also expanded their understanding about how knowledge is created. Knowledge sharing emerged in many forms. Several of the students spoke of the ways in which they planned to share their learnings within their practice environment upon returning to Canada. This included a change in the way they perceived and wanted to practice social work.

Advocating for social change is a cornerstone of the profession of social work, particularly in pursuit of social justice (Canadian Association of Social Workers [CASW], 2020). Consistent with social work values, Friesen and Scott (2013) found that when using inquiry-based teaching strategies, students can become advocates for social change, since they not only develop their own perspectives, but also have a degree of control over their learning through inquiry questions and research. The authors posit that the teacher's role, therefore, should be facilitator and guide (Friesen & Scott, 2013). Teacher or instructor guidance with IBL might include helping students generate questions, investigate, construct knowledge, and reflect (Friedman et al., 2010), thereby achieving dramatic improvement in terms of academic achievement (Friesen & Scott, 2013) by including authentic pedagogy and assessment (Newmann et al., 1996); authentic intellectual work (Newmann et al., 2001); and interactive instruction (Smith et al., 2001).

Students on the GSP reaped the benefits of IBL, such as flexibility in the learning process, in terms of developing their own inquiry direction, what to learn, and how to go about their discoveries; an increase in critical thinking and critical reflexivity; and greater focus on social justice. Specifically, IBL within the GSP provided opportunity and an intense learning environment in which to think, reflect, and interact with others; time for one-on-one interactions with instructors; real-life occasions to compare systems (Canada and United Kingdom); direct experience (experiential learning opportunities); and access to multiple sources of information. Dialogue with colleagues and reflection provided students with multiple opportunities to consider their own understanding and process of learning, both of which Sawyer (2006b) noted as requirements for deep learning.

Upon our return to Canada, five students chose to participate in a major national social work education conference (Archer-Kuhn et al., 2016) to share their experiences of IBL. Following participation in the conference, two students and the instructor then coauthored an article. This experience exemplifies IBL in providing preparation, knowledge building, and experiential learning to allow for varied student engagement. The findings support the work of Zubaroglu and Popescu (2015) and contrast with Kirschner et al.'s (2006) assertion that IBL lacks sufficient guidance to students for engagement.

One aspect on which the IBL literature appears to be silent is implementing IBL with students who have varied learning preferences. During the GSP, IBL enhanced student interest in research and, for some, accommodated students with disabilities; one student identified that this experiential learning and inquiry approach had particular relevance to learning preference because of specific learning (reading and writing) and physical (hearing and vision) challenges. This experiential learning opportunity supported the student's self-identified kinesthetic learning preference, augmenting the visual-spatial challenges and enriching social-interpersonal strengths. For example, the GSP provided multiple opportunities for one-on-one discussions with presenters, professionals, and colleagues, allowing the student to pursue inquiry utilizing self-directed learning. For other students, having the experience of excitement and enjoyment with research was viewed as novel and reportedly enabled a greater understanding of the relevance of research to practice, which reflected less the actual topic of discovery and more how the learning process unfolded (Little, 2010).

A question that remained after returning from the GSP was whether context was the reason for such a positive student experience, or to what degree IBL deserves the credit. In other words, did students praise IBL so highly because they enjoyed study abroad, or could this kind of euphoric learning experience be replicated back home? Could a similar learning experience be organized with similar components to offer a like experience? To assess this question, I designed a theory course utilizing IBL that was offered on campus.

Implementing an On-Campus Course Including Community and IBL

The on-campus course occurred in the summer immediately following the GSP return. The course was offered 1 day a week for 6 hours over 6 weeks. As we had done in the GSP, we used the same assessment tasks and supported students to navigate through the same process of learning using IBL. For example, after introductions and an overview of the course, we jumped right into an overview of IBL, as well as a lesson on some course content before beginning our first assessment task, Structured Controversy. As with the GSP, ahead of the first class, students were provided with the online module and some prereadings about IBL. In class 2, we spent some time on course content and moved into creating inquiry questions (assessment task 2). This time we added a checklist of "good" inquiry questions based on the work of Roy et al. (2003). Part of the peer feedback included assessing their peers' inquiry questions against the checklist. Students could see more concretely where they were strong and where they needed to strengthen their work.

In classes 3 through 5, students pursued their inquiry questions with guest speakers, those either invited into the class or those we met on site on our field trips to community agencies. This meant that the community agencies were varied and the speakers could offer information that might touch on the students' inquiries. The students were responsible to make the connections between what they were learning and their specific inquiry questions. During these three classes, students were responsible for completing their blog and reply posts (assessment tasks 3 and 4). Dissemination occurred through student presentations in class 6, allowing students to share the knowledge they had created while pursuing their inquiry questions. Their final analysis papers reflected their respective learning journeys throughout the course. It was not possible to replicate the opportunity to present at a national conference and coauthor a paper. See Appendix D for curriculum structure.

Student reflections through their assignments and our observations of them in the course revealed high engagement in the course material. Having more choice over their learning was a significant motivator. Students appeared to enjoy interacting with the guest speakers, both within the classroom and in the community. The positive student experience both abroad and locally encouraged me to look deeper into certain aspects of IBL. One area that seemed to remain challenging for some students and where they seemed to require further support was in creating their inquiry questions. Additionally, some students remarked that they would have liked further guidance in peer feedback. I have further added to these components in IBL teaching.

Summary

IBL can be applied in various learning environments and courses. The course can be designed around the principles of being student driven and student led, albeit there may be more structured or guided elements, and can work for online courses as well as in face-to-face delivery. Students are granted more choice as to what to learn, and the instructor supports students to engage deeply with their learning while taking greater responsibility for it. Peer feedback must be integrated throughout the process to provide support for students and allow them to gain confidence in their knowledge creation. Dissemination of knowledge can be in class, using presentations to peers and instructors, or at a larger venue, such as a conference presentation. Important is the student's ability to share new knowledge with others.

Questions for Reflection

1. What linkages do you have with community organizations in your area, for example service groups, social justice organizations, museums, media outlets, private companies in your field, research development organizations? How might they contribute to student inquiry in your course?
2. To what extent do you have peers providing formative feedback to students in your course? Are the benefits of peer feedback acknowledged by you and by students?
3. How might you envision a role for Structured Controversy in your course? Could you see the value as a learning activity or possibly an assessment task?

HOW DO I FIND MENTORING AND BUILD A COMMUNITY OF PRACTICE?

Beth Archer-Kuhn and Stacey L. MacKinnon

What to Expect

- Role and value of mentorship
- IBL projects utilizing mentorship
- Faculty mentoring faculty
- Mentoring student facilitators and student facilitators as mentors
- IBL facilitates communities of practice
- Peer support through small group work
- Peer support through large group work

In this chapter we discuss the role and value of mentorship in IBL-HE. Although neither of us authors had a mentor when we began IBL-HE, we have learned a number of lessons that we believe are helpful for faculty as they get started with IBL-HE. We have developed ways and created an instructor guide to mentor faculty who show interest in getting started. We have also created a mentorship program for students to ease the adjustment to IBL-HE, with an accompanying student introductory guide to IBL-HE. These resources come from our experiences implementing IBL-HE and through the support of student research assistants.

We share, in the section that follows, a project that included access to a faculty IBL mentor, who supported instructors throughout the teaching and learning experience. Instructors reported this type of professional development as helpful. The literature concurs with this finding, indicating that designating a mentor to support faculty through planning and debriefing meetings is important (Spronken-Smith et al., 2011; Woolf, 2017). Baker and LaPointe Terosky (2017) acknowledge benefits for the mentor, mentee, and wider organization. We also discuss, in the IBL mentorship project description, another strategy to support colleagues getting started with IBL, modeling. The IBL mentor (Beth) actively modeled the IBL approach in several of the classes during the course, while the other faculty members on the project team observed. This particular strategy is not yet exemplified in the IBL literature, though scholarship on teaching education suggests that peer observation is an effective approach to professional development (Carroll & O'Loughlin, 2014; Hendry & Oliver, 2012; Tenenberg, 2016).

Role and Value of Mentorship

We know that mentorship has been shown to have many benefits to students in academia, including growth in self-development, skills development, and career development (Haber-Curran et al., 2017). Mentorship has been studied from the perspective of students who are mentored by faculty at the undergraduate level (Castellanos et al., 2016; Fuentes et al., 2014; Kramer et al., 2018); students mentored by students at the graduate level (Lorenzetti et al., 2019); and types of mentorship that are effective with doctoral students (Katz et al., 2018; Linden et al., 2013; Paglis et al., 2006). More recently, Morales et al. (2021) considered the effects of heterogeneity on undergraduate students and found student satisfaction with mentoring was not affected by mentoring relationship heterogeneity. Finally, Schuman et al. (2021) explored e-mentoring with at-risk students and found that students showed significant improvement in grades and graduation rates. It seems that mentoring students during their time of new learning holds many benefits, provided the mentor/mentee relationship is a good match.

We also know that IBL can be challenging to implement in the beginning stages and wondered how mentorship might enhance instructor implementation of IBL to help guide the process and be available for support. If mentorship in academia has been found to benefit students during their time of learning, then how might faculty benefit from this same type of supportive strategy?

IBL Projects Using Mentorship

The following two case studies provide examples of mentorship in IBL-HE; the first reflects mentoring of faculty with faculty, and the second is students with students.

Faculty Mentoring Faculty

Faculty can take on the role of mentor or mentee depending on the context of the learning environment. The project focus was implementation of IBL in three sections of an undergraduate social work practicum seminar course taught in fall 2017. The students were all in their final year of the undergraduate program. Our study focus was on the faculty experience.

This seminar course provides students opportunities for reflection on their authentic field practicum experiences and runs concurrently with student field practicum placement. The traditional approach for this course has not been inquiry based, with the exception of a pilot project the previous year and our study conducted in fall 2017. The original course outline provided information about practicum-related dates, assignment details, and deadlines for the seminar course. Weekly topics for discussion were based on emerging issues arising from practicum experience. The integration of theory and practice were based on specific practicum experiences but were not grounded in an inquiry question. Adjustments were necessary to the syllabus.

We had four social work faculty members collaborate in this mentorship project (see Archer-Kuhn, Lee, Hewson, & Burns, 2020). One faculty member was identified as the mentor, given that instructor's extensive knowledge and experience implementing IBL in multiple courses. The remaining three faculty members agreed to implement IBL in their seminar course. Only one of the three faculty members had implemented IBL in a course, once in 2016; one faculty member had many years of student-centered pedagogy, yet not IBL; and one faculty member was new to IBL and academia. It was important that the mentor had prior positive working relationships with two of the faculty, because the challenges of implementing IBL can strain relations, especially at the beginning of the process while faculty get comfortable sitting in discomfort. These course instructors carried out the dual roles of faculty liaisons (i.e., link between the student, the agency that has engaged the student in field training) and course instructor, giving them familiarity with the practice contexts from which inquiry questions were derived.

Based on a research agenda that considered IBL in social work education, the IBL/faculty mentor had already created an instructor guide to getting started with IBL and a brief module for students to watch prior to the seminar course beginning to familiarize them with IBL as pedagogy. Both resources were shared during two preliminary project team meetings of general discussion about the process. In this way, the instructors were learning about IBL (engaging with the instructor guide) at the same time as the students (engaging with the module). Prior to the beginning of the course, we also discussed a proposed implementation process similar to what had been developed and utilized the prior year: a review and adaptation of the course syllabus, assessment tasks, rubrics, and course materials to support the IBL process. Part of the mentorship included a discussion of faculty comfort level in changing the course syllabus. Although it can be a challenge to ask instructors to give up their ways of teaching a course, adapting the syllabus is a necessary part of helping faculty to focus on the principles of IBL. We spent some time asking questions, sharing concerns, and generally creating an implementation plan for mentorship. There were many, many questions.

We agreed that one way to support faculty in their learning of IBL would be to have the mentor model implementation of IBL during classes 2 and 3 of the seminar course to inform the instructors' practice in subsequent classes. We brought together students from all three sections of the course for combined classes to ease pedagogical modeling. For some, understanding IBL is easier when it can be observed in action. We decided to bring all three sections together twice for combined classes and to model structured and guided inquiry (Spronken-Smith & Walker, 2010). During class 2, we engaged students in a structured controversy, an active learning activity to prepare students for IBL (Archer-Kuhn, 2013). A guided IBL approach was used in class 3 to support students in their development of an inquiry question. This meant that students were able to choose their area of interest and three related peer-reviewed articles. The three instructors in our project provided a template for students to document their findings and to subsequently share with peers. Faculty also facilitated a process of peer and instructor feedback to guide and support students in developing their inquiry question.

Had you been an observer, you might have seen the instructors using YouTube videos on how to create good inquiry questions, students using an accompanying checklist based on research literature (Roy et al., 2003) that helped them decide on their inquiry questions, and small group activities that provided opportunities for students to share their areas of interest and research findings with peers, all grounded in their practicum experiences. Another step was for students to both give and receive formative peer feedback. The skills students learned through this process included information literacy, a critical component to support social work student IBL (Yesudhas et al., 2014).

The project team met to debrief the process after class 2 and 3. The IBL mentor was responsible for creating notes from the debriefs, which we would later use as an additional layer of our reflection process. The three instructors were also asked to note their learning experiences and to send a summary to the IBL mentor. We decided to use a template containing a series of questions to capture faculty experiences, since we thought it would be interesting to consider the shared and varied experiences of each faculty member.

Throughout the remainder of the course, the instructors continued to support the students as they explored their inquiry question; for example, instructors supported students to engage critically with the material (Yesudhas et al., 2014), and the final assignment was a presentation of their inquiry process with a focus on their learnings in the field. When the semester was completed, the team met to discuss their overall reflections about their IBL teaching experience and their perceptions about the learning experience for students. We used a thematic analysis to analyze our data, which included faculty and mentor reflections and notes.

Three themes emerged from the data analysis: (a) deepened learning experiences; (b) adjusting to a new approach; and (c) peer support and learnings. Each theme reflects our growth process and is consistent with Elo et al.'s (2014) suggestion that findings need to be reported with clarity, using a figure to show the overall conceptualization. For further information about the findings, see Archer-Kuhn, Lee, Hewson, & Burns (2020). In general, the process of learning varied with instructor and IBL-type experiences. For example, the faculty member who had experienced mentorship the prior year was very confident in the IBL process, whereas the faculty member who was new to academia and who had no prior relationship with the mentor found the discomfort of the unknown very challenging throughout the course. An important lesson for us was that faculty need to be able to trust the mentor or, at a minimum, the IBL process, to be able to implement IBL with confidence and be a necessary support to students.

Mentoring Student Facilitators and Student Facilitators as Mentors

Mentorship in IBL-HE extends well beyond the traditional "senior faculty mentors junior faculty" model and may often include faculty mentoring senior-student learning facilitators (i.e., senior undergraduates) and these latter facilitators mentoring junior students. When IBL-HE is functioning at its highest capacity, peer-to-peer student mentoring also emerges. This mentoring structure helps to perpetuate the use of IBL both inside and outside the classroom by preparing students to serve as facilitators for their own learning and that of others. Stacey describes this type of mentoring more fully in Appendix B.

Traditionally, students who are helping in the classroom fall into one of two categories: teaching assistants (often graduate students) who teach or grade on behalf of the primary instructor, or participants in peer-assisted learning, in which all students act as peer teachers and help each other to learn while also themselves learning by teaching. Both approaches have received support in HE research, particularly in the medical field and the sciences (e.g., Furmedge et al., 2014; Groccia, 2018; Grover et al., 2017; Hughes, 2011; O'Neal et al., 2007; Wheeler, Maeng, & Whitworth, 2017).

From a student-centered IBL-HE perspective, the role of a senior student is less that of a teacher and more of a role model and support. In that sense, a student learning facilitator differs significantly from a teaching assistant (TA) or even a peer assistant, in that a facilitator's job is to model being naturally curious, becoming curious when needed, asking questions, and spurring discussion. By contrast, students expect a TA or a classmate serving as a peer assistant to have the "right" answers they need. The impact of this shift in terminology was palpable when, in The Curiosity Project (MacKinnon, 2017), the position held by the senior undergraduate volunteers was changed from TA to learning facilitator (LF). Once the senior undergraduates were seen as LFs, the junior students began interacting with them more as mentors in the inquiry journey rather than teachers who were judging them and their performance. Under these circumstances, students' confidence as academics appeared to increase as the junior students saw these senior undergraduates take their work seriously, invest their time in supporting their learning, and support them as they moved toward and hopefully past the outer barrier of their comfort zone. In this circumstance, wherein the senior students had themselves been students in The Curiosity Project (one junior student referred to them as "the survivors"), the LFs also reinforced the importance and impact of the project on them personally, given their decision to share their time to help others have a positive learning experience and their aim to inspire the junior students to value the experience as well. When engaging in assessment approaches such as contract grading, specifications grading, or ungrading, the LFs help the junior students maintain their trust in the class instructor and faith in the IBL process and can alleviate fears about these alternative forms of assessment.

Not only are the LFs beneficial to the junior students in IBL, but the senior students themselves also benefit from participating. While the LFs for The Curiosity Project had their training as former students in the project, they also requested a senior seminar course entitled "Curiosity: Theory and Practice" so that they could learn more about why the project was so successful (FP 1). Research by Wheeler, Maeng, Chiu, and Bell (2017) concluded that even without personal experience, professional development training significantly improved their TAs' content knowledge, and that finding was maintained over the entire semester. The TAs' beliefs about learning also shifted to be more in line with inquiry-based instruction. Hughes and Ellefson (2013) determined that training graduate student teaching assistants (GTAs) not only improved TAs' teaching (as evaluated by both undergraduates and the GTAs themselves), but also resulted in gains in academic performance in undergraduate science labs, particularly with respect to scientific reasoning.

There are several resources available for developing LFs/TAs in IBL-HE, including work by Linenberger et al. (2014) and Marion (2013). The research on TAs and formal professional development suggests including at least the following:

- giving the LFs/TAs the opportunity to experience the course as students themselves, either naturally, as occurs in The Curiosity Project, or by having the instructor model positive student TA interactions and then giving the LFs/TAs time to practice those skills themselves (Kurdziel et al., 2003; Rushton et al., 2011)
- discussion of teaching beliefs and allowing time for the LFs/TAs to reflect on their teaching beliefs (Kendall & Schussler, 2013; Rushton et al., 2011)
- understanding how the process of learning works and how to teach effectively in order to enhance that learning (Luft et al., 2004; Sandi-Urena & Gatlin, 2013; Sandi-Urena et al., 2011)

Regular check-ins with LFs/TAs can help by offering opportunities to raise issues, problem solve, and feel supported. Check-ins also help the primary instructor keep their finger on the pulse of what's happening in the course from a different perspective. For example, in our experience with The Curiosity Project and implementing IBL practices in pedagogy, students were often more likely to share any concerns they had about their projects with their LF who, after asking permission, shared it with the primary instructor. Often, changes to the assignment or course resulted from suggestions that LFs shared with primary instructors, based on the facilitators' immediate interactions with and observations of the junior students.

However, it is important to recognize that, as with so many pieces of the IBL puzzle, you do not need to have access to senior undergraduates or graduate students in order to employ a mentoring process in your classroom. In a cooperative environment such as IBL-HE, the students in the class themselves can act as mentors for each other. This could mean fostering a supportive mentality during small group work, in which students are all contributing to the same project, or creating small discussion groups that meet regularly to discuss each member's individual project.

These meetings can involve each group member summarizing and sharing their week's learning on their topic, as well as their reflections on it. The other group members then are charged with giving them feedback, such as asking questions for clarification, extending or narrowing their thinking, playing "devil's advocate" for critical analysis, and/or sharing resources from their own academic and personal lives (e.g., someone they know personally to talk to or a relevant reading from another class). They learn how to enjoy being curious through topics they are naturally drawn to and how to become curious about things they know nothing about. In both scenarios (i.e., common group project versus group meeting to discuss individual projects), students tend to become invested in each other's work, watching for emerging resources they may be able to share, and encouraging each other to take intellectual risks in their learning. In our experience, they also share their skills, offering a comparison point for growth in writing and critical thinking. This is particularly valuable when a student becomes bogged down by life stressors or hits a roadblock in their learning. In those cases, we have seen groups actively get involved in helping the floundering student get back on track, either by role modeling their own knowledge and experience or by directly offering to help them develop the skills they need to succeed (e.g., time management). When the opportunity to interact in small groups includes both face-to-face discussion (in person or online) and written feedback, every member of the group has the chance to share for the betterment of all.

Our experience shares similarities with work by Asghar (2010), who uses what she calls "reciprocal peer coaching" (RPC) as a formative assessment strategy in her classes. In addition to learning about each other's areas of inquiry, students who engage in RPC experience autonomy in learning, the social aspects of learning, and an environment in which learning is shared. This mirrors our observations in our own classrooms, whereby this kind of cooperative interdependent learning benefits all who participate. At its most extensive level of engagement, whereby every student in the group is working on a completely different topic, the emphasis on mentoring each other and working cooperatively to enhance everyone's learning experience means that every student becomes invested in helping every other student garner the most learning they can over the course of the term. In essence, a student's grade is not dependent on that student's contribution, but each student can learn from what other students have to share, and if they do, they will likely receive a higher grade. A norm of reciprocity is formed that keeps the group invested in supporting each other's work throughout the term. In the case of The Curiosity Project, this interdependence and peer-to-peer mentoring environment is what brought about the end-of-term Curiosity Fair. Students who had contributed to each other's projects over the course of the term asked to be able to have a gathering at the end of the semester so that they could find out how the project ultimately turned out and celebrate "their" accomplishment in this cooperative learning environment.

Whether you have more experienced students to rely on or you are trying to create a peer-to-peer mentoring environment in your IBL-HE classroom, remember that a shift in mindset is all that is absolutely required. Collaborative, not competitive, interdependent learning, and being/becoming curious regardless of who is working on what topic, is possible. Explicit reminders about the importance of these mindsets throughout the term is key. Once the mindset is firmly in place, use what resources you have to create as much positive mentoring as possible, both for students and for yourself!

IBL Facilitates Communities of Practice

Implementing IBL encourages a community of practice whereby students work in small and large groups to support a deepened learning experience. This is particularly important given the novelty of the pedagogy sometimes for both students and faculty. The excitement of IBL is in the self-discovery; however, the process of student self-discovery can create anxiety for instructors who are not accustomed to such uncertainty. We have found that the level of experience with active learning or IBL seemed to determine instructors' levels of anxiety and confusion; the more experience instructors had utilizing IBL or active learning activities, the less they experienced anxiety and confusion (Archer-Kuhn, Lee, Hewson, & Burns, 2020). Additionally, faculty also note an increased workload inherent in the IBL process for themselves and students.

To develop confidence in the IBL pedagogical method, faculty require support in understanding the inquiry process. We have shared several ways by which to mitigate confusion and anxiety for instructors and students. Providing materials, such as a handbook, videos, and readings, have been beneficial and can establish the foundational knowledge necessary for those new to IBL and feeling ill-prepared for the new approach (Little, 2010; Plowright & Watkins, 2004; Woolf, 2017). For example, students' anxiety was reduced when they were able to give and receive support from peers when creating their inquiry question. Similarly, as noted earlier in the chapter, our mentorship project included peer support for faculty by way of team meetings during planning, implementation, and evaluation of this teaching and learning strategy (Archer-Kuhn, Lee, Finnessey, & Liu, 2020).

Creating Community

Over the past 2 decades, communities of practice, sometimes called learning communities, have become more common in HE environments. Faculty join communities of practice, a space where they share a common interest with others and have a place to discuss common and diverse understandings. Environments of HE have traditionally encouraged and rewarded independent work, until, as Boyer (1990) noted in his seminal report on advancing teaching, *Scholarship Reconsidered: Priorities of the Professoriate*, researchers discovered the benefits of working with peers across disciplines to make connections and expand knowledge. Similarly, communities of practice, or learning communities, typically comprise peers who can support faculty so that they might have opportunity for critical reflection and critical thinking (FP 6). In his study on professional learning communities, Cranston (2011) writes, "The discourse of learning communities, the notion of trust is articulated as being relational in its orientation and developed around group norms of safety, risk-taking, and change orientation" (p. 59). Remarkably, we found the same is true of IBL when used as pedagogy in HE (Archer-Kuhn & MacKinnon, 2020). For both students and faculty in HE, trust, risk-taking and an action orientation are required within an IBL classroom. IBL provides this natural setting of peer support and feedback and, depending on the course, may be within or across disciplines.

IBL Requires a Community for Instructors

We have learned, and as demonstrated in the faculty mentorship project described earlier, that faculty can find it initially challenging to implement IBL without support (Archer-Kuhn, Lee, Hewson, & Burns, 2020). Not unlike implementing IBL with students for the first time, we have also learned that there are some necessary components for an effective IBL experience for faculty. Our findings suggest that first-time IBL facilitators require support to implement this pedagogical method successfully in HE, despite potential prior use of experiential learning. A number of authors have found that for instructors who are new to IBL, the change in teaching approach can be intensive and time-consuming (Justice et al., 2009; Lee, 2012; Woolf, 2017), with considerable upfront planning (Archer-Kuhn, Lee, Finnessey, & Liu, 2020; Little, 2010; Mackinnon, 2017) and increased student demands (Friedman et al., 2010; Vajoczki et al., 2011). We found, as did Woolf (2017), that these additional pressures can lead to increased levels of fear, stress, and anxiety for faculty.

The inclusion of a community of practice proved to be an essential support to faculty. Educational literature on academic careers holds that collaborative learning communities are effective in faculty growth, motivation, effectiveness, and retention (Bozeman & Gaughan, 2011; Gappa et al., 2007; Neumann & Terosky, 2007). We instituted a community of practice as we met regularly to reflect, debrief, and build on our learnings. This experience is supported by Little (2010), who describes IBL communities of practice as a form of dedicated support for staff. Other studies describe similar approaches through the formation of networks and special interest groups (Levy, 2012).

Another important component supported our positive shared experience as a community of practice implementing IBL: institutional support. Our team had departmental support through a teaching and learning grant and access to our larger teaching and learning center at our institution, whereby we could access large classroom spaces to bring three classes of students together in the faculty mentorship/seminar course project. We found that by providing institutional support, faculty were encouraged to experiment, take risks, and trust engaging in IBL practices.

Small Group Work

Whether you are a group of instructors, groups of peer leaders, or students new to IBL, the ability to work in small groups is critical in creating community. Students sit together in their small groups during class time. Time is designated during each class for small group work activities; students learn to rely on and trust their group members to support their learning. Typically, students have small group time to share information they have found related to their inquiry question and to receive formative feedback from peers. As such, small group work allows students to engage deeply in their learning. This process requires positive working relationships and understanding.

One activity that I have found helpful at the beginning of group development for creating community is the use of the Tao of Groupwork.

QR Code 12.1. The Tao of Groupwork contract.

(https://teaching.unsw.edu.au/group-work-when-groups-first-meet)

This requires students to think about what they want their learning experience to be and propose a written contract with their small group members. Students set expectations for themselves and each other, and each team member signs the contract. The contract includes items such as group purpose, ground rules, individual members' roles, individuals' responsibilities, and guidelines for group meetings (see the Tao of Groupwork for further detail). The final component is a plan for addressing potential challenges; for example, when establishing ground rules, members commit to tasks being completed by agreed-on dates. Because we know that doesn't always happen in life, what then will be the plan? All discussions then lead to a plan for addressing potential challenges. Students are asked to establish this contract during their first class together.

Large Group Work

Another layer of peer support in creating community in an IBL classroom is large group work. Opportunities are designated throughout the course for students to present their work to the whole class. This additional layer of support means that students are able to provide and receive critical questions and critical feedback from others who have not been as closely related to their inquiry process. Allotting time for class-wide reflection means that students can discuss challenges and revelations and brainstorm with peers to help fill knowledge gaps and learn about additional resources. This kind of learning, collectively reflecting and providing/receiving specific constructive feedback, prepares students for future inquiry activities (Tutt, 2021). Peers can ask essential questions that can help students consider alternative ideas and strategies to try during their ongoing inquiry process. Some students struggle in the more intimate setting of small group work, and larger groups provide an alternative that can promote ongoing learning. Students develop their inquiry questions with the support of peers in small groups; however, once they begin exploring evidence in the literature or through other sources, students present their findings to the larger group. This allows students to present quantitative articles that inform their inquiry. Then, later, qualitative articles can be presented to the larger group to inform their inquiry and to wrap up the course, the final analysis presentation of their inquiry process. A requirement at each student presentation is written critical constructive peer feedback. In these ways, through small and large groups, students receive a number of varied ideas to consider along with instructor feedback to enhance their inquiry process.

Summary

This chapter provides ideas about the kinds of support that are helpful for faculty and students while engaging in IBL-HE. We have learned through experience that these strategies are necessary when implementing pedagogy that differs from traditional teaching and learning. The process of learning through IBL is similar for instructors and students, which is why mentorship and modeling is so important for both groups. Engaging in support as a faculty member may be the difference for you in gaining confidence in your ability to successfully implement IBL-HE.

Questions for Reflection

1. Who do you have on campus or in your online community who could serve as an IBL-HE mentor?
2. What would you like your mentor to do for you? Do you have specific questions or needs they could address?
3. Are there others on your campus or in your online community who are interested in starting an IBL-HE "beginners support group" where you could invite experienced IBL-HE practitioners to come and answer questions?

13

WHAT KIND OF INSTITUTIONAL SUPPORT DO I NEED TO BE SUCCESSFUL AT IBL-HE?

Stacey L. MacKinnon

What to Expect

- Knowledge and the willingness to learn
- Immediate support
- Classroom supports
- Funding is nice, but not necessary
- IBL-HE as SoTL research
- Memberships and networking support
- Classroom design
- Career advancement
- Reflection
- Teaching and learning center

In this chapter we discuss the role of institutional support in incorporating IBL into HE classrooms, courses, and programs. We address both the monetary, space, and technical support that make IBL-HE easier to implement (though we are living proof that such challenges aren't necessarily barriers to successful IBL implementation). We also address the professional support that makes taking a leap into IBL a less risky venture, particularly in an early or precarious career. We discuss ways in which to document the instructor's own learning and growth as an IBL facilitator, to network with colleagues to implement complementary IBL experiences and support each other, and to garner the support of the relevant chair/dean/vice president (VP) and students in expanding campus IBL-HE.

As you know, our goal in writing this book is to give you a realistic look at getting started with IBL-HE in your own classrooms. This chapter is dedicated, not to research findings or theories, but the most practical advice we have for you based on our years of experience. Beth and Stacey are in very different universities: Beth's is large and research intensive, and Stacey's is small and balanced between teaching and research; Beth's faculty is systematically embracing IBL-HE as its primary teaching and learning approach, and Stacey's work is being adopted and adapted by professors from various faculties across her campus; Beth has the support of the Taylor Institute for Teaching and Learning, while Stacey's university has only a part-time teaching and learning development coordinator. You get the picture. What we have in common is our desire to support students to engage, take ownership of their learning, and ask a lot of good questions. What's important about this comparison of our circumstances is that it emphasizes that no matter what type of educational institution you are in and no matter how much support is readily available, you *can* get started with IBL-HE and be successful!

Knowledge and the Willingness to Learn

The first and most important thing you need to get started is *you*. Remember, as we discussed in chapter 5, the importance of your own belief in the IBL-HE process and your willingness to take on a new role in your students' academic lives. In chapter 7, we shared with you our research and experience on building trust in the IBL-HE classroom, and recall it also started with you and your mindset. So, the first thing you need to get started is to learn about IBL, particularly as it pertains to HE, and you are doing that by reading this book. We've given you many good resources to continue to expand and deepen your understanding of IBL-HE (chapter 1) so you can continue to learn and experiment in your own practice, and we will continue to update our website with more resources as they become available. Feel free to contact us to make suggestions of your own as well!

Immediate Support

The second thing you need to get started is immediate support. By immediate, I mean two things: people around you who will be supportive even if they aren't into IBL themselves and people who are into IBL that you can connect with to talk through (Friedman et al., 2010). In chapter 12, recall that we talked about mentorship, but this support can also come from within or without your department, in person or online. If you have a faculty development office or a teaching and learning center, make sure you find out what they offer, how you can access these services, and if they can set you up with others who share your interest—after all that's how Beth and Stacey got started. If your university or college doesn't have one, then you can lobby with other interested colleagues to have one created (Miller, 2014). Everyone benefits from having dedicated teaching and learning support, especially when curveballs like COVID-19 emerge.

Classroom Supports

The question most new IBL-HE enthusiasts ask me at this point is "What institutional support do I need *in* my classroom to be successful with IBL-HE?" Ideally, you want to be in a room large enough to have breakout groups that will allow students to hear themselves talk. Stacey has never had that since her classes are larger (60–90 students), and this usually means her classes are held in a lecture hall where they can't move the seats or packed into a small room where students can't hear themselves think. At her students' suggestion, Stacey started allowing them to meet during their regular class time for their small group discussions *outside* the classroom. Some stay, but most go to sit in the quad during nice weather, book a study room at the library, or claim tables in the campus coffee shop. Students will be creative. One group was desperate when they lost their library reservation and had their discussion on a set of stairs in the back hallway where it was guaranteed to be quiet! Regardless of where they land, they are always willing to engage fully and support each other's learning.

Having a classroom management system that allows for students to work together and give online feedback on one another's work is a big help. In the early days of The Curiosity Project, Stacey's students hand wrote or printed out their learning logs and kept them in brightly colored folders, which were shared with classmates. This wasn't sustainable long-term, however, as the class grew and the local stationary store's supply of bright folders diminished (no one ever wants the gray ones). Stacey found that switching to using Moodle discussion forums to upload thoughts, papers, and learning logs for feedback is much more effective and maintains a reliable record of every student's work and responses to it in real time. It also allows the students to share and store materials and resources they find outside the classroom as well. Any classroom management system will do; the key is everyone having access to everyone else's work for feedback purposes.

Since COVID-19 became a driving force in our teaching preparation, Stacey took her IBL-HE work online and has found it is still very successful. She prefers to keep it simple as she is not a technology aficionado, so she maintained the use of the course management system, Moodle, for learning logs and online feedback, but also gave students the option to meet via Zoom in their small groups for discussions. One third of the 2021 cohort decided to participate in this way, and it has been very successful; they simply join the Zoom session, Stacey puts them into prearranged breakout groups, they open a Google doc to track their discussion ideas (sharing it with each other and with Stacey), and away they go for 50 minutes. This has been a fascinating experience for Stacey as she can jump in and out of the breakout rooms exactly as she could when the discussions were in person, but in addition, she can also watch as their discussions unfold via the Google doc. She often keeps several of their Google docs open on her two screens and as something interesting or concerning shows up in their notes, she can go into their breakout room to see what's up. Her students call it "lurking," but they don't mind it, and they say they enjoy having her pop in like that. They say it feels good to know she's giving them their space to learn but that she also has their back if discussion lags or issues emerge.

That is it. That is the bare minimum you need to get started: the right attitude, the willingness to try, physical or virtual space in which your students can have discussions, and colleagues you can count on to bounce ideas, give honest feedback, and support you over the challenging times. Now we get to the bells and whistles!

Funding Is Nice but Not Necessary

Never tell your administrators that you can do something on a shoestring because you know they will be happy to watch you try. There are several things you can use to make the IBL-HE journey a bit more smooth: funding for LFs, classrooms for group work, research funding, and funding for memberships and conferences. Note the common denominator here: funding. This will often have to wait until you've proven to them that IBL-HE is worth their investment, but there are also small grants that can get you started. Stacey's initial IBL-HE work started with a small "Students Come First" teaching development grant sponsored by her university. She used it to hire four TAs to help her facilitate small group discussions and give the students written feedback on their work. The money didn't last long, of course, but it was enough for her to be able to see the value of having senior undergraduate students facilitating the learning of her junior students. It was also long enough for some of those junior students to decide they wanted to be facilitators even if it was strictly on a volunteer basis (with a good reference letter at the end of course). Stacey also

dealt with the lack of funding issue by creating (at the students' request) a
senior seminar course, Curiosity: Theory and Practice, where the applied
component involves facilitating. Funding is wonderful for getting started,
and if you can maintain it, that's even better, but getting creative is
sometimes necessary.

IBL-HE as SoTL Research

We strongly encourage you to look at your IBL-HE adventure as a source of
research data as well. The SoTL is growing exponentially, and if you have a
story to tell, then collecting the data to support it is key. In Stacey's case, she
happened into an unusual set of circumstances wherein she had two sections
of the same course to teach, 1 hour apart, and while doing a full-on Curiosity
Project with 90 was possible, it wasn't going to happen with 180 students.
So, her department chair suggested she teach one with The Curiosity Project
and one without to determine if the time and effort to incorporate IBL into
her classroom was making a difference. So she did. And it did make a difference (MacKinnon, 2017). Being on the university's research ethics board for
15 years, Stacey was well aware of the challenges of doing SoTL in your own
classrooms. In this case, she received approval to design meaningful assessments that would serve double duty as research data (e.g., final written reflection papers) and only after the final grades were official did she email the
students to ask their permission to (a) analyze their work, and (b) send them
a brief survey. Over 90% agreed to have their material used and appreciated
that she hadn't said anything about it before the course was officially finished
so they could feel free not to participate. She had one volunteer research
assistant de-identify the work and two others do the coding to maintain
as much anonymity as possible. Stacey has found this to be the most effective way to collect unbiased data from the students in her classes. Beth uses
similar ethical data-collection strategies.

The beauty of looking at your IBL-HE practice as SoTL research is that
not only can it help increase your knowledge and publication record and
help you connect with like-minded others, it also opens the door to finding funding from granting agencies. By harnessing our IBL-HE practice,
research, and publications, Beth and Stacey were able to successfully attain
funding from various sources; UPEI, the University of Calgary (Taylor
Institute for Teaching and Learning), our own university departments, and
the federal SSHRC. It also brought us here, to the point of writing this
book! Connect with those of us who have experience in making the case for
SoTL research funding and use the 21st-century competencies described in
chapter 17 to support the argument for IBL-HE as a facilitator to increased

reflective and integrative learning, increased higher-order learning (Archer-Kuhn, Wiedeman, & Chalifoux, 2020), and a significant path to lifelong and life-wide, sustainable learning (MacKinnon, 2017).

Memberships and Networking Support

At the very least, ask your institution to support an individual, or better yet, a group membership to the International Society for the Scholarship of Teaching and Learning.

QR Code 13.1. Welcome to the International Society for the Scholarship of Teaching and Learning (ISSOTL).

(www.issotl.com)

Or, ask your institution to support the Society for Teaching and Learning in Higher Education.

QR Code 13.2. Welcome to the Society for Teaching and Learning in Higher Education (STLHE).

(www.stlhe.ca)

Another option would be to support the SoTL section of your primary professional organization. This will not only help you connect with others interested in teaching and learning but will keep you abreast of grant opportunities and conferences where you can network. And speaking of conferences, find out if your institution funds (fully or partially) SoTL conferences. While the conferences in your own field of expertise will often have sections and presentations dealing with teaching, attending a more general SoTL conference will broaden your perspective to see not only what others in your field are doing but also how people in other fields are using the same teaching practices as you. It is a wonderful way to find experts and those who are just beginning, as well as people like you who are looking for collaborators—after all, many hands make light (or at least lighter) work! The more multidisciplinary and multinational your SoTL practice and research groups, the more interesting and viable your teaching, learning, and grant writing experiences will be. Sometimes you can find internal funding to host a small research symposium on IBL. You may be surprised to find the number of people from various disciplines who want to present their work!

Classroom Design

We left classroom design for last simply because for some of us there is often very little we can do to impact it. We can request already existing rooms with moveable chairs and tables, big enough to house small group discussions. If a new building is being planned, we can lobby for these types of rooms to be included (especially if your university, like ours, has active, experiential learning as part of its stated focus). And for those who don't have appropriate space, we can ask for technology and tech support that allows for more reliable online interaction between groups of students. Creativity on our part only takes us so far, so don't be afraid to ask for what you need (and for what you want). The research on the effectiveness of these pedagogies found throughout this book can help to support this kind of investment request. We also know that some of you will have institutions with much focus on teaching and learning, perhaps even a center for dedicated human resources to carry out the function of a teaching and learning specialist, or simply ample space to use as you need. Make use of those resources as much as you can; there is no need to reinvent the wheel when you have people like these in your contact list!

Career Advancement

Now let's get personal and talk about career aspirations. Many people hesitate to embark on new pedagogies when they are pretenure or untenured contract or sessional instructors. Stacey was already tenured when she began, but Beth was a pretenure assistant professor when she started incorporating IBL in her classrooms. We know it is difficult to ignore the risk that a low teaching evaluation can have on our career trajectory, especially for those who work under precarious employment or a merit system for pay. There are ways to help ameliorate some of this risk at any level of employment though.

The first line of support is within your own department or faculty. Who else in your immediate academic field engages in IBL-HE or even another type of nontraditional pedagogy? Not only could they be a potential mentor or collaborator, they may be able to give you insight on how to approach using new pedagogies when you are untenured. This is also the person or people who will be able to write a detailed reference letter for you as needed, supporting your innovative approach to teaching and learning. Secondly, who else on your campus could you connect with who is experienced this way? What can you learn from their experience?

Most of us who mentor colleagues who are trying IBL-HE give similar advice regardless of institution or field: reflect, reflect, reflect, and collect data whenever possible. Keeping a journal has certainly been a very useful tool in Stacey's professional toolbox. Every time she tries something new, she notes what she was going to do and why she thought it was a good idea, then she takes note of how it turned out and how she feels about how it turned out. She also notes alternative ideas that emerged and possibilities suggested by students. This metacognition about her own pedagogical approaches has allowed her to keep an ongoing record of her attempts (both successes and not yet succeeded) to innovate in her teaching (FP 6). As we noted in the very beginning of this book, IBL-HE is something you start and then grow. It takes time, effort, and tweaking (or all-out overhauling) to get to a point where it is running smoothly—and even then new challenges will present themselves for you to deal with (hello COVID). If you walk the talk and treat IBL-HE as your own inquiry project, it should never be "done," because each class, each cohort, and you yourself will change, and that's just fine. Growth requires change for our students and ourselves (and our institutions!).

Both Beth and Stacey have found it important to collect data on our new teaching and learning practices, from the perspective of ourselves and our students. Engaging in high-quality SoTL work gives further weight to your own decisions in the classroom and can inspire others to join in as well. If this type of research isn't something you're particularly adept at, turn to your mentors and community of practice to find those who can guide you along the way. Data collection and dissemination can strengthen your tenure/promotion/hiring file and increase the likelihood of receiving grant funding by demonstrating that you are taking this shift seriously and want to encourage others to follow along—double win!

If you are about to get started incorporating IBL-HE into your class-room practice, let your immediate supervisors know. Show them you are well versed in the method, share your plans, and let them know you will be monitoring the rollout of those plans as they progress over the term. Let them know you have engaged experienced mentors to guide and support you as you begin and that you are excited to share your experience with colleagues. Better yet, have this conversation face-to-face and then follow up with a detailed email so your higher-ups are aware of what you're doing. Keep any response you receive for your tenure/promotion/hiring file. In chapter 11 Beth shared her experiences of informing others of her IBL practices; first with a GSP by creating an IBL course, then by engaging colleagues to join in, and all the while applying for funding to support the systematic collection of data to inform our teaching and learning practice.

Reflection

Once you've finished your semester, take the time to reflect in writing on the experience as a whole. What worked well and what did not? Why is that? What do the students say about the experience? If it was wonderful, great! Do it again, though we would bet there are things you're still going to tweak and change. We certainly have. On the flip side, there may be times when things are not all positive, so it will be important to document your efforts to understand what happened for not only your next attempt but also for your tenure/promotion/hiring files. Discussing this with your immediate supervisor (who you made aware you were going to be attempting this) can go a long way to ameliorating a less-than-stellar student evaluation. Presenting your experience to your colleagues can also put the focus where it rightly belongs, on your growth and development as a teacher, rather than on a single difficult semester's evaluations.

Teaching and Learning Center

If you have one, get your teaching and learning center or faculty development office on board. They are invested in improving the teaching and learning on your campus and often have insight, support, and yes even funding that can help you navigate this new chapter in your teaching. They can advocate for you when things are challenging and celebrate you when things go well. At the University of Calgary, for example, Beth is part of an IBL community of practice. If you are part of unionized faculty you should also look into how innovative teaching and SoTL research are treated at your institution.

If they need further consideration, take it up with those who represent you. Ensure that your work is recognized for the quality contribution that it is. If you are not in this position, discuss with colleagues how innovative teaching and SoTL research are viewed during key career processes. If necessary, lobby with other like-minded people to raise the status of teaching innovation and SoTL to reflect the quality of work being done on your campus. Don't hide your light: If you publish in SoTL, let everyone know; if you are presenting innovative teaching work at a conference, let everyone know; and if you're getting ready to try something new, let everyone know—maybe you'll find an unexpected collaborator among your colleagues.

The more seriously you take your new adventure and the more positive you are about not only its success but your ability to navigate any choppy waters that emerge on the journey, the more likely it is that your colleagues, immediate supervisors, and administrators will be behind you in support. At the least, your institution will see your students engaged and learning more broadly and deeply using IBL-HE; add in the possibility of conference presentations, publications, and grant funding and your institution will be very pleased to enhance its reputation for teaching excellence by highlighting your work with IBL-HE in the classroom.

Is that then a guarantee that your colleagues and perhaps even the larger institution will take on the cause of IBL-HE across the board? Probably not. But it is the first step toward bringing more IBL-HE into your institutions' classrooms in a purposeful way. While some institutions have indeed gone full IBL-HE (e.g., McMaster University), others have full buy-in within certain faculties (e.g., Faculty of Social Work at the University of Calgary), and still others have pockets of IBL-HE sprinkled around campus either as courses (e.g., UPEI inquiry studies) or parts of courses (The Curiosity Project). What is important is that IBL-HE is done well and that whenever possible we share our learning with others. Feel free to start small with a single project, or if you're feeling ambitious, redesign a full course to incorporate IBL and build from there. Inspire others to try the approach for themselves, mentor them when they do, demonstrate its value to your administration, and anything is possible.

Summary

What do you need to get started?

- your own knowledge of and belief in the process of IBL-HE
- local support and experienced mentors

- a room with movable chairs/tables and/or an online environment that allows for breakout room discussion
- a classroom management system that allows everyone access to everyone else's work for feedback and resource sharing
- the willingness to try, reflect, adapt, and keep trying

How can you increase your institution's buy-in for your inclusion of IBL-HE?

- Share your knowledge with everyone.
- Be open about your plans and findings with your immediate supervisors; find champions to support you taking chances on innovative teaching approaches for your tenure/promotion/hiring file.
- Take advantage of your institution's teaching and learning center.
- Reflect regularly.
- Collect data whenever possible.
- Share your findings locally and through SoTL conferences.
- Apply for funding.
- Demonstrate the benefits of IBL-HE to your students' competencies in 21st-century lifelong and life-wide learning.

Once you have started the ball rolling, enjoy the ride! You will never have a boring moment in the classroom if you and your students are engaged in IBL-HE! Let us know how it goes!

Questions for Reflection

1. Who within your institution or discipline do you think might want to join you and begin utilizing IBL in their course?
2. In what ways will you plan to share your intentions with your administrator or trusted colleagues?
3. Are there resources that you think your organization might be able to provide if you were to identify what you need from them?

PART FIVE

WHAT DOES SUCCESSFUL IBL-HE LOOK LIKE IN THE END?

A t this stage, you have considered the fundamental principles of IBL-HE and the importance of developing a curiosity mindset. We have discussed the choices you need to make when designing your IBL path and talked about how to get your students started on their IBL-HE journey. You're thinking about the relationships you have and those you need to build to make your IBL practice successful and sustainable over the long term. After all these pieces are in place, what will success in IBL-HE look like for you and your learners?

In this part of the book, we will discuss some of the key indicators of and goals for success in IBL-HE that we have experienced in our practice and that are echoed in the research literature, namely the following:

- student engagement and pride in learning (chapter 14)
- increased social justice focus in and out of the classroom (chapter 15)
- adopting a lifelong and life-wide learning mindset and skills (chapter 16)
- academic and personal transformation (chapter 17)

Let's start with examining the first key outcome: increased student engagement and pride in learning!

14

STUDENT ENGAGEMENT IN LEARNING

Beth Archer-Kuhn

What to Expect

- IBL and student engagement
- IBL in social work education
- Seven cohort study: What we found and how our teaching practice is informed

Engaging students in their learning can be challenging given the various demands facing the contemporary student. This increased focus is due in part to what Friesen and Scott (2013) note as students' current need for different skills, such as the ability to think critically, synthesize, analyze, collaborate, and communicate effectively. The increase in technology that has given rise to a more connected global economy requires employees who are creative and collaborative to respond to contemporary complexities (FP 3; Friesen & Scott, 2013). Student engagement has been noted to increase when using IBL (Parsons & Taylor, 2011; Saunders-Stewart et al., 2012). In this chapter, we examine the student experience of IBL in undergraduate and graduate education when it is introduced in a structured way, then supported with guided and open inquiry for the remainder of the courses.

IBL and Student Engagement

Engaging students in their learning can be challenging given the various demands facing the contemporary student: work, family, and other responsibilities. Students' engagement in their learning has become a much more focused topic in the research literature. This increased focus is due in part to what Friesen and Scott (2013) note as students' current need for different skills, such as the ability to think critically, synthesize, analyze, collaborate, and communicate effectively. IBL is likely to give students more benefit in terms of deep learning and understanding through increased student engagement than traditional teaching approaches (Dunleavy & Milton, 2009; Healey, 2005; Hudspith & Jenkins, 2001; Yesudhas et al., 2014). Student-focused approaches such as IBL allow learners to construct their own knowledge through active participation, such as undertaking their own projects or gaining experience through applied research or consultancy through work-based learning (Healey, 2005). Aditomo et al. (2013) have found that the educators hoped that IBL would allow students to think critically about their personal paradigms and the impact on their practice.

In HE, Little (2010) suggests that IBL is perceived as fostering students' perception of themselves as part of a professional community and academic professionals rather than students of a subject. Further, studies reveal that when students are presented with IBL, they require deep engagement with subject material and the inquiry process (Justice et al., 2009), which often lends itself to improved relationships and partnership between teacher and student (Buckner & Kim, 2014; Little, 2010). As a pedagogic tool, IBL is a process of discovery and moving systematically to higher and deeper levels of understanding. Students are able to explore individual interests and develop critical thinking skills that lead to personal discovery and deeper understanding of their central question (Alberta Education, 2010). A number of researchers (Hudspith & Jenkins, 2001; MacKinnon, 2017; Parsons & Taylor, 2011; Saunders-Stewart et al., 2012) report finding an increase in student engagement when IBL is used as a teaching method.

Social Work Education: A Detailed Example of IBL and Engagement in Action

Although IBL has been adopted in various disciplines in HE, there is limited documentation in the research literature of its use in social work education. Our findings on social work student experiences add to the research literature on IBL with students in HE.

Our review of the literature revealed only four publications on the use of IBL in social work education. We searched a number of databases, including Social Service Review, Social Work Abstracts, Sociological Collection, PsycINFO, Google Scholar, SocINDEX, and ERIC, specifically for IBL in social work education or HE. We further searched targeted social work journals (*British Journal of Social Work, Journal of Social Work, Canadian Social Work Review, Journal of Teaching in Social Work, Journal of Social Work Education*) and a variety of journals that focus on studies in HE.

Of the four studies, Plowright and Watkins (2004) examine IBL in a social work program in the United Kingdom. Braye et al. (2003) report on an examination of IBL within social work law. Yesudhas et al. (2014) reflect on the application of IBL outside the classroom in field education, among social work students in Mumbai, India, noting the advantage of IBL as a teaching and learning strategy that permits students to participate in the cocreation of knowledge. In Germany, Zorn and Seelmeyer (2017) used IBL with information and communication technologies in a social work seminar course. In our study, we intended IBL as a student-centered approach promoting student freedom, choice, and decision-making about their own topic and question formulation (MacKinnon, 2017; Wright, 2011). Understanding the need for initial guidance, we provided structure and guided inquiry to the point of development of the inquiry question.

The Seven Cohort Study

This chapter addresses a mixed-methods study of how we have engaged students successfully in their learning using IBL-HE across seven cohorts, seven social work courses within the classroom. The GSP aspect of this study can be viewed in full details of the study (see Archer-Kuhn, Lee, Finnessey, & Liu, 2020). We examine the student experience of IBL in undergraduate, graduate, and doctoral education when it is introduced in a structured way, then supported with guided and open inquiry for the remainder of the courses.

What We Did

Following the recommendation of several authors, we began to construct an IBL course. Yesudhas et al. (2014) suggest that students be introduced to IBL prior to beginning their experience, while Friesen and Scott (2013) identify three key strategies of IBL that lead to deep learning, including scaffolding; formative assessment; and powerful, critical, and essential questions. Dunleavy and Milton's (2009) three criteria for increasing student engagement in the learning environment include (a) learning from and with each other and people in their community; (b) connecting with experts and expertise; and (c) providing opportunities for dialogue and conversation. Together these criteria and strategies made up our IBL course. For example, to accommodate the prior-knowledge component, we created an online module that students viewed prior to the beginning of the course, along with some readings. Together these provide opportunities to gain a basic-level understanding of IBL.

We then integrated strategies within each of the seven courses, including scaffolding assessment tasks and formative feedback to support the inquiry process, such as the development of powerful, critical, and essential questions, known as the central question (Hudspith & Jenkins, 2001), utilizing a structured controversy (Archer-Kuhn, 2013), videos, brainstorming, and a checklist for the development of an inquiry question (Roy et al., 2003) to take in the lessons from Friesen and Scott (2013). Finally, we provided access to multiple sources of information, including many peer consultations and field trips into the community for varied types of knowledge. In this way, students from all seven cohorts received not only information and education about IBL and the process of developing inquiry questions to pursue, but they also enacted their own teacher-supported, student-directed learning. Further, Justice et al. (2002) propose a five-stage pedagogical process: (a) engaging with a topic through a review of the literature, (b) developing questions, (c) gathering and analyzing data, (d) synthesizing and communicating the new knowledge, and (e) evaluating the output. Our IBL process, tied to each of the seven courses, also incorporated these strategies. Hudspith and Jenkins (2001) add that IBL is artful and creative, allowing students to develop critical thinking skills. We also observed creativity in the student learning journey with IBL. Regardless of how it is defined, the purpose of inquiry as a pedagogical tool is to help students develop the necessary skills to enable them to explore and find answers to their central question (Hudspith & Jenkins, 2001). The focus of the IBL instructor is to support each student in the learning journey.

Our Methodology

We used an explanatory mixed-methods research design, collecting both quantitative and qualitative data. Explanatory mixed-methods designs begin with the quantitative strand of data collection and add the qualitative component to help explain the quantitative results. This type of design is used when the results of one data set require further explanation (Creswell & Clark, 2011) and is supported in previous social work research (Engel & Schutt, 2016). Study participants were recruited from seven social work courses in two study sites. The courses included two international GSPs for both BSW and MSW students, a 6-week master's-level summer course, an intensive master's-level summer block-week course, two bachelor's-level 13-week semester courses, and a doctoral 13-week semester course. Members of our research team taught all courses.

Study participants who completed the pre- and post-course surveys (National Survey of Student Engagement [NSSE]) for their given courses among the seven courses were invited via email to participate in focus groups following completion of their courses. Our research assistants and researchers facilitated the six focus group interviews (one per course) to help explain the results of the quantitative data. The seventh cohort did not participate in the focus group given the low course enrollment of a doctoral course. Using a semi-structured interview guide, the focus groups allowed for exploration of participants' understandings of IBL and student engagement in social work education. Research assistants audio recorded and transcribed the focus groups verbatim. We used thematic analysis for data analysis (Braun & Clarke, 2006). Two research assistants compared these themes independently within and across cases, reviewing the transcripts from each focus group and recording on a table the raw data (comments) that represented the themes.

What We Found

Results of the quantitative data show that an overall main effect for time was significant: Wilks's lambda = .88; $F (1, 41) = 5.92$; $p < .05$; and partial eta squared = .12, which indicated an increase in higher-order learning among students after participating in the IBL course, regardless of their levels of education and gender. Similarly, there was a significant increase in students' resulting reflective and integrative learning after participating in the IBL course: Wilks's lambda = .79; $F (1, 41) = 11.21$; $p < .01$; partial eta squared = .22. Four themes emerged from the qualitative data: (a) experience of IBL; (b) adjustments required for the learning process; (c) impactful facilitation to learning; and (d) developing deep learning (See Archer-Kuhn, Lee, Finnessey, & Liu, 2020 for further details).

The experience of IBL across all cohorts reflected a new kind of learning for students, whereby they experienced increased awareness and metacognition: They were more conscious of what and how they were learning. Students noticed this awareness in stark contrast to traditional teaching strategies. Many students also described their IBL experience as freedom in learning (theme 1), noting the control and choice they had, which honored the uniqueness of each student. This was most apparent in students' peer consultations and during presentations as students noted the excitement, passion, and energy reflected in their colleagues' work. Rather than being led, students said they were supported by the instructor, whom they experienced as being in the trenches with them. It was here that students experienced a shift as they described shared power in the learning environment. IBL was also acknowledged to be more work for students (theme 2), requiring much preplanning and reflection time. Sometimes the reflection time occurred during interactions with others, and at other times the "aha" moments were apparent for students when they were reflecting on their own. Either way, there was agreement among students that IBL requires more reflection than traditional learning environments.

Students identified a number of impactful facilitators to their learning with IBL (theme 3), such as the intentional nature of the learning, the real-world and experiential learning process, the value of peer support, and the previously mentioned power sharing within the learning environment. Deep learning was achieved through IBL (theme 4), as the students described a broadened learning environment from multiple sources. These facilitated linkages in understanding, between the pursuit of their inquiry and their everyday experiences. Their curiosity was sparked.

We found an increase in students' reflective and integrative ability in learning (theme 4). For example, participant comments reflected that the experiential learning involved in the inquiry-based process; the dialogue with others through valuable peer support; and the engagement with their environment, or real-world experience, supported their ability to reflect and integrate former and new knowledge into their practice. Participant experiences supported the theorizing of Miller-Young and Yeo (2015): Learning comes from interactions with others, and during the inquiry process students construct knowledge from new and former knowledge to create new subjective realities. Participants' integration of their new understanding of learning as intentional learning showed their adaptation from recipients of knowledge to cocreators of knowledge, from passive students who do not know the answer(s) to actively engaged students pursuing answers through continual questioning.

Participants also shared the ways IBL helped them to engage in their learning and increased their higher-order learning (theme 4). For example, participant comments suggested they were making linkages to the everyday, meaning that they illustrated an ability to apply, synthesize, and analyze, delving deeper into their learning and seeking opportunities to apply their new knowledge to former knowledge to create new knowledge. It was clear from student comments that critical thinking skills were developing, reinforcing what has been found in grades K–12 (Alberta Education, 2010; Friesen & Scott, 2013). This was further evidenced when a participant shared noticing how they applied this new way of learning across contexts as the student made connections in other courses where previously the participant had not. Participants reported an awareness of an evaluative component to their learning, expressing thoughts about learning together and coming to understand their role in creating knowledge.

How Our Study Informs Our Practice

During the inquiry process, students construct knowledge from new and former knowledge to create new subjective realities. Situated within the constructivist tradition, IBL recognizes multiple ways of knowing and positions students as coconstructors of knowledge and instructors as facilitators and learners (Apedoe & Reeves, 2006; McKinney, 2014; Saunders-Stewart et al., 2012; Spronken-Smith & Walker, 2010; Woolf, 2017; Yesudhas et al., 2014). We studied student engagement in social work education through IBL and then applied IBL as the theoretical framework to examine student engagement in their learning.

We have learned from our students' experience of IBL that it encourages greater engagement through choice and freedom in their learning. We have also learned that students require guidance, support, and clarity about IBL so that they can build confidence in their skill development. As a pedagogical practice, IBL comes with an inherent teaching and learning partnership, with student feedback informing the teaching and learning process. To be successful, IBL does require instructors to be intentional in designing courses to imbed IBL and specific about it as a teaching and learning strategy. For most students, IBL is new, so it is important in the course design to include opportunities for engagement with multiple sources of knowledge producers and a positive peer support system. Finally, we learned that IBL can thrive when attention is given to power relations within the learning environment. Students were encouraged to take greater ownership of their learning such that power is shared between instructor and students and teaching and learning are more of a partnership.

Summary

We have learned that HE students need to be invited to engage in their learning. Doing so can result in greater commitment to their learning process, an increase in higher-order thinking, and an increase in reflective and integrative learning. These are important outcomes for today's students, whom employers expect to have the skills of critical thinking and the ability to synthesize and analyze. An intentional learning environment and course design that include the IBL criteria and strategies can provide students with the support and encouragement they require to achieve these important goals, through greater student engagement in their learning.

Questions for Reflection

1. Think of someone you know in your institution who utilizes IBL in their course. In what ways do they implement it? How do they talk about it? How do the students appear in the course?
2. What are your intentions for the students who take your courses? How do you envision them applying the knowledge they gain in your course to their future self?
3. When was the last time you spoke with professionals working in your substantive field of practice? What do they say about new graduates who join their team? In what ways do their comments inspire you in your teaching?

15

SOCIAL JUSTICE FOCUS IN AND OUT OF THE IBL-HE CLASSROOM

Beth Archer-Kuhn

What to Expect

- IBL as a socially just pedagogy
- IBL and social work education/professional alignment
- Indigenous ways of knowing and IBL
- Relationships of change, with examples
  - Teaching/research
  - Knowledge/praxis
  - Student/teacher
  - University/community

IBL-HE can be understood as a socially just pedagogy. For example, integrating IBL into the classroom would be a means of advancing social work's commitment to social justice (Pulliam, 2017). That is, studies reveal that IBL problematizes the traditional student–teacher relationship and instead promotes a more egalitarian relationship, whereby both positions share the role of knowledge creation such that a student (learner) can be a teacher and a teacher can be a (learner) student (Levy & Petrulis, 2012; Little, 2010; Saunders-Stewart et al., 2012). While we use an illustration in social work, a socially just pedagogy can be applied across disciplines (Summerlee, 2018).

Further, social justice is achieved using IBL-HE to manifest relationships of change. These various relationships are described later in this chapter, but we will focus on one manifestation of these aspects here, that of student and teacher. From a constructivist perspective, IBL aims to change the traditional classroom relationship and, in doing so, the power between student and teacher (Levy, 2012; Saunders-Stewart et al., 2012). This shift in practice can result in shared power between student and teacher (Saunders-Stewart et al., 2012). Within a traditional classroom, teachers transfer information and knowledge to students, and students receive it. As a result, student questioning is limited, with little space for student engagement (Buckner & Kim, 2014). You will recall that student engagement is what motivated Stacey and Beth to pursue IBL and curiosity in HE. In contrast, IBL challenges this didactic relationship by promoting and fostering students' engagement as partners in knowledge creation; as such, their direct and active role is encouraged (Little, 2010). As roles shift, through the freedom, choice, and student-led learning that IBL affords, students can come to appreciate their own abilities in cocreating knowledge.

We can, therefore, see that IBL can be implemented as a strategy to promote and foster social work principles in teaching and learning, thereby aligning with the value (social justice) of the profession of social work. Mullaly and West (2017) suggest that students are able to observe and experience relational teaching through shared power (i.e., power with versus power over) and partnership, two important concepts for professional practice. It stands to reason, then, that enacting social justice in the classroom as a live process is critical to exploring the topic of social justice for social work practice (Sensoy & DiAngelo, 2009). Despite this, relatively little explicit connection to social work exists in the academic literature, with the noted exception of Pulliam (2017). The core value of social justice in social work is about working toward equitable treatment for all (CASW, 2020). This includes social justice, whether understood from a liberal perspective, including self-determination, empowerment, and personal freedom (Reisch & Garvin, 2016), or from a critical practice perspective, such as through education, consciousness raising, and social change (Baines, 2017). Our national association, CASW (2005), indicates that "social workers promote social fairness and the equitable distribution of resources, and act to reduce barriers and expand choice for all persons" (p. 5).

Exploring the Link: IBL and Social Work Education

There are several other logical connections between IBL and social work. For example, both share related conceptual frameworks with respect to the construction of reality. While there is no one form of social work, Payne (2015) positions social work within social constructionism. This means that social work as a profession is socially constructed through our interactions with service users, social processes, and social influencers. While constructivism in the context of IBL refers to a learning theory that advances students' construct knowledge and meaning from their experiences (University of Sydney School of Education and Social Work, 2018), constructionism is closely related, since it asserts the coconstruction of reality through our interactions with each other and through one's experiences (Payne, 2015).

While constructivism and IBL are concerned with issues of power, so too is social work. Power is highly relevant to social work across a range of situations, including with service users, marginalized populations, intergroup relationships, social service providers, and interactions with institutions and structures (Dominelli, 2004; Nadan et al., 2015; Ranz & Korin Langer, 2018; Reisch & Jani, 2012). Anti-oppressive practice is a core social work approach, which aims to counter privilege and power in all social work contexts (Baines, 2017). Though issues of power and anti-oppressive practice in the social work classroom are less frequently discussed in the literature, related ideas, such as teaching intersectionality (Crenshaw, 1989); the interconnected nature of social categorizations, such as race, class, and gender, as they apply to a given individual or group; categorizations that are regarded as creating overlapping and interdependent systems of discrimination or disadvantage; antidiscrimination (Abrams & Moio, 2009); and social justice (Pulliam, 2017), have been described. Integrating IBL into the social work classroom would be a means of advancing social work's commitment to anti-oppressive practice since IBL problematizes the traditional student–teacher relationship by design. Continuing with the theoretical stance of social construction that social work takes, the profession and IBL also acknowledge, mutually, multiple ways of knowing and multiple realities. This expansiveness is most evident in IBL when the construct of "knowledge" is critiqued explicitly and alternative ways of knowing are explored and valued (Levy & Petrulis, 2012).

Indigenous Ways of Knowing and IBL

Social work as a profession also recognizes multiple ways of knowing as part of an anti-oppressive stance (Payne, 2015), calling for us to challenge dominant-culture knowledge creation at the institutional level. One example might be Indigenous ways of knowing—a field gaining greater momentum in mainstream social work (Baskin, 2006; Gray et al., 2013; Sinclair, 2004). Indigenous ways of knowing aim to incorporate these cultures' traditional knowledge and Indigenous worldviews into social work education and practice, such as those related to land, spirit, and ritual, as well as traditional roles, laws, and values (Hart et al., 2009). Scholars, including those who identify as Indigenous, have highlighted social work's history as perpetuating colonial and structural oppression against Indigenous students and communities (Baskin, 2006).

Some academic institutions are moving toward the challenging task of incorporating anticolonial practices through including Indigenous worldviews (Tamburro, 2013). Postcolonial concepts explicate and critique othering (placing the dominant culture as superior) and hegemony (placing the worldview of dominators as the only reality) and value re-membering (reconnecting to the past; Tamburro, 2013). In Canada, for example, the University of Calgary (2018) implemented *ii' taa'poh'to'p* Indigenous strategy. As an approach, IBL would complement this shift since it makes space and supports alternative viewpoints and diverse ways of generating knowledge.

Similarly, in the United Kingdom service user participation in social work education is standard practice and mandated within the curriculum (Anghel & Ramon, 2009). IBL may be a natural fit with the UK approach to social work education given the latter's principles of supporting multiple ways of knowing, coconstruction of knowledge, and attention to power relations in the classroom. For example, IBL aligns with service users being experts of their own lives and, through their provision of direct feedback to students (Dill et al., 2016), working as partners in teaching social work knowledge, values, and skills. Within this model, service users are included in decisions about student admissions and teach specific social work skills in the classroom on designated skill days.

The IBL knowledge–practice nexus is the final connection that we would observe with social work. Through its emphasis on field placements and critical self-reflection practices, the profession is driven toward merging theory and practice. In fact, in the United States, social work education accreditation standards require programs to provide field education experience with the intent to "integrate the theoretical and conceptual contribution of the classroom with the practical world of the practice setting" (Council on Social Work Education, 2015, p. 12). In a complementary way, IBL creates the opportunity for students to design and lead their own projects, developing transferable skills, thereby gaining practical experience (Justice et al., 2009). In some cases, students already do IBL-type work, especially those enrolled in MSW leadership and international development programs; some practicums are student created and driven, and supervisors act as facilitators.

In a doctoral course at the University of Calgary, in which IBL was the teaching and learning strategy, the five students and instructor collaborated on two conference presentations to look at the fit of IBL with Indigenous knowledges. Figure 15.1 is an example of how the connection between IBL and Indigenous ways of knowing was understood by our group so that IBL might support a decolonizing framework (Archer-Kuhn et al., 2018). The

Figure 15.1. Connecting IBL and Indigenous ways of knowing.

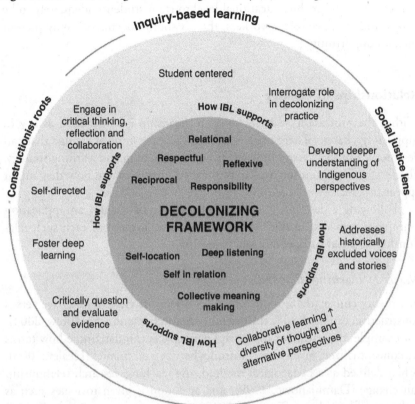

perimeter represents IBL, conceived as fostering social justice, the dark gray center, aspects of a decolonizing framework. The light gray band in between identifies the ways in which IBL can support the decolonizing framework, for example by questioning critically and evaluating evidence and, as a result, enabling collaborative learning, increased diversity of thought, and alternative perspectives. IBL's student-driven learning process can support a postcolonial approach in which knowledge is community based and derived from the people and student learning is about self-determination (Battiste, 2013).

Integration and formalization of IBL in social work would be a natural fit for all the reasons presented here. The approach aligns with many core social work principles, as outlined, which value multiple ways of knowing, anti-oppressive practice, and concern with use and misuse of power. As we prepare social work students for the future and success in the field, IBL approaches would greatly enhance the opportunities for linking theory with practice and building strong transferable skills. If there is more work that can be done at the educational level to train students adequately to be strong and effective social workers, then it should occur. IBL may present such an opportunity.

Relationships of Change

Within the profession of social work, relationship is understood as key to supporting change. There are a number of relationships of change that can be observed in the classroom when IBL is the teaching and learning strategy. Figure 15.2 illustrates the overlap of these relationships and how they might appear in a social work course.

Following a description of each relationship of change, an application example is provided to illustrate the possible occurrence of each such relationship in social work education, using IBL.

Nexus 1: Teaching–Research

In a theory course, the ways in which knowledge is viewed, objective versus constructive, can determine the teaching–research relationship (Brew, 2003). For example, the nature of the disciplinary spaces can determine how terms are conceptualized, given varied attitudes between disciplines (Healey, 2005). When defined as a pedagogical method, the teaching–research relationship can change (Damnjanovic, 1999), and attention is given to issues such as authority of knowledge (Fougner, 2012) and content versus social processes (Healey, 2005). Wood (2003) suggests that navigating this tension can be challenging in HE institutions, because the reward system in research is often

Figure 15.2. Relationships of change.

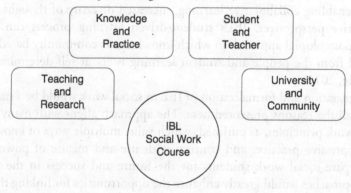

greater than the value placed on teaching. The teaching–research nexus can benefit student learning when it reflects the drive toward creating opportunities to merge teaching and research.

Healey and Jenkins (2009) present a four-quadrant matrix of the research–teaching nexus. At the top half, students are situated as participants in the process, while in the bottom half they are receivers of information. The authors assert that much more attention to the top half of the matrix is needed in HE, wherein students are either engaged in research discussions or undertaking research and inquiry. IBL (and its associated activities) are some of the best ways to achieve this culture of learning (Healey, 2005) since it positions students as coresearchers (Woolf, 2017).

Spronken-Smith and Walker (2010) investigated whether IBL does, indeed, strengthen the research–teaching nexus. Through analysis of three cases with three levels of associated inquiry (structured, guided, and open), the researchers found significant variation among levels of relationship. They determined that if IBL is striving for the optimal point of the research–teaching nexus, then an open, discovery-oriented approach, through which students create a robust research question and are able to complete the full cycle of inquiry, is best. Further, structured and guided approaches were found to be less significant in terms of arriving at the nexus but still were useful in developing specific inquiry skills.

An example of a teaching–research nexus includes graduate social work students who are enrolled in a theory course using a combination of structured and guided inquiry. Inquiry is explained as the pedagogical method, and students are encouraged and supported, through a variety of individual, small, and large group activities, to develop a question related to the course topic and an area of student interest (structured inquiry).

Each subsequent class is designed to provide students with opportunities to give and receive peer and instructor support and feedback while also engaging with research literature and brief field trips to community agencies. There students can interact with service providers and service users as a means of pursuing their question (guided inquiry).

Nexus 2: Knowledge–Praxis

IBL has implications for the knowledge–practice nexus. Cochran-Smith and Lytle (2001) unpack the ways in which inquiry relates to knowledge and practice when these are generated from a teaching perspective. Academia, through publication/dissemination, produces formal knowledge and theory for teachers to use—knowledge for practice. Knowledge in practice relates to the knowledge generated from practical experience; in other words, teachers gain knowledge when they practice teaching. Finally, and of greatest relevance to IBL, Cochran-Smith and Lytle (2001) describe knowledge of practice, whereby one seeks to understand the relationship between knowledge and practice. This is achieved when teachers treat their own sites of practice as spaces of inquiry.

According to these authors, teachers are coconstructing both their knowledge and their practice and, thus, present a space where "knowledge making is understood as a pedagogical act" (p. 48). The authors term this approach *inquiry as stance*. Teachers play a central role in knowledge creation by engaging students in their classes as coconstructors in knowledge creation. Inquiry as stance, therefore, can be viewed as a political act. Knowledge, practice, and inquiry intersect, and critical discourse can occur that problematizes, deconstructs, and reconstructs knowledge in order to bring change, produce context-specific understanding, and provide a richer conceptualization of learning (Cochran-Smith & Lytle, 2001).

Let's apply this knowledge–praxis nexus by using A GSP (such as study abroad) as the example of context for undergraduate and graduate students enrolled in a 2-week international social work course. The students traveled throughout the United Kingdom and constructed their inquiry question on the first day. Students learned about the origins of social work practice through a visit to Toynbee Hall (where, some argue, social work began); attended research seminars; practiced specific skills of reflexive practice; and engaged with service user groups, service providers, students, and academics while pursuing their inquiry question (combined structured and guided). Students were then encouraged to present their new knowledge at conferences.

Nexus 3: Student–Teacher Nexus

In all sites of IBL work, the student–teacher nexus is key. Expanding even beyond the point raised earlier in the chapter about the student–teacher relationship as a rebalancing of power, emblematic of social justice, this rebalancing also has important functional implications for roles in learning. When teaching and learning become more relational under IBL (Brew, 2003; Wood, 2003), the roles naturally shift as the teacher—no longer the sole expert—becomes a facilitator, and the student assumes responsibility for establishing a knowledge base (Damnjanovic, 1999). There is a sharing of power and an openness to challenge and critique (Brew, 2003). Language is an important tool to express authenticity and empowerment (Mangione et al., 2011), while the permanent tension of dialogue becomes taken for granted (Narayan, 2000).

The student–teacher nexus is evident in all sites of IBL in social work education. Students learn to provide and receive constructive feedback from both colleagues and instructors (guided inquiry). This process encourages students to view themselves and their colleagues as knowledge cocreators as they come to understand the instructor as a guide in the inquiry process. Despite the common initial experience of uncertainty, students tend to quickly embrace their "choice" and "partnership," created within the shared-power relationship.

Nexus 4: University–Community

The relationships between universities and communities change with IBL, as they become transitional learning communities (Fougner, 2012). Students can create communities of inquiry (Healey, 2005) through processes of situated learning (Fougner, 2012). As these university–community relationships change, so too does the opportunity to change the context for scholarship (Brew, 2003), since service user perspectives can be incorporated into curriculum development and knowledge creation (Green & Wilks, 2009). Within this service learning context (Thomson et al., 2010), service users share power in decision-making (Green & Wilks, 2009). Attention to social justice is observed through balancing mutual and competing interests (Thomson et al., 2010).

A field practicum seminar is the site for the university–community relationship to change. Students engage their field supervisor and service users at the community field site in their inquiry question, opening up learning communities (guided or open inquiry). Students then learn about their practice and advance their perspectives through interaction and feedback from service users. Within the UK context, the university–community relationship has broadened to include formal service user advisory groups in all social work programs. This protocol provides service users with decision-making power in various areas of the social work program, including admissions, curriculum, and research. In this context, students benefit from service user input about their lived experience, and from service users' feedback on student skill development.

Summary

IBL is a socially just pedagogy. It promotes and inspires student choice, agency, and independence in learning while also embedding the value of caring for others, respecting various perspectives, and honoring multiple ways of knowing. Many professions, including social work, engage with vulnerable populations whose voices have been silenced, overlooked, or ignored. These same populations are our students in HE! IBL is one means of supporting their unique learning needs as a socially just pedagogy. In this chapter we shared how relationships of change inherent within HE can apply IBL as a socially just pedagogy.

Questions for Reflection

1. Within your profession, field, or discipline, how is social justice enacted within the classroom?
2. How important is it to your profession that you consider social justice in your teaching?
3. In what ways do the relationships of change (teaching–research, knowledge–praxis, student–teacher, university–community) apply to your discipline in HE? How might IBL support you in enacting these relationships within your course?

16

ACADEMIC AND PERSONAL TRANSFORMATION

Stacey L. MacKinnon

What to Expect

- Identifying transformational learning
- Instructor transformation leads to student transformation
- IBL encourages transformation
- How students talk about transformation

In this chapter, we discuss the idea that IBL-HE is not simply about improving students' skills in asking questions and searching for answers, but also about the possibility for academic and personal transformation, derived from both the students' own foundational orientations, their IBL experience, and considering academic constraints that may be present. More specifically, the broader and more long-term goal is to help students make the shift to becoming strong, independent learners across areas of interest, as a path to encouraging transformation over their life spans. Students' transformation into holistic and engaged learners begins with uncovering the beliefs we, as instructors, hold, and the impact of those beliefs on who we are in the classroom.

> I gained so much more than just the credit to fill my degree requirements. Through the curiosity project I developed a greater understanding of how I learn, and the skills I possess . . . not just an assignment that I had to complete for credit, but it became a personal journey and investment that meant something to me. (Third-year undergraduate student in The Curiosity Project)
>
> The conversations, ideas, and words of encouragement that were shared in those meetings were very impactful. I couldn't help but stop and think several times throughout the process that "this is what university is all about." This mutual learning and respectful dialogue worked to challenge and strengthen our curious minds. (Third-year undergraduate student in The Curiosity Project)

Are there sweeter words an instructor can hear from a student than "my experience in this class changed me for the better"? For so many of us, the goal in our classrooms is more than just the sharing of content information. It includes providing the building blocks for academic and personal transformation. We want to create an experience in which our students begin, or continue, their journey toward being effective, invested, critical, open-minded, and intrinsically motivated learners. It is a tall order; however, the philosophy and practice of IBL-HE is ideally suited to helping our students, as academics and citizens of the world, start on this road to transformation.

Mezirow (2000) refers to the importance of "learning that transforms problematic frames of reference to make them more inclusive, discriminating, reflective, open and emotionally able to change" (p. 22). When we talk about transformation, we are referring to two different but mutually reinforcing groups of theoretical orientations (Taylor, 2007, 2008). Stemming from the work of Cranton (1994), Daloz (1986), Dirkx (2006), Kegan (2000), and Mezirow (1991), the first orientation focuses on personal transformation and growth, emphasizing self-critique of closely held assumptions and beliefs, the result of which is greater personal awareness in relationship to others. We will refer to this orientation as "personal transformation." The second orientation, which finds its roots in work by Freire (1984), Johnson-Bailey & Alfred (2006), and Tisdell (2003), focuses as much on social change as it does on personal transformation. From this theoretical perspective, personal and social transformation are linked intimately. We will refer to the second orientation as societal transformation. The societal transformation orientation focuses more on ideological critique, encouraging learners to develop greater awareness of power and to strengthen their own and others' sense of agency or ability to transform society.

For some of us, the initial attraction to IBL-HE comes from personal reflection and critique of our own practices in the classroom, including feedback from students (FP 8) and feelings that we need to play a stronger role in preparing our students for life in an ever-changing and challenging world. Because of these personal transformations, many of us expand our focus to embrace the idea of using IBL-HE to inspire societal transformation. Certainly within our classrooms and institutions we use our personal transformational learning to guide others toward critique of the status quo of teaching and learning. We lead by example to demonstrate how power exists in unhealthy ways and in showing how, as instructors, shifting these power dynamics can change passive students into intrinsically motivated learners. By doing so, we can inspire our colleagues, administrators, and students to be more reflective, flexible, and able to navigate the assumptions that impede societal growth. We begin to question the perspectives long accepted and explore even the classic concepts or theories held to be gold standard in order to understand where they began and if they still hold true. We see the world and the information we share with our students through a wider variety of lenses, modeling critique, inquiry, and respectful disagreement wherever possible.

IBL-HE is positioned uniquely to encourage transformative learning. There are six core elements to transformational learning: individual experience, CR, dialogue, holistic orientation, authentic relationships, and awareness of context (Taylor, 2009). Individual experience includes what the learner brings to and what they experience within the classroom. It is the foundation upon which both CR and dialogue rest. When the world can be seen as socially constructed, it can be deconstructed and examined for assumptions and biases. For example, when the education system is seen as socially constructed, we, as members of that society, can question its philosophies, pedagogies, and purposes, with an eye toward improving the human condition. Rather than focusing exclusively on external knowledge sources, IBL-HE incorporates the experiences of the learners themselves and uses those as the starting point for learning. When coupled with CR, experience can open the door to new perspectives.

Critical reflection can then lead to dialogue that further enhances the individuals' understanding of key issues. This dialogue, whether it occurs between peers, student and instructor, or students and stakeholders, is much more than just a point/counterpoint exchange. In order for dialogue to be successful in putting CR into action, trust must be built so that people are able to speak their truth without fearing personal judgment (FP 7; Archer-Kuhn & MacKinnon, 2020). This is particularly important, both when engaging in dialogue that encourages using a "devil's advocate" approach, wherein someone in the group is designated to question everything, or in the case of eliciting authentic dissent (Nemeth et al., 2001). Mezirow et al. (2000) suggest that successful reflective dialogue will be based, among other things, on freedom from intimidation and self-deception, open-mindedness toward other points of view, and empathy, all of which are enhanced by the development of trust. This sense of trust in the process of engaging in dialogue with others allows learners to embrace the discomfort of new learning while they are at what Berger (2004) refers to as "the edge of knowing" (p. 338), gaining new insights and broadening and/or deepening their understanding of the topic at hand. Janik and Daniel (2005) share that

> What [we] call transformative learning occurs as the result of mentor actions and attitudes [that reflect] that learning discovery is rarely easy. It is at best, discomforting, especially just prior to discovery. When learning feels

uncomfortable, TL [transformative learning] reinforces learner persistence, until discovery finally pops up or out. (p. 145)

Part of the reason why this dialogue is so important is that learners rarely change through a rational process yet are impacted by more holistic personal engagement. Kotter and Cohen (2002) refers to the rational process as "analyze-think-change," versus holistic "see-feel-change" (p. 11). Having a more holistic orientation means that the whole person, including their affective, intuitive, thinking, physical, and spiritual self, is present in the classroom (Yorks & Kasl, 2006). The presence of the holistic self in the learning environment encourages the development of community, a key component of IBL-HE. Although many found it challenging to share their work publicly, participants often mentioned that the support and feedback from their community of peers and LFs helped them overcome when they were struggling. As one student in Stacey's social psychology class observed:

> Another big challenge that I had from time to time was trying to think of things to write about; coming on the end of the semester I had great difficulty with this but with the help of my group and lab instructor I managed to find something to write about each time that interested me and was relevant to my topic.

For these relationships and communities to be successful, not only do you need to have the holistic self present, you must also ensure that the self that is being presented is authentic. Again this starts with you, the instructor, serving as a role model for your learners. Cranton and Carusetta (2004) identified five facets of authenticity in the context of teaching: (a) self-awareness; (b) awareness of the needs and interests of others and how they may differ from yours; (c) encouraging others to be genuine and open; (d) becoming aware of how context impacts your practice; and (e) engaging in CR and self-reflection about your practice (FP 6). As you saw in chapter 10 of this book, our research into IBL-HE and trust supports these facets as well (Archer-Kuhn & MacKinnon, 2020).

One of the biggest speed bumps we face as instructors using IBL-HE and encouraging transformation in ourselves and our students is time (Boyle & MacKinnon, 2016). Some students are, through nature or nurture, better predisposed to transformative change. Some will be inclined to trust quickly, while others will be more hesitant, and some will not get there at all. Some will excel at CR but may cringe at the thought of engaging in dialogue. If you are operating within the constraints of a typical university or college schedule, your time with your students may be limited to short class periods in single-semester courses. Does this mean you shouldn't strive for transformation? No. But it does mean you have to keep your expectations reasonable. In a single activity, or a single course, you may only be able to open the door to the possibility of transformation, but every door that opens gets the student closer to becoming a more invested, intrinsically motivated learner.

How Students Talk About Transformation

So what do students say about the role of IBL-HE in transformative learning? Let's use Stacey's experience with The Curiosity Project as an example. (You can read all about how it works in Appendix B and get more details at their website.)

QR Code 16.1. Welcome to The Curiosity Project.

http://projects.upei.ca/curiosityandinquiry/the-curiosity-project/

She and her master's student, Sarah MacLeod, collected these reflections from The Curiosity Project students about their experiences. Let's hear from them in their own words, in the series of quotes that follow, on what was, for all of them, their first time engaging in IBL-HE and link their experience to Taylor's (2009) six core elements to transformational learning: individual experience, CR, dialogue, holistic orientation, authentic relationships, and awareness of context.

Individual Experience

For many in The Curiosity Project, they were unnerved by the freedom to choose their own topic and the lack of guidelines on how much to write, because they did not have anything to reassure them that they were on the right track to getting a good grade. They began to use social comparison as a way to overcome their discomfort and believed that if they wrote around the same amount and researched using the same types of sources as their peers, then they would be doing it "right." However, many learned throughout the project that this was not necessary and stopped examining what their peers were doing and started to focus on their own learning.

> At the start of the semester I would have recommended more guidelines in the [project] because no guidelines scared me to death, but now looking back I realize that putting constraints in would defeat the point of the project, which is to just let your curiosity take you and learn openly.
>
> In all honesty, near the fifth learning log, I really didn't care anymore. I didn't care if my learning logs were what my professor expected or about the grade I would receive, I only cared about what I was learning. This was a drastic change compared to other projects I have done. It allowed me to consider myself in my own learning. Ultimately, I was the leader of my learning, and I got to decide my fate.

One of the benefits of the lack of guidelines in The Curiosity Project was that grades became less of a focus for students and, for many, their own learning became the motivation to do the work every week. The students began to exhibit intrinsic motivation rather than extrinsic motivation in doing their work. According to Ryan and Deci (2000), intrinsic motivation occurs when "doing something because it is inherently interesting or enjoyable," while extrinsic motivation refers to "doing something because it leads to a separable outcome" (p. 55), such as course marks.

> The Curiosity Project was pretty daunting initially, because I'm definitely a mark-oriented person. It felt very foreign to go into a project with no final goal in mind other than to learn. It was definitely an adjustment, but I've made it there. Life's too short to constantly worry about grades, and this project, along with some other aspects of the semester, have helped me realize that.
>
> I found it really hard to just write and not worry about grades. Everyone said to just let it flow and write and it will all work out. It took till the fourth or fifth log for me to start getting more comfortable about just writing. Other than getting used to it I loved it.

Not surprisingly, once students took this leap of faith, the quality of their work and, as a result, their grades improved, often dramatically. In addition, many students continued their learning after the course had ended:

> Since finishing the project I have actually gone back and continued to research a few of the topics even further just because I thought what I had already found had just been so interesting I wanted to know more.
>
> Finally, I conclude that although I have spent three months on this topic, there is so much more to learn. I do not feel this is the end of my curiosity project, but that it is just the beginning.

Authentic Relationships, Dialogue, and CR

The support offered by their peers and LFs was discussed as being the anti-dote for many of the challenges the participants mentioned as causing them difficulty over the course of the semester. For example, some participants found that the groups helped them overcome such challenges as speaking in groups due to social anxiety or shyness:

> Being with other students that were supportive in these discussions allowed me to feel more comfortable with sharing my ideas about my own project. Even though this may not seem too important, I feel very proud about being able to share the information that I had gathered because I am usually too shy to share my ideas with others.
>
> The group discussions are another part of the curiosity project that has been wonderful in developing my critical thinking and researching skills. Getting feedback from other interested, curious learners with a wide range of background views has been really helpful and has encouraged me to approach my topic in different ways. Hearing about and discussing other people's topics has also made me more open-minded.

Awareness of Context

The theme of pride surfaced again and again in the participant reflections and focused on three major aspects of which they were most proud. The participants mentioned being proud of themselves, the learning that they accomplished, and also their final curiosity projects. All three are linked; however, they were discussed separately often enough to warrant distinguishing them. When participants discussed their pride in themselves, they talked about it in terms of the amount of effort they put into their projects: "I am extremely proud of this project. My final project is a good representation of the hard work I dedicated to this project the last ten weeks"; "Overall, I am proud of the work that I did on this project; especially in my ability to complete a creative project since creativity and art work have never been my strong suit."

When the participants referred to the pride they had in their learning over the course of The Curiosity Project, they weren't referencing merely their own topic, but some mentioned feeling proud of how much they learned about their peers' topics as well. In the end, students who participated in The Curiosity Project realized they had begun the process of transformation both academically and personally:

> I have learned so much this semester. It has been wonderfully exciting to rediscover my interest in education and to realize that no matter what I do with my life, this is a passion I will have for the rest of my life.

Wow, I cannot believe the distance I have come when comparing my thoughts on this project and myself as a student since the beginning of January. I am truly surprised that a class could spark such a change in me in such a short period of time.

It goes to show that you can develop skills without explicitly teaching them in a class. I believe that we (or at least some of us) have learned more about critical thinking this semester than if we had been lectured about what critical thinking is and were instructed to try and apply it.

The Curiosity Project has been an incredibly demanding and incredibly rewarding part of my semester. It has prompted me to engage in truly critical thinking, both outward to the world and inward into myself.

Holistic Orientation

Personal transformations were discussed a bit differently than the academic transformations, and often participants began these with what they've learned about themselves throughout the process:

What I learned about myself through this experience is how vulnerability really can change (and already has in some ways) my life drastically. I am so happy that I chose this topic because I learned so much and I can't wait to continue practicing everything I've learned and applying these new things to the relationships in my own life.

It has taught me to learn in different ways and to keep an open mind when it comes to new ways of doing things—such as The Curiosity Project. It is amazing that as I was doing my project and learning new things about [Asperger's] syndrome that I was thinking back to times when I had first-hand experience with someone with AS and how I acted differently because of the lack of knowledge I had on this syndrome.

Transformation can even be seen in those who expressed regrets at the end of their experience in The Curiosity Project. When the participants discussed their regret at not putting more work into their projects, much of it stemmed from difficulties with time management and procrastination:

I wish I had have allowed myself more time to write my logs and find better sources. As a typical university student, I am known to lack in the time management department. This shortcoming stunted my ability to get top quality information/findings for my logs.

Others mentioned the things that they regret not having done, such as researching a particular area of their topic or not having used certain research methods, either through not identifying different sources or by not conducting interviews:

> There are certain things that I do regret over the time spent on the learning logs and the project in general. I feel that I could have reached out more to other people who have experience in diagnosing children with ADHD and see the approaches that they take.

Some participants also regretted not having put the effort into attending the Friday discussions:

> Something I really regret about this project and wish I would have put more effort into is going to the Friday discussions. . . . I really regret it not because of marks, but more because I didn't get to hear as many people's projects as I would have liked to.

For some participants, The Curiosity Project was so novel that they held back for a significant amount of time, rather than letting go, to the process itself or they censored themselves because they knew others would be reading their learning logs.

> Looking back, I also wish that I would have just let go a little bit more and just said everything on my mind. Sometimes I would filter myself because I knew others would be reading it but now I wish I would have just said it all.

Finally, an interesting item that some participants listed as a regret was in not taking this course and The Curiosity Project sooner. One participant even went a step further and made a recommendation to the university: "My only regret after this course was that I waited until my third year of studies to take it, as I could make a strong argument as to why this course should be required to graduate from UPEI."

In keeping with FP 8, Stacey always considers students' thoughts and suggestions into consideration and learn from them. As a result of the previous comment, in 2015, she used The Curiosity Project as a model to design a first-year undergraduate course called "Inquiry Studies." This new course explicitly teaches students how to inquire and addresses the challenges they face in being and becoming curious and how to navigate the speed bumps they will encounter in their IBL. "Inquiry Studies" is now one in a suite of three first-year experience courses (including university studies and academic writing) that UPEI students can choose from to fulfill their graduation requirement (see Appendix C).

As well, former Curiosity Project students asked Stacey to provide a senior seminar in which they would be able to explore what it was that made The Curiosity Project so seemingly effective. As such, the fourth-year undergraduate seminar called "Curiosity: Theory and Practice" was born, wherein senior students used IBL to explore how and why IBL was working so well for the junior students in their discussion groups (FP 1). Other professors on campus have since taken up The Curiosity Project banner, adapted it for their own needs, and incorporated it into their own teaching methods (you've read some of their stories in previous chapters). Inquiry-based projects such as this can now be found not only in other psychology courses, but also in biology (Otfinowski & Silva-Opps, 2015), English, environmental studies, and family studies.

Speed Bumps and Roadblocks

We promised you this book would be a realistic guide to getting started with IBL-HE, so we also have to acknowledge that the road to transformation isn't always a smooth one, nor do we suggest that once a transformative experience has been had it isn't possible to backslide into old habits. Research by Boyle and MacKinnon (2016) suggests that even students who have a highly positive and self-labeled transformative first experience with IBL-HE can face "speed bumps" and "roadblocks" on their way to knowledge and skill transfer in subsequent experiences. Ironically, many of the difficulties that students saw as roadblocks in their second IBL project resembled or were related to those they had experienced and successfully overcome during their first IBL project. These include a temporary regression in curiosity mindset, an absence of passion, a lack of novelty, and feeling overwhelmed by self-inflicted social comparison. Some participants also experienced difficulties surrounding the lack of structure of The Curiosity Project, a desire to do the project "right," and the experience of hitting the wall and not knowing how to move their learning forward during their second Curiosity Project.

Initially participants expected that the second projects would be essentially repeats of their first experiences (Boyle, 2015). These expectations not only left some participants feeling disappointed and frustrated, but also hindered their ability to be curious within the project. In hindsight participants were able to acknowledge that their expectations had a negative impact on their projects but were unable to see the crippling effect during their second project.

> I went into my second [project] really anticipating that kinda life changing experience again and I didn't have that. . . . You can never re-experience something for the first time. (Boyle, 2015, p. 44)

In addition, these students had expectations relating to their personal performance and identity as curious individuals (Boyle, 2015). The students participating in this second project were individuals who accurately identified themselves as curious individuals. They had participated in the first project and had positive, successful experiences. In addition, they had acted as LFs and had actively guided other students successfully through the process. However, this success and sense of identity led to a perceived pressure to be curious within the second project.

These "speed bumps" don't have to become full on roadblocks. When participants who indicated that they had expected that their second projects would be smooth sailing and immediately successful were asked to reflect on their first projects they mentioned having experienced difficulties and challenges and talked about how they had been able to overcome them (Boyle & MacKinnon, 2016). This reflection allowed participants to see the totality of their first IBL experiences more clearly rather than focusing only on the transformative outcome and therefore relieved them of the pressure they perceived to have a flawless learning experience the second time around.

In addition, as students get closer to graduation, it is easy to allow the pressures of the prevailing academic system and a hyper focus on their future—both academic and professional—seep into every aspect of their IBL projects. Unlike their experience in their second year, now that they were nearing graduation some students found it difficult to focus on the learning process rather than the mark that they would receive for the outcome. In some cases, this interfered with their willingness to fully exercise their curiosity and engage in self-directed inquiry. Regular reassurance that quality work results in quality grades is sometimes necessary for even experienced IBL-HE students to be able to ensure that these speed bumps don't become roadblocks to their learning and continued transformation.

Lastly, the group in which participants completed their second Curiosity Project naturally had a significant influence over how they experienced it. This group had a positive impact on some, who described the group as "tight knit, supportive and 'therapeutic'" (Boyle, 2015, p. 48); however, others experienced a change in attitude due to a perceived social comparison.

One student repeatedly spoke of the pressure that she felt from the group, an expectation from others to be curious. While she knew that this pressure was actually self-inflicted, she felt this social comparison had a dramatic influence on her project.

It was like there was all this pressure on me that hadn't been there before, but it wasn't directly on me. I just put it on myself because I felt like there was a lot expected from what other students knew about me. (Boyle, 2015, p. 49)

Other students also felt themselves "putting more value in what they [the other students] thought" (Boyle, 2015, p. 50). This self-inflicted pressure to impress their peers meant that instead of relying on the group for support and feedback, participants in some cases isolated themselves from the group. Regular reminders that IBL is an interdependent process of learning wherein everyone is responsible for supporting each other and helping each other succeed can alleviate this kind of unnecessary social comparison and encourage continued transformation.

It is also important to remember that the same is true for instructors. The road to transformation for us can include many of the same types of speed bump experiences our students encounter. Remembering that both learning and transformation are journeys, giving ourselves and others grace when things do not go smoothly, reflecting when the road gets bumpy, and seeking out the support of others (including our students) are key to continuing our own transformative learning as IBL-HE practitioners.

Summary

IBL-HE can play an important role in helping instructors become LFs and role models, while encouraging passive students to become invested, active, intrinsically motivated learners. The road to achieving and maintaining academic and personal transformation will not always be straightforward or smooth. You and your students will encounter speed bumps and roadblocks along the way (Boyle & MacKinnon, 2016). But by investing in the core elements of transformative learning using IBL, we can create a learning environment that will encourage lifelong and life-wide (across different areas of one's life—family life, work, school broadly, volunteerism, etc.) critical exploration, of and for ourselves and our learners.

Questions for Reflection

1. What goals do you have for your students' learning beyond content acquisition?
2. How could you incorporate more of these into your time with your students? Even if you can't do it all the time, where are the places where you can encourage more learner-centered approaches that embrace these goals?
3. Who else in your professional circle may be interested in or experiencing transformation in terms of their teaching practice? Could you get together to support each other through the ongoing process?

ADOPTING A LIFELONG AND LIFE-WIDE LEARNING MINDSET AND USING YOUR INQUIRY SKILLS BEYOND THE CLASSROOM

Stacey L. MacKinnon

What to Expect

- The skills and mindset needed for success
- Graduate preparedness
- IBL can prepare graduates for life by addressing wicked problems

Many students have become obsessed with getting the "right" answer as defined by an authority figure as opposed to focusing on how to learn, investigate, evaluate, understand, and question skills that would serve them well throughout their lives (Mussel, 2013). Bottino (as cited in Berger, 2014) suggests that as our world becomes more complex and dynamic, the value of questions and critical and creative thinking increases as the value of "right" answers decreases, due in large part simply to the accessibility of information. Our students need the skills to be able to sort through the quagmire of information available at their fingertips, to question it, to deconstruct it to determine its veracity and usefulness, to put it together in new ways. Employers indicate that the ability to ask questions, gather information, and solve problems are three of the key characteristics they are looking for in future employees but that recent graduates are lacking (Coplin, 2012; NACE, n.d.; Rancourt & Archer-Kuhn, 2019).

The Skills and Mindset Needed for Success

If society's success depends on well-thought-out innovation, creativity, problem-solving, and lifelong and life-wide learning in everyone, from ditch diggers to research scientists (Berger, 2014), then we have to create an environment in which students can learn to question, explore possible answers, see the big picture, and try things without constantly being afraid of being "wrong" (Adams, 2016). To do that, students need to feel invested in their learning, believe they have the support to learn the appropriate skills, and come to understand that persistence and resilience in learning are essential life skills. What are these key skills, and how does IBL-HE support the development of lifelong and life-wide learning skills? What exactly do we mean by lifelong and life-wide learning?

Most of us are familiar with the term *lifelong learning* (Parmelee et al., 2020). It simply refers to remaining engaged in learning throughout the life span. This includes keeping up to date on the latest changes in your employment field, reading about and discussing new ideas, and taking courses of interest to you. It emphasizes that leaving school is not, nor should it be, the end of learning, particularly in a world that is in a constant state of change. Lifelong learning is so important in today's world that it is included in the United Nations' sustainable development goal number four, which is to "ensure inclusive and quality education for all and promote lifelong learning" (goal 4).

QR Code 17.1. United Nations sustainable development goals.

(https://sdgs.un.org/goals)

Initially, lifelong learning referred mostly to the workplace, and because of this, its impact was measured in terms of economic productivity. Much of the research over the past 2 decades has focused on the importance of lifelong learning and developing critical thinking skills in these work settings (Blaschke, 2021; Calma & Davies, 2020; Froehle et al., 2021; Maluleka, 2021; Roohr & Burkander, 2020; van Woezik et al., 2020). More recently, lifelong learning has also taken a more "life-wide" approach, thereby also emphasizing personal development, active citizenship, volunteering, and community activism. Life-wide learning adds value to lifelong learning by recognizing that people exist simultaneously in a number of different spaces: work or education; home; being a family member; caring for others; being involved in clubs or societies; traveling; and looking after their own well-being and personal growth on mental, physical, and spiritual levels. However, the key mindsets and skills associated with lifelong and life-wide learning are very similar and center on the idea of knowing how to learn.

The benefits of lifelong and life-wide learning are well supported: job success, improved brain health as you age, staying connected with others, experiencing fulfillment, improved emotional balance, and avoiding depression (Dede & Richards, 2020; Drewery et al., 2020; Liu et al., 2019; Narushima et al., 2018; Obhi et al., 2021; Pstross et al., 2017; Rüber et al., 2018; Yamashita et al., 2017). Now scholars have begun to explore the ways in which learning must become not only life wide, but also sustainable over the long-term (Ben-Eliyahu, 2021; Billett, 2018; Hays & Reinders, 2018, 2020; Taranto & Buchanan, 2020).

Graduate Preparedness

Consider, for example, the key 21st-century workplace competencies identified by three international bodies. In 2016, the WEF asked employers to indicate the top 10 skills they believed would be needed by 2020. According to the WEF's "Future of Jobs" report (Gleason, 2018), by order of priority, these skills included complex problem-solving, critical thinking, creativity, people management, coordinating with others, emotional intelligence, judgment and decision-making, service orientation, negotiation, and cognitive flexibility. In 2020, the European Commission hosted a blog post indicating the 10 most useful competencies for learning in the 21st century.

QR Code 17.2. European Commission Key Competencies for Lifelong Learning.

(https://eur-lex.europa.eu/legal-content/EN/TXT/PDF/?
uri=CELEX:52018SC0014&from=EN)

The WEF and the EC, along with NACE, all agreed on five key areas: solving complex problems, critical thinking, coordinating with others, leadership, and communication.

However, the extent to which students are embracing, transferring, and utilizing the skills in these five areas is less impressive. In research conducted by NACE (as cited by Gray, 2022), employers were asked to indicate which of the competencies they deemed essential for university/college students to enter the workforce. They were also asked to rate recent graduates as either "very" or "extremely" proficient in each competency. Table 17.1 shows that while employers considered professionalism/work ethic, critical thinking/ problem-solving, teamwork/ collaboration, and communication essential for entering their workforces, recent graduates were perceived to be seriously lacking in these competencies.

As you can see from these percentages, less than 55% of employers indicated that recent graduates were "very" to "extremely" competent in the most essential competencies of work ethic and communication. A mere 55.8% were deemed "very" or "extremely" competent in critical thinking/problem-solving, and only 33.3% in leadership. Perhaps even more concerning is the

TABLE 17.1
Percent of Employers and Students Rating New Grads Very/Extremely Proficient in Key Competencies

Competency	Percentage of employers who rated recent graduates as "very" or "extremely" proficient in this competency	Percentage of students who rated themselves as "very" or "extremely" proficient in this competency	Difference in perspectives
Professionalism/ work ethic	44.2%	84.9%	40.7%
Critical thinking/ problem-solving	55.8%	79.8%	24.0%
Teamwork/ collaboration	77.5%	86.9%	9.4%
Oral/written communication	54.3%	79.9%	25.6%
Leadership	33.3%	66.8%	33.5%
Digital technology	79.8%	64.7%	-15.1%
Career management	35.7%	61.6%	25.9%

(Source: National Association of Colleges and Employers Job Outlook 2002 and 2021 Student Survey)

percentage of students who rated themselves as "very" or "extremely" competent in these areas, compared to employers' ranking.

As you can see in Table 17.1, there were significant discrepancies in comparing the perceptions of employers and recent graduates in terms of their proficiency in these key competencies. Most egregious is in work ethic, whereby 84.9% of recent graduates rated themselves "very" or "extremely" good, while only 44.2% of employers agreed. 79.8% of students rated themselves as "very" or "extremely" good at critical thinking and problem-solving, while employers indicated that rating applied to only about 55.8% of recent graduates. While a lower percentage of students rated themselves highly on communication (79.9%) and leadership (66.8%), they were still far more positive in their evaluations than employers, who rated only about 54.3% and 38% of recent graduates highly in these categories respectively.

This data tells us two very important things: (a) We know what the work world is looking for in terms of mindsets and competencies in recent graduates, and (b) we know that while recent graduates believe they are performing strongly on these competencies, employers do not agree. If graduates are not exhibiting these key competencies for success in the work world, how can they apply them to their lives more broadly?

It isn't a leap to see how these key competencies would translate to life-wide learning circumstances as well. Whether you are at work, volunteering for a nonprofit, or deciding how to vote in an upcoming election, complex problems must be addressed using critical thinking, often in concert with others with whom you will need to communicate and possibly lead. Often real learning objectives cannot be fully realized within a single context. Instead, learning and skills are distributed across diverse settings and areas of expertise (González-Sanmamed et al., 2019; Hays, 2015).

Taking this logic one step further, many if not most of the big problems or issues we encounter in everyday life (including, for many of us, in our work) are not just complex, but also cross over into being "wicked" problems/issues (Head, 2019). Wicked problems are especially difficult to solve because of incomplete, contradictory, and changing requirements that are often hard to recognize. Examples of wicked problems we are facing today include poverty, climate change, judicial reform, health care, and economic disparity (Lintern et al., 2020; Petrie & Peters, 2020). Each of us lives in a world full of wicked problems, most of them urgent challenges calling out for creative, democratic, and effective solutions (Weber et al., 2017). What we need to remember is that we have to work at solving them one piece at a time, even when a problem is truly wicked and it may not be possible to resolve it fully, since every solution to a piece of the problem creates new issues to be dealt with (Elia & Margherita, 2018). But making progress on wicked problems matters.

IBL Can Prepare Graduates for Life by Addressing Wicked Problems

One of the main issues underpinning these lower competencies, as assessed by employers, may simply have to do with students' not having enough exposure to and experience with them in HE. When it comes to critical thinking/problem-solving, for example, most students have been educated in a lecture-based environment, and when there were opportunities for more active learning, these have been presented as activities (e.g., labs or case studies) that had a single correct answer. If you follow the steps, you will find the "right" way. Having the opportunity to wrestle with more real-world wicked problems or issues is far less common. For example, a 2-week or 1-month unit on "the causes of World War II" in no way leads to a full understanding of the cultural, geographical, political, economic, psychological, and sociological factors that help to explain, not only what occurred, but also how to avoid this wicked problem from happening again.

Why are our students not getting regular exposure to wicked problems? There are likely several reasons. Addressing wicked problems takes time, more time than most teachers have in the run of a single class three times a week. It is also very challenging to grade students who are engaging in attempts to understand, let alone solve, wicked problems. Wicked problem work also doesn't lend itself to content testing, so if you are teaching in an environment that lives and dies by test scores (which includes most grade schools and institutions of HE), wicked problems likely will not be on your radar.

If life (and possibly work) is full of complex and/or wicked problems, then in order for lifelong and life-wide learning to be sustainable, there are mindsets and skills that students must adopt. Here is where IBL-HE can help! As we discussed earlier in this book, developing students' metacognition and promoting self-regulated learning are key issues in IBL (Justice et al., 2007; Spronken-Smith & Walker 2010). In addition, IBL experiences focus explicitly on developing students' cognitive skills, such as critical thinking and complex problem-solving, both in terms of the content under examination and the interaction of the learning group via the development of students' collaborative learning skills (Justice et al., 2007). Justice et al. (2007) suggest that IBL can develop and strengthen students' ability "to think critically and reflectively about the production of knowledge" (p. 203), not just its acquisition. Spronken-Smith et al. (2007) agree, describing IBL as a

pedagogy that allows "students to experience the processes of knowledge creation" (p. 2). Given the necessity of engaging in clear communication in both
the workplace and in real-life interactions, IBL-HE can also aid in developing students' oral and written communication, which the Boyer Commission
(1998) refers to as "the hallmark of clear thinking as well as mastery of
language" (p. 13). Perhaps most importantly, though, IBL-HE helps students
develop and strengthen their enjoyment of learning and the intrinsic motivation to want to learn, which is the first key to lifelong and life-wide learning
(Justice, Rice, & Warry, 2009; MacKinnon, 2017).

IBL-HE is an ideal time and place to engage students with real-world
wicked problems and gives students the skills and confidence to tackle lifelong and life-wide learning. For example, several years ago, Stacey introduced the concept of wicked problems and life-wide learning into UPEI's
"First Year Inquiry Studies" class. This was intended to be a simple class
exercise in generating, refining, and prioritizing questions, using the QFT
(Rothstein & Santana, 2011; see chapter 6). The class was divided into
groups of four and given easel paper and colorful markers. She showed
them a visual of two signposts in a farmer's field, pointing in opposite directions, one labeled "GMO" (genetically modified organisms) and one labeled
"Organic." She then asked them to come up with as many questions as they
could about this issue, using the steps of the QFT.

Once they began writing down their questions, she asked them to stop
and consider the perspective from which these questions stemmed, in this
case, first-year undergraduate students. While she valued their questions,
Stacey then challenged them to consider what other perspectives should
be present "at the table" to address this issue. They suggested scientists,
farmers, government officials, dieticians, plant biologists, doctors, pregnant
women and parents, economists, and marketing specialists. She then suggested each group take on one of these perspectives to see how the questions
and their relative priorities would shift. She also gave them the opportunity
to add further questions they needed to best represent their chosen perspective's concerns. Because they did not themselves belong to these actual
groups, they were able to take the lesson one step further and compare the
questions each perspective would bring, to see where the perspectives would
be aligned and where the divergences might cause conflict.

This introduction to wicked problems was the first time the students
had really considered a controversial issue from the perspective of a variety
of stakeholders, and they saw how the questions they asked and their prioritization of them could make or break attempts to resolve or at least make
progress on the issue. These skills in perspective taking, critical thinking,
asking and refining questions, and working together to fill out the corners

of a wicked problem are exactly what they will need to be able to do, moving forward into the work world and beyond. Were they able to apply these competencies in complex questioning and perspective taking beyond their studies? We don't know, but we do know that several upper-year professors have asked us what happened in the inquiry studies course that got their students asking so many more varied questions and incorporating issues from other areas of study into their classes. This is a very good sign that students are beginning to embrace the idea of life-wide learning, which, over time, can grow into lifelong learning as well.

This is just one example of how IBL-HE can encourage the kind of "deep learning" (Sawyer, 2006a) that leads to lifelong and life-wide engagement with ideas, particularly complex and wicked problems. Sawyer (2006b) suggests that "students learn deeper knowledge when they engage in activities that are similar to the everyday activities of professionals who work in a discipline" (p. 4). Many students, however, particularly in the beginning of their HE experience, are comfortable learning passively. But with encouragement most can be nudged outside their comfort zone to learn with greater depth. What does deep learning look like?

According to Sawyer (2006b), deep learning requires that learners

- relate the new information they are acquiring to ideas and concepts they already have knowledge of and experience with
- integrate their new knowledge into their existing conceptual systems and link those systems to one another
- search for patterns and underlying principles and assumptions
- evaluate new ideas critically and relate them to possible conclusions
- understand how knowledge is created and examine the logic of arguments
- reflect on not only their own understanding of the ideas and concepts but also on their own process of learning

Sounds a lot like IBL-HE to us!

Summary

Deep learning melds significantly with the goals and process of IBL-HE. Indeed, after participating in a GSP in the United Kingdom, students reflected on their experiences of deep learning using Sawyer's model (Archer-Kuhn, Wiedeman, & Chalifoux, 2020). The competencies in deep learning also coincide with the description of the key competencies employers deem essential for 21st-century learning and the characteristics of lifelong and life-wide learners who are actively engaged in the wicked problems of life. By incorporating IBL-HE experiences in our classrooms, we are giving our students the opportunity to build mindsets and skills that will not only benefit them in the long run, but also give our society its best chance to move forward in positive, healthier ways.

Questions for Reflection

1. What lifelong and life-wide learning skills are you interested in fostering in your students? How do you already do so? Where is there room for further enhancement?
2. Do you explicitly discuss with your students how the skills they are learning in your classroom are relevant to their lifelong and life-wide learning? How could you reinforce this idea in your classroom interactions?
3. Which of these skills are you still developing in your own life and learning? How can you continue this growth through your teaching?

CONCLUSION

The End of This Book Is Just the Beginning

Stacey L. MacKinnon and Beth Archer-Kuhn

Truer words were never spoken as "the end is just the beginning." While this book draws to a close, it is just the beginning of your IBL-HE adventure! Let's reflect for a moment on the messages we hope you take with you into your classrooms.

Curiosity and the Development of a Mindset

Modeling and encouraging a mindset of curiosity is key to making IBL-HE more than just a classroom exercise or a set of skills, but a way of thinking that can result in lifelong and life-wide learning for you and your students. Show them your natural curiosity and model how to become curious when you are inherently interested in a topic. Let them see your enjoyment of exercising your curious mindset and inquiry skills so that a norm of valuing curiosity becomes the gold standard in your courses, in and outside of the classroom. Follow their curiosity whenever possible, particularly if it relates to the content of the course. If you don't know the answers to a question, let them know, find it, and share it at a later time, or better yet, engage them in finding the answer. They will thank you for valuing their ideas and taking the time to follow up.

Student-Driven Learning

You are shifting the landscape in HE when using IBL-HE. Students are encouraged to lead their learning, to make choices about what and how they want to learn. They drive their learning process while the structure facilitates and supports their learning journey. Anticipate some challenges initially as everyone adjusts to this new way of learning. Listen, support, and project confidence in the IBL-HE process and in students' abilities.

Collaboration not Competition

Possibly for the first time in their HE career, students are being asked to collaborate first and put competition aside (FP 3). They are being asked to give constructive feedback to peers, to encourage peers to move in other directions; they are sharing helpful resources with peers. In other words, they are joining as a group of collaborators to support one another on their individual inquiry questions. It is truly beautiful to observe!

Balancing Content and Process

Successful IBL-HE comes from a desire to not only have students learn facts but to think critically and creatively about the content and about their own learning. Finding a balance between content understanding and metacognition is the goal in an IBL-HE course. The skills students learn and practice while engaging in IBL-HE will serve them well long after they have left our classrooms. Their inquiry skills will allow them to determine what questions need to be asked and how to find the answers, consider multiple perspectives, and communicate their findings—a task worthy of a course in any discipline.

Scaffolding

There are many ways to include IBL in your practice (activity, course, program) and different levels of structure (structured, guided, open) you can choose from. It is fine to start just outside your comfort zone and grow your practice of IBL from there. Starting small is recommended. Remember this is a long-distance event, not a sprint. Some things will go smoothly, and others will result in speed bumps, but by continuing to be reflective and using your own inquiry skills you will figure out what the issues are and come up with new ways to do things that will be more successful.

Reflection and CR

Reflection is key for success, both for yourself and your students. Make note of what works and do it again; reflect on why things did not go according to expectations, make some changes, and try again. Learn from your students' reflections on their experience and consult them on ideas you are considering (FP 8). Be explicit in asking which activities facilitated their learning and which did not, and why. Let them know that you adjust the course based on student feedback. Don't be afraid to share how you are experimenting with your students. As long as they trust that you "have their back" they will be willing to take intellectual risks with you.

CR becomes second nature when implementing IBL. CR as a skill brings students to a deeper level of knowing—about self, about other, and about self in relation to other. Students learn to interrogate that which is known and taken for granted to become more independent thinkers. Helping students to develop this skill will enhance their learning in other courses and in other areas of their life. Employers are seeking curious, independent thinkers who bring new ideas and ways of knowing into their work environment. As an instructor who utilizes IBL well, you can help support the needs in society for well-prepared, entry-level employees.

Embracing the Discomfort of New Learning

If you are not feeling uncomfortable, you are not learning. Know that you are engaging in pedagogy that will have moments of discomfort for you and for the students. These moments will be the most intense just before transformation occurs.

Anxiety

Anxiety is to be expected in IBL-HE initially. After all, we are asking students (and ourselves) to do something new and unfamiliar: lead their own learning. Know that this will ease with time and likely after the first assessment task is done, so you may want to consider implementing your first assessment task early in the course. Be open and transparent about IBL-HE, provide lots of resources, talk openly about how they might feel, and let them know you are there to support them through the process.

Relationships and Trust

Relationships matter in IBL-HE. They are indeed a cornerstone of the IBL process. Building and maintaining trust in yourself, between you and your students, between the students themselves, and each student's trust in themselves is worth spending time and energy on. Enlist students as you go to share their experiences with incoming classes. Build community within your classroom for your students and in your professional network so you too can have the support of mentors and collaborators. Consider how professionals, agencies, and organizations in your local community can support student learning. Interdependent learning and collaboration are key to successful IBL for both students and faculty.

Peer, Instructor, and Outside Support

IBL-HE is built around the premise that students can lead their own learning journey and that they will have support along their path. Support comes from peers, instructor, and outside sources, so be sure to consider how you will incorporate each of these components into your course design.

Expect to Learn From Your Students

Take every opportunity to learn from your students and make your classroom your own IBL project. Use what you are learning to customize the IBL-HE experience for each cohort, to plan for future cohorts, to test out new ideas, and to track your successes as well as your challenges. Remember that if you are doing inquiry well, finding answers spurs the next round of questions. This is exciting because it keeps your IBL-HE practice fresh; you will never be "done" given that, as your students grow and change, so will your IBL-HE knowledge and practice. IBL-HE is meant to be dynamic, so each experience brings you new insights, opportunities to try something different, and new questions to explore with your students. This means your course might look a bit different each time you teach it because you have learned from your own experiences and from the students' experiences.

IBL-HE and SoTL

There is far less SoTL research on IBL-HE than you may imagine. Much of what is available is concentrated in computer science, professional training programs, and mathematics, leaving the rest of the sciences, arts, humanities, and social sciences with little to guide them. Join us in remedying this imbalance by making a point of collecting data on your IBL-HE experiences whenever possible. Find an interested colleague in a different course, department, or faculty and try the same IBL-HE activity in more than one discipline, looking for commonalities and differences in students' experiences. Consider using quantitative, qualitative, or mixed methods in your exploration. If you don't usually do research with human participants, enlist the help of a colleague who has the experience to help you design your approach, get ethics approval, and engage in the analysis. Then write it up and share it with the rest of us in a peer-reviewed journal, conference presentation, newsletter, blog post, or a good old brown-bag lunch talk. This keeps your ideas fresh, your knowledge expanding, and your interest high while adding to the strength of your CV and inspiring others to incorporate IBL-HE into their own practice.

Perhaps most importantly, have fun and enjoy the ride. IBL-HE happens moment by moment, taking you places you never thought to go and raising questions you would never have considered asking. Learn to embrace the discomfort of new learning because IBL-HE will excite you, it will frustrate you, it will surprise you, and you will have the pleasure of guiding your students toward becoming more independent, capable, invested learners through curiosity and inquiry.

We hope that this book inspires you to delve into IBL-HE and provides you with a realistic guide to getting started. We also hope you will share your ideas and experiences with us through our website; after all, you and your practice are part of our IBL-HE project too. If you have enjoyed what you have read in this book, keep an eye out for our edited book, which looks at a variety of ways in which IBL has been implemented in HE across disciplines. Or, if you want to contribute to our edited book with your experience of implementing IBL, please feel free to contact either Stacey MacKinnon (smackinnon@upei.ca) or Beth Archer-Kuhn (beth.archerkuhn@ucalgary.ca).

Outstanding Questions to Consider

Now that you have had time to reflect on the book as a whole, what questions remain for you about IBL and how you might get started? Take a minute and write them down. This will be your first step in taking the IBL journey.

Question 1:

Question 2:

Question 3:

Our Final Questions For You

1. Which course would you like to consider while you begin to plan your IBL journey? When will you next teach this course?
2. Are there any activities in the book or on our website that you would like to try out? Can you think of an activity or assessment task that you currently utilize that you think you may be able to tweak to reflect the values of IBL?
3. How will you assess this new approach versus your former approach?

4. Which of your three questions will you address first? How will this question support or hinder your planning?
5. When will you consider the remaining questions, and how do they fit into your IBL plan?

All the best with your IBL journey! We will be thinking of you as you go forward in your planning.

APPENDIX A

Beth's Example of Implementing Structured Controversy

Beth Archer-Kuhn

Structured Controversy helps prepare students for IBL. I use it as the first step in the IBL process. Students explore a theme as a member of a group of students. Each group in the class presents arguments for its position and against an opposing team's arguments. I have used Structured Controversy in many types of courses, including community practice or a macro course as a teaching strategy that fosters social action, in a research course, a theory course, and as a field seminar course. According to Hudspith and Jenkins (2001), Structured Controversy is an active and deep learning activity that goes beyond the achievement of learning outcomes from traditional group presentations to "help the student get some background in a particular area, become familiar with disputed issues, and to spark starting points for inquiry" (p. 27).

Hudspith and Jenkins (2001) describe IBL as an art and a creative process that requires critical thinking skills. IBL differs from problem-based learning (PBL) in that

(a) the student explores a subject or theme and chooses a focus for the research; (b) a central research question for inquiry is formulated; (c) the student develops a plan of research, based on critical questioning and the attempt to anticipate findings; and (d) these research findings are brought to bear on the central question. (Hudspith & Jenkins, 2001, p. 10)

I have used structured controversy (Archer-Kuhn, 2013) as a means to help students begin to explore a theme (https://ojs.lib.uwo.ca/index.php/tips/article/view/3645).

QR Code A.1. Structured Controversy: Inquiry-based learning in place of traditional group presentations.

Depending on how large the class is, the group may require splitting into several smaller groups. I have used Structured Controversy with up to 60 students, whereby each group comprised 30 students, or with as few as 18 students in a class. To complete their tasks, each group of 30, in the one example, then subdivided further into smaller groups before joining back together in a large group of 30. When introducing a structured controversy, I tell students ahead of time about the activity and provide a handout that describes the activity, so they have a chance to review and reflect on what the expectations are. The following link will take you to the "Inquiry-Based Learning: A Guide for Social Work in Higher Education" manual that contains all of the resources referred to in this chapter (https://live-ucalgary.ucalgary.ca/inquiry-based-learning/template-basic-page-detailed-info-2-clone).

QR Code A.2. Inquiry-Based Learning: A Guide for Social Work in Higher Education.

Typically, a structured controversy in IBL has the following format: I read a scenario that involves a vulnerable population that the students may have some knowledge of or may have worked with in their field practicums or employment. For example, in focusing on the homeless population, I rely on authentic situations in the local community to set up a controversy, such as a gentrified neighborhood in which some stakeholders (politicians, business owners, community leaders) want to move the homeless people out of the community, while other stakeholders (homeless people, homeless coalition, allies) do not. The class is divided into two groups. Students must work together in their groups to identify three to four arguments they want to make about their position. One group argues on behalf of one side of the argument (community leaders), and the other group argues on behalf of the other side (homeless). After deciding on their arguments, each team develops a research plan about how they will explore their topic, whereby they must report on the evidence they find in the following areas in relation to the topic: historical, social, cultural, political, and economic (see rubric, https://docs.google.com/document/d/1sFHaw60OEMgfCC2RiC3BVjioOOHmt mnh/edit).

QR Code A.3. Structured Controversy rubric.

They also provide demographic information, present relevant statistics, articulate the relationship between need and social justice, and identify the implications for the community.

Teamwork and organizational skills are emphasized, and the activity is timed. I use the amount of time in a class and divide the many tasks into time allotments. This is presented as a visual for students and as a reminder of expectations throughout the activity. For example, in a 3-hour class the timing looks something like Table 4.2.

In Structured Controversy, although it is similar to a debate, the goal is not for one group to win and the other to lose. Instead, we want students to present arguments and then listen to the other group's arguments. In their teams students are exploring a topic, developing critical reflection and research and teamwork skills, practicing giving and receiving constructive feedback, and most importantly, learning to understand alternative perspectives. They also work in small and large groups. You will notice from the timeline that each team presents its arguments, listens and takes notes on the other team's arguments, reflects as a group about the opposing team arguments, and reflects back to their opponents what they heard the other group say. Students often report that in traditional debates they are so focused on winning that they don't bother to hear the other points of view, whereas with a structured controversy these essential components of listening and reflecting are built into the process. During the exploring-a-topic phase, we want students to consider alternative perspectives while also considering their own so that they enhance critical reflection skills. At the end of the process and having considered all sides, they are left to choose how they want to present their final comments.

An important component is for students to debrief on the process of the structured controversy, which allows students the space to voice their learnings, their challenges, and their emotions about the learning process. It also provides them further information as they consider the experiences of their peers. A final component is for students to reflect on their role in the activity. How did they contribute specifically to the work of their team? Students then submit a one-page reflection on their role and experiences. The skills developed from this activity (encouraging a curiosity mindset, learning and practicing inquiry skills, focus on process, critical analysis, interdependent learning, application of mindset to real-world issues) are then used in the next phase of the inquiry process, when students create their inquiry questions.

APPENDIX B

The Curiosity Project

Stacey L. MacKinnon

William Arthur Ward (n.d.) said, "Curiosity is the wick in the candle of learning" and that, more than ever, students must be encouraged to venture forth into the land of intrinsically motivated learning (Deci & Ryan, 1992, see also Baranes & Oudeyer, 2009; Csikszentmihalyi, 2014; Gottfried, 1985, 1990). In my view, The Curiosity Project is an opportunity for students to investigate topics that interest them and follow those topics down long and often winding roads, places where U-turns, hidden side roads, and venturing off the map are cause for excitement, not a distraction from the destination (MacKinnon, 2017; http://projects.upei.ca/curiosityandinquiry/the-curiosity-project/).

QR Code B.1. Welcome to The Curiosity Project.

Specifically, my goals with The Curiosity Project are to

- model and foster independent and collaborative learning
- allow students the opportunity to exercise their intrinsic curiosity in the fullest manner by having them choose a topic from any area of the course to investigate

221

- encourage students to think about what they already know, believe, or think about this topic and why, before they start researching. I encourage them to think about what they don't know about the topic as well, valuing this information as a positive starting point for curiosity, as opposed to a personal intellectual shortcoming to be rectified
- allow students the flexibility of using, valuing, and analyzing critically multiple formal and informal inquiries/resources. These could include but are not limited to academic and nonacademic literature searches; web-based searches; documentaries; and talking with other professors, students, family, friends, or community members
- encourage students to think critically about what they are learning and how they are learning and engage in regular sessions of "writing to learn"
- create an ongoing dialogue among the students, professor, librarian, and other project facilitators in order to increase self-directed learning and self-efficacy as learners and budding researchers
- encourage students to tolerate and hopefully value the ambiguity inherent in the topic and in the learning process itself, viewing it as a positive sign of intellectual growth and curiosity

While The Curiosity Project can be used in any discipline (indeed it has been picked up by biology, food science, English, and a transdisciplinary inquiry studies course), I originally designed it for incorporation in a second-year Introduction to Social Psychology class. This course is taught to 60–90 students in 50-minute sessions on Mondays, Wednesdays, and Fridays in a single semester. Mondays and Wednesdays involve lectures and in-class activities, while Friday's classes are dedicated to this project. Each component of this project is grounded in the structure of PBL (Blumenfeld et al., 1991), the focus of IBL (Friedman et al., 2010), intrinsic motivation (Ryan & Deci, 2000), proximal self-motivation (Bandura & Schunk, 1981), guided discovery theory (Brown & Campione, 1994), writing to learn (Fry & Villagomez, 2012), freewriting (Li, 2007), and metacognitive reflection (White & Frederiksen, 2005).

Everyone has a role to play in The Curiosity Project. The students' jobs are to attend classes and discussions, to submit their work on time after they have deemed it to be the best they are capable of, to ask for support when they need it, and to participate actively in supporting and furthering the learning of others. As the instructor, I am in charge of the logistics of managing the groups, ensuring that the systems are functioning, providing a safe and supportive learning environment, trouble-shooting unexpected learning needs and (contrary to the ideal version of this project, but in accordance with university requirements) having the final say on grades.

Whenever possible, I have also engaged volunteer senior undergraduate LFs. Most semesters I have a team of senior undergraduates who facilitate the in-class discussions, help guide the conversations, make suggestions, ask questions, and provide support to small groups of junior students. These volunteers have themselves been students in The Curiosity Project in previous semesters, so they understand how it works and how it feels to be embarking on this adventure. When we have been unable to have facilitators involved in the live discussions, they have volunteered their time to give written feedback online for students' projects.

The Curiosity Project unfolds over the semester in three recurring and two final end-of-term steps:

- weekly learning logs
- weekly online peer and facilitator feedback
- weekly small group discussions facilitated by senior undergraduate students
- a final submission shared with classmates and the public at The Curiosity Project Fair
- a final reflective write-up

It all begins with intrinsic motivation, or the doing of an activity for its inherent satisfaction. In the first class, students are asked to browse through their social psychology textbook, consider their life experiences, talk with friends, and then choose a topic that naturally sparks their interest and begin learning.

Weekly Learning Logs

The purpose of the learning logs is to enable students to

- spread out their learning over time, allowing for the kind of both breadth and depth of thinking that is one of the keys to success in university and the work world
- develop their ability to find information through online searches, journal articles, documentaries, conducting interviews, surveys, and other sources of learning
- improve their ability to summarize information

- develop their ability to express their ideas clearly in writing as they "think on paper" and to know when they have finished without being told how much to write
- give students time to think about/analyze what they are learning, rather than just summarizing other people's thoughts
- reflect on their past ideas, creating a bigger picture/context for their topic
- find links between weekly course work, other classes, other students' projects, and their chosen topic
- learn to determine for themselves when they have done their very best work, have said everything they have to say, and when they have finished without being told how much to write

The first learning log is unique. Students are asked to write in detail about the topic they are interested in learning more about. They discuss why they are interested in it, what they already believe or think they know about it, what they don't yet know about it, using the QFT (Rothstein & Santana, 2011; see chapter 6) to determine what questions they may be interested in pursuing over the semester.

There are no minimum or maximum word or page limits in the learning logs. Students are instructed to write until they have nothing more to say and they feel that they have given their very best thinking. Written in the first person, the language of learning logs is very much of the "writing to learn" variety (Fry & Villagomez, 2012), a conversation with oneself and one's readers in which ideas are explored, considered, reconsidered, dissected, and put together into a meaningful whole. In the event that they change their mind, begin to disagree with something they've written about earlier, or experience an "aha" moment, students are strongly encouraged, in an approach similar to freewriting (Li, 2007), to continue writing instead of editing or deleting their previous thoughts. The metacognitive process of watching thinking unfold is a vital component of The Curiosity Project, whereby we celebrate students' efforts to follow their thinking where it takes them without pretending it was the destination they had in mind all along.

In their subsequent nine weekly learning logs, students discuss in depth what they are learning; how they came up with the information; their critical assessment of the information; and their ideas, questions, and potential answers to questions concerning the topic they have chosen for their project. Each week these learning logs are uploaded to our course management web page, where they are accessible to the professor, senior undergraduate LFs, and most importantly, a small group of their peers in the class for detailed online feedback.

Online Feedback

The purpose of the online feedback is to enable students to do the following:

- share their learning and get considered feedback from their peers and experienced senior undergraduate LFs
- improve their ability to give and receive feedback that also helps improve and expand others' learning; they learn how others express themselves and ask questions in ways that differ from their approach, taking ideas that can improve their own skills
- share their life experiences and learning from other courses with others for the purpose of enhancing other people's projects
- look for links, connections, or discrepancies between their projects and those of their small group members

Each student reads and makes detailed suggestions/critiques of at least two classmates' online learning logs. Each senior undergraduate LF does the same for every student in their group (usually five to eight logs per week). Using the RISE feedback framework (see chapter 9 and Appendix E), peers and LFs are encouraged to ask the learner for clarification, suggest other ways to look at something, suggest some "it depends" ideas, ask "why" and "how" questions, recommend a reading/documentary they've seen themselves or heard about that may interest the learner, or suggest someone they could speak to about the topic. Since the goal is to increase and expand each other's learning, the more attention students give to the process, the more each student benefits. This means that simply agreeing with the writer or saying "That's interesting" will not suffice. Students are strongly encouraged to read the feedback they receive regularly and use it whenever possible to enhance their own learning.

These online feedback groups remain the same for the entire semester, allowing students to help their group mates grow and develop their projects over the long term and support each other when things get challenging. It also allows the senior LFs to get to know their students' work over time and note when significant leaps forward (or backward) are made. These are then communicated to the professor, who will bring them to the attention of the student for praise or concerned inquiry.

Small Group Discussions

Every Friday the students meet face-to-face during our usual 50-minute class time to talk with each other and their senior undergraduate LFs in small groups (five to six students) about what they are learning and how they are learning it. The purpose of the in-class discussions is to enable students to do the following:

- improve their listening skills
- share their learning and get spontaneous feedback from both peers and experienced LFs
- develop their ability to speak about topics that matter to them in public and be open to questions and critique from their conversation partners
- improve their ability to think on their feet and question, helpfully and respectfully, others people's ideas or interpretations
- learn more about other topics and find links among the group's projects
- give and receive from others constructive suggestions, guidance, and resources

To accomplish these goals, students and facilitators question and clarify what has been learned, respectfully debate points of contention, consider possible intersections among students' areas of interest, and share ideas about ways to collect and understand information and opinions. The senior undergraduate facilitators not only monitor students' progress and the effectiveness of the approach, but also model curiosity, tolerance for ambiguity, and flexibility in learning that is the cornerstone of this project.

For the first 4 weeks of the semester, the in-person discussion groups and the online feedback groups include the same people, giving students and facilitators an opportunity to put a face to their online colleagues. This first grouping is created quite randomly, and the projects do not necessarily, at least on the surface, have any relation to one another, allowing for a breadth of ideas and perspectives. While the online groups remain the same all semester, at week 5 the face-to-face discussion groups change completely, bringing together a different group of students and a new facilitator. This allows for fresh perspectives on students' topics, a new pool of potential resources, and avoids the development of tunnel vision within the group. With this second grouping, I try to bring together groups of students and facilitators whose interests or experience have something in common (e.g., stereotyping, media, and bullying) to encourage the transmission of in-depth learning among students and linkage of topic areas. In week 8, the face-to-face groups change completely for the final time, again being created somewhat randomly to encourage "big-picture" thinking and to begin the process of deciding on the appropriate audience and format for the final submission.

The Curiosity Project Fair

In response to students' interest in knowing more about how their peers' projects evolved over the semester, I instituted in 2016 the end-of-term Curiosity Project Fair. At the end of the semester, each student creates a final submission that integrates or applies what they have learned all semester, in a format that can be shared with the general public or a specific target audience (e.g., not a formal academic paper). This fair has grown from 50 minutes of mingling at the front of a lecture hall to a 3-hour interactive display time between the end of classes and start of exams, whereby students participate in each other's interactive projects and see how others have dealt with their topics, ask large numbers of questions, eat large quantities of baked goods, and explore links among their topics. Students also share their findings with the general public (e.g., visiting high school students, relevant community organizations, media interviews). The purpose of the Curiosity Project Fair is to enable students to do the following:

- compile, analyze, apply, and share the key points of their learning with the most appropriate or widest possible audience in the most effective way
- be creative in sharing their learning and to learn new approaches to presentations
- realize just how much they have learned all semester and how it combines to form a bigger picture of their topics
- take pride in the work they have done all semester and celebrate the multitude of ways in which they have helped others with their projects

For the final submission/presentation and the fair, students need to reflect on all they have learned over the semester and distill from it the key points they feel the general public (or target audience) needs to know. Students should not include everything they've learned all semester in their final submission; their choice of what to include is an essential part of the process. Then they consider the best way to share this information with their target audience so that the audience will be maximally receptive and willing to consider the students' positions on their topics. Finally, students have to get creative and have fun! The rationale for the "no formal research papers" requirement stems from my realization that there are many opportunities for students to hone their formal research dissemination skills and that most of my students will be going on to positions in the workforce that require experience in producing high-quality but less-formal dissemination tools. Final submissions are assessed on the appropriateness of the mode of delivery for reaching the target audience, depth of thought, creativity, and clarity (for examples, check out the final project gallery on our website https://projects.upei.ca/curiosityandinquiry/final-project-gallery/).

Detailed Final Reflection

In concert with the final submission, students submit a detailed final reflection about their experience in The Curiosity Project. The purpose of the final reflective write-up is to enable students to

- reflect on how far they have come in their learning and how much there remains to learn, viewing that as a positive, not a personal failure in learning
- reflect on their learning process over the semester and what they have learned about how they learned
- give me feedback about the overall process that I can use to improve The Curiosity Project for future classes

This final reflective write-up again has no minimum or maximum word/page limit. It includes the students' justification for the approach they chose to take for their final submission and the fair, both in terms of content included and mode of delivery; conclusions they feel they can (or cannot) now draw about their topic; any initial ideas that they found not to be valid; and questions that remain unanswered and new questions that formed. Most importantly, though, this final write-up focuses the students on the transformative properties of The Curiosity Project, such as the

- skills they acquired or honed in their exploration of their topic
- challenges they faced, overcame, and/or wish they had tried to overcome over the course of the semester
- lessons they learned about themselves as students and people
- what they are proud of themselves for and what they regret from their experience in this class

This metacognitive, reflective exercise is, for many, the first time they have really considered their process of learning and exploration in academia. Frequently, the most meaningful strides they make are in terms of who they are as learners and their attitude toward learning (see chapter 16), rather than simply recognizing the improvement in their basic research skills. This write-up allows them to explore in depth these changes in themselves. Though

I was initially concerned that the students would paint a uniformly rosy picture of their experiences in The Curiosity Project, they have consistently honored my request to talk about "the good, the bad, and the ugly" of their experience, often making great suggestions for changes to the project, which I often try.

The Curiosity Project's innovation in IBL-HE lies in its approach to bringing pieces together in a programmatic way, as detailed previously, to form a cohesive pedagogical tool that can be transferred to and adapted by any discipline on a university campus. The project is also unique in that its utility is not limited to a particular size of class or year of study. It is based solidly on academic research on learning (Bandura & Schunk, 1981; Blumenfeld et al., 1991; Brown & Campione, 1994; Friedman et al., 2010; Fry & Villagomez, 2012; Li, 2007; Ryan & Deci, 2000; White & Frederiksen, 2005); the students' needs as they move through their programs and into the work world; and their previous academic experiences (the good, the bad, and the ugly). In this way, The Curiosity Project goes beyond being an effective way to learn content or practice skills to being a game changer in students' attitudes toward and beliefs about their own learning. The Curiosity Project, as a version of IBL-HE, emphasizes the critical importance of actively creating a "fearless" or less "fearful" learning environment and reciprocal learning relationships between students and the larger community and building a community on campus, breadth, depth, divergences, and interconnections in learning, and is living example of lifelong and life-wide learning (as we discussed in chapter 17 of this book).

How Successful Is The Curiosity Project?

Despite having one third less time focused on testable content in class and traditional content-based writing assignments, students who completed The Curiosity Project matched their peers on cumulative exam scores on testable material (MacKinnon, 2017). They achieved this despite having spent no greater amount of time studying course content independently but having devoted upward of 2.25 more hours per week to their written assignments (learning logs versus instructor-provided content-based assignments). In the end, 90% of students indicated that this project should remain a part of the class, while 100% said that based on their experience they would recommend others take the course. Perhaps most telling, though, is the fact that 90% indicated that they would seriously consider taking another Curiosity Project–type course in the future, based on their experience in this class.

We faced our greatest challenge to date with the arrival of COVID-19 and our switch to online learning. I admit, in the beginning I had serious doubts about the chances of a project of this magnitude to be successful in a wholly online environment. But true to form, I decided to approach the upcoming online term as my own IBL project. I spent the summer learning as much as I could about e-learning, consulted with the e-learning team on my campus, and gave it a try with a class of 60. I am pleased to say that it was indeed a successful two terms, and in truth, The Curiosity Project needed only a few changes to make it work. Students still wrote their 10 weekly learning logs; however, I gave them the choice to engage in weekly small group discussions via Zoom breakout rooms or to give each other weekly written feedback on their logs via the course management system. Senior undergraduate LFs gave written feedback on all logs regardless. One third of the class chose live small group discussions, keeping their discussion notes in a Google doc, which they shared with me each week. Two thirds chose written feedback in which they responded to at least two peers' logs every week. Both approaches were equally successful in stimulating learning and questioning, and I am heartened to see the level of connection and community students created in the online environment.

We were unable to have a virtual Curiosity Fair with a class this size, but students still completed a final reflection paper, and in a new twist, I asked them to self-assess their work on the project all term, including the quality of their logs, group discussions, and written feedback, ultimately suggesting a grade for themselves based on their portfolio of work and in-depth reflection on their learning experience. With these simple changes, we were able to maintain the core goals of The Curiosity Project in an online environment in a meaningful way, and I would not hesitate to offer it again this way in the future.

Since we began in 2011, we have had more than 1,500 students complete The Curiosity Project, with more than140 of them returning for multiple semesters to serve as volunteer senior LFs. Both the students and undergraduate facilitators, in order to improve the delivery of this project, frequently approach me with ideas and issues that they observe. These students are dedicated to being curious, to enhancing their own learning and that of others, and embody the spirit of The Curiosity Project. This is of particular note, given that because they originally experienced The Curiosity Project primarily in their 2nd year, they are not all psychology majors. We also have had senior students from other majors, such as sociology, English, math, history, religious studies, music, biology, chemistry, and physics return to the course as LFs, bringing a wonderful variety of knowledge and experience to their feedback and mentoring. This has also helped us spread the word about The Curiosity Project across our campus and, to date, this project has been adopted and adapted by professors in biology, food sciences, English, and business and now forms the basis of our redesigned UPEI 102 Inquiry Studies course (see Appendix C).

In short, the feedback from students has been overwhelmingly positive for more than 10 years. The students who became LFs remain close even after they have graduated, and many have shared with me the impact of their IBL-HE experience on their postgraduate studies. As one former student-turned-facilitator said in a social media message to me from their master's program,

> We have been given an assignment in class where we have to create a presentation. We are given very little info to go on and most of the people in my class are freaking out because they don't know what to do with the freedom. One person actually asked if the prof could make more restrictions that this freedom was not good. . . . I was amazed that people were asking for more restrictions. I feel so lucky to have taken your class.

APPENDIX C

First Year Inquiry Studies

Stacey L. MacKinnon

The UPEI 1020 "First Year Inquiry Studies" course explicitly teaches students how to inquire, addresses the challenges in engaging in inquiry, and gives students practice inquiring using structured and guided inquiry projects throughout an entire semester (http://projects.upei.ca/curiosityandinquiry/inquiry-studies-upei-1020/).

QR Code C.1. Welcome to Inquiry Studies at UPEI.

It could be argued that I should discuss the inquiry studies course first as it is intended for first-year students and focuses explicitly on teaching inquiry-based learning skills, while The Curiosity Project (Appendix B) tends to occur in second-, third- and fourth-year courses. I have chosen instead to present them in accordance with the timeline in which they were developed so you can see how it is possible to use IBL as your own learning project, making changes and developing new approaches as needs are identified. I believe this approach shows the dynamic nature of IBL development and can serve as a model for not only getting started but growing the use of IBL in your classrooms.

Inquiry Studies: UPEI 102

One of the first things I noticed when I began The Curiosity Project (see Appendix B) was that students were initially petrified at the idea of the freedom they would have to learn. Most indicated that they were highly uncomfortable with the idea of being responsible for asking questions instead of simply answering those proposed by others and, indeed, did not have a clear view of how to determine what questions to ask. In response to this, I went to the VP and proposed UPEI 102, Inquiry Studies, a course that would explicitly address the question "What do our incoming students need in order to become successful lifelong and life-wide inquirers, and how can we make sure they participate in first year?" By making this one of the three "First-Year Experience" courses our students have to choose from to fulfill their graduation requirements, they would be better able to launch successfully into further inquiry-based projects in upper-year courses such as the The Curiosity Project in my second-year social psychology class.

In deliberately meeting students where they are at entry and supporting them to achieve the goals of excellence in inquiry, we have created an engaging first-year experience (FP 8). Through theory and practice in divergent and convergent thinking, as well as metacognition, this new approach to UPEI 102 strives to explicitly teach students the mindsets and skills they need to be successful inquirers, such as

- developing a curiosity-based learning mindset: naturally occurring and intentional curiosity
- developing effective questioning skills
- dealing with "wicked questions"
- being your own "devil's advocate"
- dealing with uncertainty
- understanding the role of failure in learning and inquiry
- integrating and finding divergence between ideas
- shifting from judgment to learning
- the art and science of giving and receiving feedback
- seeing the bigger picture and considering the implications of what is learned

Most importantly, we give students regular opportunities to practice these skills in the larger class sessions, using assigned topics, and in smaller group sessions, exploring individual topics of intrinsic interest to them. The instructors model and allow for the practice of giving, receiving, and using formative feedback effectively. We strongly encourage students to focus less on social comparison (me versus you) and more on temporal development (me now versus me then), using reflective practices throughout the semester. This gives them a stronger sense of their own capabilities and ownership of their learning, as well as an increased desire and ability to learn in a variety of situations (Boud et al., 2013). We address, head on, the issues students bring with them into IBL-HE by teaching students why effective questioning is important; how to ask questions and determine what questions are a priority for their purposes (primarily using the QFT; see chapter 6); and how to find reliable answers to them, all with the goal of jump-starting their transition from "student" to "learner" in HE.

To enhance this experience of learning critical thinking skills, we use a two-level "learning over time" approach to assignments, designed to encourage students to learn only from formative feedback rather than judging themselves by a number grade. This decision was based on the success of a similar model in The Curiosity Project: the learning logs described in Appendix B, wherein students get detailed feedback on each week's learning log but no numerical grade until the end of term. The final grade for the course is based in part on their growth in thinking and use of feedback for improvement over the course of the 10 logs. We found that not giving a grade on each log initially increases stress (due to its novelty); however, as students begin to appreciate the learning that happens over time, they begin to realize that taking the detailed feedback seriously will lead to superior learning (and eventually a good grade).

Not surprisingly, the inquiry studies course has more structure and guidance than the open-inquiry Curiosity Project. The purpose of each exercise and assignment is to strengthen students' inquiry skills and help them use metacognition to begin to take ownership of their own learning process. Each assignment in the course is done twice so that students can demonstrate improvement in their skills over time. No marks are given for the first go-round, only formative feedback. The second go-round receives both summative feedback, encouragement to use this feedback to continue improving, and (because the institution requires it) a grade.

Myself as an Inquirer: Past/Present

In inquiry studies, we begin reinforcing this growth mentality with the first assignment in the course. It is a "Myself as an Inquirer: Past/Present" paper, whereby students discuss their history with asking questions at home, in the community, and at school, as well as what they perceive to be their strengths and weaknesses in curiosity and inquiry. Not only does this give us an opportunity to get to know our students' needs better at the beginning of term, it is also often the first time the students have considered what has brought them to be who they are as inquirers. This is particularly important for students who have a negative or complicated history with questions, such as students raised in fundamentalist religions, in which questioning is a basis for shunning, or international students from countries where, as one put it, "asking questions will get you shot." The assignment is also important for students who are coming out of high school very confident in their academic capabilities but whose strengths are really in absorbing material, not questioning it. This paper begins a discussion that is referred to throughout the semester, which ends with the students writing a "Myself as an Inquirer Now" paper, discussing what they have learned about themselves, the process of inquiry, and the multifaceted nature of learning. Students receive formative assessment on their ability to reflect back to where they started, assess where they are now, and analyze where they need to focus next.

Curiosity Conversations

The same pre/post approach is taken in our popular Curiosity Conversations assignment, which begins early in the term when we have students choose someone with whom to speak about something that interests them. With no formal preparation, students have the conversation, summarize it, and analyze the process of having the talk. This is all written up and submitted for detailed formative feedback from the instructor, but no numerical grade is assigned. Later in the term, students are asked to complete a second Curiosity Conversation with a new person, reviewing their previous feedback and personal observations, and this time using the QFT (Rothstein & Santana, 2011; see chapter 6) to prepare. Once the conversation is completed, students are again asked to summarize what they learned about the topic of conversation and to compare the quality and experience of learning between their first and second conversation. They are asked to discuss the extent to which preparation and attention to feedback impacted their experience. At this point they receive a numerical grade (summative feedback) that is based on their comparisons and analyses of their experience from time 1 to time 2 of the conversations. This becomes part of their final grade for the course. The key here is that for many, this is the first time they have taken seriously and actively used feedback on how to learn and improve, and it is eye-opening for them.

This approach reinforces the idea that everyone can experience growth as a learner (even those who habitually achieve grades in the 90s) and that even if an attempt is truly a catastrophic failure, there are ways to use feedback (both offered and requested), reflection, and metacognition that can result in more meaningful learning and future success. The "Myself and Inquiry" paper and "Curiosity Conversations" assignment reduce the fear of trying because there isn't only one correct answer. Rather, students demonstrate the importance of preparation and reflection and learn explicitly about their values, growth, and development.

Wicked Questions

We superimpose these lessons about inquiry in HE on a foundation of "wicked questions," or issues that have no single answer, and such that even when a portion of the puzzle has been solved, it shifts all the others, so the quest for resolution is ongoing. Instead of focusing on topics of personal interest such as The Curiosity Project example, we use the same structure of inquiry (weekly learning logs and feedback; group discussions) to have the entire inquiry studies class address a wicked question. In this case, we use an approach in which the instructor chooses a broad "wicked" topic from which each small group of students chooses a piece and forms their own inquiry projects. For example, in 2016 we addressed gender stereotyping and discrimination, and over the past 3 years we shifted our focus to the Truth and Reconciliation Commission's report, residential schools, and other issues facing Indigenous peoples in Canada. This brings together an opportunity for practicing the skills of inquiry being taught explicitly in the course using the real-life, multifaceted global issues that we face in our modern world.

Most recently students were asked to choose one of the 94 recommendations made by the Truth and Reconciliation Commission report to learn about in more detail and design an implementation plan for that recommendation. Working in small groups, students discussed what they knew about the issue and worked to help each other create, refine, and prioritize questions, raising points of interest/convergence/divergence, offering suggestions for resources, searching for answers, and coming up with more questions, all in service of expanding their understanding of the issue before they attempted to determine how best to implement the recommendation. This also required them to adopt several different perspectives in determining their questions (e.g., Indigenous peoples, policymakers, financial professionals, teachers, parents, Elders, etc.), which highlights the multifaceted nature of these challenging issues.

Assessment

The students' final grades are derived from (a) pre-post in-class activities/ assignments, whereby they are graded on their ability to exhibit and reflect on the skills taught; (b) a pre-post formal assessment of their inquiry skills to determine how much their skills have improved and been retained over the course of the semester; (c) weekly learning logs, participation in discussions, and online feedback for their wicked problems project; and (d) a detailed reflection on the inquiry process and their position within it. Remember, no numerical grades are shared with the student during the semester to avoid focusing on numbers rather than the formative feedback. In my experience with The Curiosity Project, students are willing to be open to the idea of not receiving numerical grades as long as they are clear that the road to high marks comes from the active consideration and appropriate use of the detailed feedback given throughout the semester. This is particularly important for those whose inquiry skills are high from day 1 and who may come into the class believing that they need not improve further, thereby disengaging from the course experience. Grading that is based on the learning process and responding to feedback is also a benefit to the student whose inquiry skills are weak upon entry, since they do not have the negative impact of initial low scores to overcome with each successive assignment. This puts the onus on students to learn to interpret feedback correctly, as formative, not just judgmental, awareness is a key component to this course and to effective learning more generally.

IBL in Block Week, Community, and GSP

Beth Archer-Kuhn

T he following are three examples of the process and content of IBL-HE, including the number of days of the course, the topics and activities covered, and the assessment tasks. These three examples reveal some of the ways in which you can adapt your course to utilize IBL-HE when it is on campus (block week), in the community (community-based IBL-HE), and on study abroad (GSP). You will notice the assessment tasks are similar in terms of accounting for the inquiry process and content. Course content is weaved into the inquiry process. The principles of IBL-HE are immersed into the structure, always allowing for student choice, peer and instructor feedback, and opportunities for presenting new knowledge. Beth provides prereadings and an IBL module for students to review prior to beginning the course.

Example 1: Block Week IBL Content and Assessment Tasks

Date: Day 1 to Day 6	Topic	Assessment Tasks
Day 1	Welcome and introductions Course overview Review of syllabus Structured Controversy	Assignment 1: Structured Controversy
Day 2	Developing good inquiry questions Peer consultation and feedback Course content Guest speaker: Librarian	Assignment 2: Inquiry question

(Continues)

239

Example 1 (*Continued*)

Date: Day 1 to Day 6	Topic	Assessment Tasks
Day 3	Pursuing inquiry question Quantitative evidence Course content Reviewing the evidence: quantitative methods Large group discussion Group consultation	
Day 4	Pursuing inquiry question Presentations Learnings on quantitative evidence Qualitative evidence Qualitative methods	Assignment 3: Presentation of quantitative evidence
Day 5	Pursuing inquiry question Qualitative analysis Group work with analysis activity Within and across case analysis Group consultations	
Day 6	Student presentations Learnings on qualitative evidence Course content Course content Student evaluation of teaching and course Consultation with peers and instructor	Assignment 4: Presentation of qualitative evidence
	Due 1 week after last class	Assignment 5: Analysis paper

Example 2: Community-Based IBL Content and Assessment Tasks

Date	Content	Assessment Tasks
Week 1	Course overview Introductions Overview of IBL Course content Structured Controversy	Assignment 1: Structured Controversy

Date	Content	Assessment Tasks
Week 2	Course content Development of inquiry question Guest speaker: Librarian	Assignment 2: Inquiry question
Week 3	Pursuing inquiry question Course content: Guest speaker—service user Course content: Guest speaker—professor	Assignment 3a: Blog 1 Assignment 3a: Reply post 1
Week 4	Pursuing inquiry question Course content: Guest speaker—service provider Course content: Field trip to community agency—service provider, service user	Assignment 3b: Blog 2 Assignment 3b: Reply post 2
Week 5	Pursuing inquiry question Course content: Field trip to community agency Course content: Field trip to community agency	Assignment 3c: Blog 3
Week 6	Group presentations	Assignment 4, in class
	One week post classes ending	Assignment 5: Analysis paper

Example 3: GSP IBL Content and Assessment Tasks

Date: Day 1 to day 15	Topic	Assessment Tasks
Day 1	Travel	
Day 2	Structured Controversy Cultural activities	Assignment 1: Structured Controversy
Day 3	Course content: International conference Creating inquiry question	Assignment 2: Inquiry question
Day 4	Pursuing inquiry question Train travel to another city Guest speaker, community tour: University professor Cultural activities	

(Continues)

Example 3 (*Continued*)

Date: Day 1 to day 15	Topic	Assessment Tasks
Day 5	Pursuing inquiry question Train travel to another country Guest speaker, professional workshop: University professor Train travel to another city	Assignment 3a: Blog post 1
Day 6	Pursuing inquiry question Course content at historic community setting Field trip to community agency	Assignment 3a: Reply posts (three) to peers
Day 7	Cultural tour and activities	
Day 8	Free day of cultural activities	
Day 9	Pursuing inquiry question Course content: Field trip to university, university professors, service users, students	
Day 10	Pursuing inquiry question Course content: Field trip to university, university professors, guest speaker, professional workshop, students Flight travel to another country	Assignment 3b: Blog post 2
Day 11	Pursuing inquiry question Course content: Field trip to university, guest speakers—university professors Course content: Cultural activities Course content: Field trip to community agency Cultural activities	Assignment 3b: Reply posts (three) to peers
Day 12	Pursuing inquiry question Course content: Field trip to university, all-day workshops Cultural activities	

Date: Day 1 to day 15	Topic	Assessment Tasks
Day 13	Pursuing inquiry question Course content: Field trip to university—university professors, students Course content: Field trip to community agencies Cultural activities	
Day 14	Free time Presentations of learnings Travel to airport	
Day 15	Arrive home	Assignment 3c: Blog post 3
Due 2 days after course ends		Assignment 4: Analysis paper

APPENDIX E

Additional Resources

Example 1: Pursuing Inquiry Question—Peer Feedback Form Sample

Colleague providing feedback:

What is the issue or claim being made in simple and direct language?

Are there any ambiguities or a lack of clarity in the claim?

What are the underlying value and theory assumptions?

Is there indication of any misleading beliefs or faulty reasoning?

How good is the evidence presented?

Is any important information missing?

Is consideration given to alternative explanations?

Are the conclusions reasonable?

global digital
citizen foundation

The Ultimate Cheatsheet for
Critical Thinking

Want to exercise critical thinking skills? Ask these questions
whenever you discover or discuss new information. These are
broad and versatile questions that have limitless applications!

Who	... benefits from this? ... is this harmful to? ... makes decisions about this? ... is most directly affected?	... have you also heard discuss this? ... would be the best person to consult? ... will be the key people in this? ... deserves recognition for this?
What	... are the strengths/weaknesses? ... is another perspective? ... is another alternative? ... would be a counter-argument?	... is the best/worst case scenario? ... is most/least important? ... can we do to make a positive change? ... is getting in the way of our action?
Where	... would we see this in the real world? ... are there similar concepts/situations? ... is there the most need for this? ... in the world would this be a problem?	... can we get more information? ... do we go for help with this? ... will this idea take us? ... are the areas for improvement?
When	... is this acceptable/unacceptable? ... would this benefit our society? ... would this cause a problem? ... is the best time to take action?	... will we know we've succeeded? ... has this played a part in our history? ... can we expect this to change? ... should we ask for help with this?
Why	... is this a problem/challenge? ... is it relevant to me/others? ... is this the best/worst scenario? ... are people influenced by this?	... should people know about this? ... has it been this way for so long? ... have we allowed this to happen? ... is there a need for this today?
How	... is this similar to _____? ... does this disrupt things? ... do we know the truth about this? ... will we approach this safely?	... does this benefit us/others? ... does this harm us/others? ... do we see this in the future? ... can we change this for our good?

globaldigitalcitizen.org

RISE MODEL

The RISE Model for Peer Feedback is a tool that structures and facilitates the giving and receiving of meaningful critiques.

By addressing a series of stems aligned with Bloom's Taxonomy, students are prompted to use higher order thinking skills in the delivery of constructive feedback to their peers.

Visit www.risemodel.com for licensing and implementation information.

ELEVATE

Raise to a higher degree or purpose in FUTURE iterations

EXAMPLE STEMS:

Perhaps you can expand this in X capacity to further address Y.
Perhaps you can re-purpose X as Y for Z.

SUGGEST

Introduce ideas for improvement of CURRENT iteration

EXAMPLE STEMS:

You might consider tweaking X for Y effect.
You might want to include supporting information from X resource.

INQUIRE

Seek information and provide ideas through questioning

EXAMPLE STEMS:

Have you considered looking at X from Y perspective?
When you said X, am I understanding you to mean Y?

REFLECT

Recall, ponder, and articulate

EXAMPLE STEMS:

I relate/concur/disagree with X because Y.
I liked what you did with X because Y.

CREATING EVALUATING ANALYZING APPLYING UNDERSTANDING REMEMBERING

Abrams, L. S., & Moio, J. A. (2009). Critical race theory and the cultural competence: Dilemma in social work education. *Journal of Social Work Education, 45(2)*, 245–261. https://doi.org/10.5175/JSWE.2009.200700109

Adams, M. G. (2016). *Change your questions, change your life: 12 powerful tools for leadership, coaching, and life*. Berrett-Koehler.

Aditomo, A., Goodyear, P., Bliuc, A., & Ellis, R. A. (2013). Inquiry-based learning in higher education: Principal forms, educational objectives, and disciplinary variations. *Studies in Higher Education, 38(9)*, 1239–1258. https://doi.org/10.1080/03075079.2011.616584

Alberta Education. (2010). *Inspiring education: A dialogue with Albertans*. https://open.alberta.ca/publications/9780778586104#summary

Anghel, R., & Ramon, S. (2009). Service users and carers' involvement in social work education: Lessons from an English case study. *European Journal of Social Work, 12(2)*, 185–199. https://doi.org/10.1080/13691450802567416

Anstey, L. M., Michels, A., Szymus, J., Law, W., Ho, M.-H. E., Qu, F., Yeung, R. T. T., & Chow, N. (2014). Reflections as near-peer facilitators of an inquiry project for undergraduate anatomy: Successes and challenges from a term of trial-and-error. *Anatomical Sciences Education, 7(1)*, 64–70. https://doi.org/10.1002/ase.1383

Aparicio-Ting, F. E., Slater, D. M., & Kurz, E. U. (2019). Inquiry-based learning (IBL) as a driver of curriculum: A staged approach. *Papers on Postsecondary Learning and Teaching: Proceedings of the University of Calgary Conference on Learning and Teaching, 3*, 44–51. https://doi.org/10.11575/pplt.v3i1.53136

Apedoe, X. S., & Reeves, T. C. (2006). Inquiry-based learning and digital libraries in undergraduate science education. *Journal of Science Education and Technology, 15(5/6)*, 321–330. https://doi.org/10.1007/s10956-006-9020-8

Apple, D., Jain, C., Beyerlein, S., & Ellis, W. (2018). Impact of higher education culture on student mindset and success. *International Journal of Process Education, 9(1)*, 59–98. https://www.ijpe.online/archive.html#9th

Archer-Kuhn, B. (2013). Structured controversy: Inquiry-based learning in place of traditional group projects. *Teaching Innovations Project, 3(1)*. https://ojs.lib.uwo.ca/index.php/tips/article/view/3645

Archer-Kuhn, B. (2020). Putting social justice in social work education with inquiry-based learning. *Journal of Teaching in Social Work, 40(5)*, 431–448. https://doi.org/10.1080/08841233.2020.1821864

Archer-Kuhn, B., Cullen, O., St. Denis, N., Halvorsen, J., & Nguyen, Q. (2018, May 28–31). *Can inquiry-based learning support a decolonizing framework to make room for Indigenous knowledges in social work education?* [Paper presentation]. Canadian Association of Social Work Education Conference, Regina, Saskatchewan.

Archer-Kuhn, B., Degenhardt, C., Wiedeman, D., Chalifoux, J., Hernandez, W., & Andrews, H. (2016, May 31–June 3). *Inquiry and experiential learning in the UK context: Social work student engagement on study tour* [Paper presentation]. Canadian Association of Social Work Education Conference, Calgary, Alberta.

Archer-Kuhn, B., Lee, Y., Finnessey, S., & Liu, J. (2020). Inquiry-based learning as a facilitator to student engagement in higher education. *Teaching & Learning Inquiry, 8*(1), 187–207. https://doi.org/10.20343/teachlearninqu.8.1.13

Archer-Kuhn, B., Lee, Y., Hewson, J., & Burns, V. (2020). Growing together: Cultivating inquiry-based learning in social work education. *Social Work Education, 41*(3), 333–353. https://doi.org/10.1080/02615479.2020.1839407

Archer-Kuhn, B., & MacKinnon, S. (2020). Inquiry-based learning in higher education: A pedagogy of trust. *Journal of Education and Training Studies, 8*(9), 1–14. https://doi.org/10.11114/jets.v8i9.4929

Archer-Kuhn, B., Samson, P., Damianakis, T., Barrett, B., Matin, S., & Ahern, C. (2020). Transformative learning in field education: Students bridging the theory/practice gap. *The British Journal of Social Work, 51*(7), 2419–2438. https://doi.org/10.1093/bjsw/bcaa082

Archer-Kuhn, B., Wiedeman, D., & Chalifoux, J. (2020). Student engagement and deep learning in higher education: Reflections on inquiry-based learning on our group study program course in the UK. *Journal of Higher Education Outreach and Engagement, 24*(2), 107–122. https://openjournals.libs.uga.edu/jheoe/article/view/2069

Arend, B., Archer-Kuhn, B., Hiramatsu, K., Ostrowdun, C., Seeley, J., & Jones, A. (2021). Minding the gap: Comparing student and instructor experiences with critical reflection. *Teaching & Learning Inquiry, 9*(1), 317–332. http://dx.doi.org/10.20343/teachlearninqu.9.1.21

Arter, J., & Spandel, V. (1992). NCME instructional module: Using portfolios of student work in instruction and assessment. *Educational Measurement: Issues and Practice, 11*, 36–44. https://doi.org/10.1111/j.1745-3992.1992.tb00230.x

Asghar, A. (2010). Reciprocal peer coaching and its use as a formative assessment strategy for first-year students. *Assessment & Evaluation in Higher Education, 35*(4), 403–417. https://doi.org/10.1080/02602930902862834

Ash, S. L., & Clayton, P. H. (2009). Generating, deepening, and documenting learning: The power of critical reflection in applied learning. *Journal of Applied Learning in Higher Education, 1*(1), 25–48. https://hdl.handle.net/1805/4579

Aumi, V., & Mawardi, M. (2021). Validity and practicity of flipped guided inquiry-based learning (FGIL) model in chemical kinetics for year 1 students. *International Journal of Progressive Sciences and Technologies (IJPSAT), 26*(2), 142–147.

Baines, D. (2017). *Doing anti-oppressive practice: Social justice social work* (3rd ed.). Fernwood.

Baker, V., & LaPointe Terosky, A. (2017). Early career faculty mentoring: Career cycles, learning and support. In D. Clutterbuck, F. Kochan, L. Lunsford,

N. Dominguez, & J. Haddock-Millar (Eds.), *The SAGE handbook of mentoring* (pp. 421–435). SAGE.

Bandura, A., & Schunk, D. (1981). Cultivating competence, self-efficacy, and intrinsic interest through proximal self-motivation. *Journal of Personality and Social Psychology, 41*(3), 586–598. https://doi.org/10.1037/0022-3514.41.3.586

Baranes, A., & Oudeyer, P. Y. (2009, June). Robust intrinsically motivated exploration and active learning. *2009 IEEE 8th International Conference on Development and Learning* (pp. 1–6). IEEE. https://doi.org/10.1109/DEVLRN.2009.5175525

Barnes, S., Brown, K. W., Krusemark, E., Campbell, W. K., & Rogge, R. D. (2007). The role of mindfulness in romantic relationship satisfaction and responses to relationship stress. *Journal of Marital and Family Therapy, 33*(4), 482–500. https://doi.org/10.1111/j.1752-0606.2007.00033.x

Baskin, C. (2006). Aboriginal world views as challenges and possibilities in social work education. *Critical Social Work, 7*(2). https://doi.org/10.22329/csw.v7i2.5726

Bata, M., & Whitney, A. (2015). Using inquiry-based learning outside of the classroom: How opportunities for effective practice can animate course-based learning. In P. Blessinger & J. F. Carfora (Eds.), *Inquiry-based learning for multidisciplinary programs: A conceptual and practical resource for educators* (pp. 233–252). Emerald. https://doi.org/10.1108/S2055-364120150000003029

Battiste, M. (2013). *Decolonizing education: Nourishing the learning spirit.* UBC Press.

Beltrano, N. R., Archer-Kuhn, B., & MacKinnon, S. (2021). Mining for gold and finding only nuggets: Attempting a rapid systematic review, on trust in higher education IBL classrooms. *Teachers and Teaching, 27*(1–4), 300–315. https://doi.org/10.1080/13540602.2021.1955672

Ben-Eliyahu, A. (2021). Sustainable learning in education. *Sustainability, 13*(8), 4250. https://doi.org/10.3390/su13084250

Berg, C. A., & Sternberg, R. J. (1985). Response to novelty: Continuity versus discontinuity in the developmental course of intelligence. *Advances in Child Development and Behavior, 19*, 1–47. https://doi.org/10.1016/S0065-2407(08)60387-0

Berger, J. G. (2004). Dancing on the threshold of meaning: Recognizing and understanding the growing edge. *Journal of Transformative Education, 2*(4), 336–351. https://doi.org/10.1177/1541344604267697

Berger, W. (2014). *A more beautiful question: The power of inquiry to spark breakthrough ideas.* Bloomsbury.

Billett, S. (2018). Distinguishing lifelong learning from lifelong education. *Journal of Adult Learning, Knowledge and Innovation, 2*(1), 1–7. https://doi.org/10.1556/2059.01.2017.3

Blackstone, B., & Oldmixon, E. (2019). Specifications grading in political science. *Journal of Political Science Education, 15*(2), 191–205. https://doi.org/10.1080/15512169.2018.1447948

Blaschke, L. M. (2021). The dynamic mix of heutagogy and technology: Preparing learners for lifelong learning. *British Journal of Educational Technology, 52*(4), 1629–1645. https://doi.org/10.1111/bjet.13105

Bloom, B. S. (1956). *Taxonomy of educational objectives, handbook I: The cognitive domain.* David McKay.

Blum, S. D., & Kohn, A. (2020). *Ungrading: Why rating students undermines learning (and what to do instead)*. West Virginia University Press.

Blumenfeld, P. C., Soloway, E., Marx, R. W., Krajcik, J. S., Guzdial, M., & Palincsar, A. (1991). Motivating project-based learning: Sustaining the doing, supporting the learning. *Educational Psychologist, 26*(3–4), 369–398. https://doi .org/10.1080/00461520.1991.9653139

Bolhuis, S. M. (2003). Towards process-oriented teaching for self-directed lifelong learning: A multidimensional perspective. *Learning and Instruction, 13*(3), 327–347. https://doi.org/10.1016/S0959-4752(02)00008-7

Botwin, M. D., Buss, D. M., & Shackelford, T. K. (1997). Personality and mate preferences: Five factors in mate selection and marital satisfaction. *Journal of Personality, 65*(1), 107–136. https://doi.org/10.1111/j.1467-6494.1997.tb00531.x

Boud, D., Keogh, R., & Walker, D. (Eds.). (2013). *Reflection: Turning experience into learning*. Routledge.

Boyer, E. L. (1990). *Scholarship reconsidered: Priorities of the professoriate*. Princeton University Press.

Boyer Commission on Educating Undergraduates in the Research University. (1998). *Reinventing undergraduate education: A blueprint for America's research universities*. State University of New York at Stony Brook for the Carnegie Foundation for the Advancement of Teaching. https://eric.ed.gov/?id=ED424840

Boyer, N. R., Maher, P. A., & Kirkman, S. (2006). Transformative learning in online settings: The use of self-direction, metacognition, and collaborative learning. *Journal of Transformative Education, 4*(4), 335–361. https://doi.org/ 10.1177/1541344606295318

Boyle, S. L. (2015). *The barriers and challenges to curiosity: Exploring the lived experience* [Unpublished honors thesis]. University of Prince Edward Island.

Boyle, S. L., & MacKinnon, S. L. (2016). Speed bumps or road blocks? Students' perceptions of barriers to learning and developing academic resilience. *Proceedings of the 2016 Atlantic Universities' Teaching Showcase, 20*, 58–67. https://ojs.library .dal.ca/auts/index

Bozeman, B., & Gaughan, M. (2011). Job satisfaction among university faculty: Individual, work, and institutional determinants. *The Journal of Higher Education, 82*(2), 154–186. https://doi.org/10.1080/00221546.2011.11779090

Braun, V., & Clarke, V. (2006). Using thematic analysis in psychology. *Qualitative Research in Psychology, 3*(2), 77–101. https://doi.org/10.1191/ 1478088706qp063oa

Braye, S., Lebacq, M., Mann, F., & Midwinter, E. (2003). Learning social work law: An enquiry-based approach to developing knowledge and skills. *Social Work Education, 22*(5), 479–492. https://doi.org/10.1080/0261547032000126425

Brew, A. (2003). Teaching and research: New relationships and their implications for inquiry-based teaching and learning in higher education. *Higher Education Research and Development, 22*(1), 3–18. https://doi.org/10.1080/0729436032000056571

Brookfield, S. (2016). So what exactly is critical about critical reflection? In J. Fook, V. Collington, F. Ross, G. Ruch, & L. West (Eds.), *Researching critical reflection: Multidisciplinary perspectives* (pp. 11–22). Routledge.

Brown, A., & Campione, J. (1994). Guided discovery in a community of learners. In K. McGilly (Ed.), *Classroom lessons: Integrating cognitive theory and classroom practice* (pp. 229–270). The MIT Press.

Brubaker, N. D. (2012). Negotiating authority through cultivating a classroom of inquiry. *Teaching and Teacher Education, 28*, 240–250. https://doi.org/10.1016/J.TATE.2011.10.002

Buckner, E., & Kim, P. (2014). Integrating technology and pedagogy for inquiry-based learning: The Stanford mobile inquiry-based learning environment (SMILE). *Prospects, 44*(1), 99–118. https://doi.org/10.1007/s11125-013-9269-7

Bunce, L., Baird, A., & Jones, S. E. (2017). The student-as-consumer approach in higher education and its effects on academic performance. *Studies in Higher Education, 42*(11), 1958–1978. https://doi.org/10.1080/03075079.2015.1127908

Burch, C. (1997). Finding out what's in their head: Using teaching portfolios to assess English education students—and programs. In K. B. Yancy & I. Weiser (Eds.), *Situating portfolios: Four perspectives* (pp. 263–277). Utah State University Press.

Burke, P. J. (2015). Re/imagining higher education pedagogies: Gender, emotion and difference. *Teaching in Higher Education, 20*(4), 388–401. https://doi.org/10.1080/13562517.2015.1020782

Butler, R. (1988). Enhancing and undermining intrinsic motivation: The effects of task-involving and ego-involving evaluation on interest and performance. *British Journal of Educational Psychology, 58*(1), 1–14. https://doi.org/10.1111/j.2044-8279.1988.tb00874.x

Cain, J. (2019). We should pay more attention to student curiosity. *Currents in Pharmacy Teaching and Learning, 11*(7), 651–654. https://doi.org/10.1016/j.cptl.2019.03.001

Calma, A., & Davies, M. (2020). Critical thinking in business education: Current outlook and future prospects. *Studies in Higher Education, 46*(11), 2279–2295. https://doi.org/10.1080/03075079.2020.1716324

Cambridge, B. L. (2001). *Electronic portfolios: Emerging practices in student, faculty, and institutional learning.* Stylus.

Campbell, D., Melenyzer, B., Nettles, D., & Wyman, R. (2000). *Portfolio and performance assessment in teaching education.* Allyn & Bacon.

Canadian Association of Social Workers. (2020). *Social work code of ethics and scope of practice.* https://www.casw-acts.ca/en/Code-of-Ethics%20and%20Scope%20of%20Practice

Capaldi, M. (2015). Inquiry-based learning in mathematics. In P. Blessinger & J. M. Carfora (Eds.), *Inquiry-based learning for science, technology, engineering, and math (STEM) programs: A conceptual and practical resource for educators.* Emerald.

Carlisle, S. (2020). Simple specifications grading. *PRIMUS, 30*(8–10), 926–951. https://doi.org/10.1080/10511970.2019.1695238

Carroll, C., & O'Loughlin, D. (2014). Peer observation of teaching: Enhancing academic engagement for new participants. *Innovations in Education and Teaching International, 51*(4), 446–456. https://doi.org/10.1080/14703297.2013.778067

Castellanos. J., Gloria. A., Besson. D., & Harvey. L. (2016). Mentoring matters: Racial ethnic minority undergraduates cultural fit, mentorship, and college and life satisfaction. *Journal of College Reading and Learning, 46*(2), 81–98. https://doi.org/10.1080/10790195.2015.1121792

Caswell, C. J., & LaBrie, D. (2017). Inquiry based learning from the learner's point of view: A teacher candidate's success story. *Journal of Humanistic Mathematics, 7*(2), 161–186. https://doi.org/10.5642/jhummath.201702.08

Clark, S., Harbaugh, A. G., & Seider, S. (2021). Teaching questioning fosters adolescent curiosity: Analyzing impact through multiple-group structural equation modeling. *Applied Developmental Science, 25*(3), 240–259. https://doi.org/10.1080/10888691.2019.1591956

Clark, S., & Seider, S. (2017). Developing critical curiosity in adolescents. *Equity & Excellence in Education, 50*(2), 125–141. https://doi.org/10.1080/10665684.2017.1301835

Chaudhuri T. (2017). (De)constructing student e-portfolios in five questions: Experiences from a community of practice. In T. Chaudhuri & B. Cabau (Eds.), *E-portfolios in higher education* (pp. 3–19). Springer. https://doi.org/10.1007/978-981-10-3803-7_1

Chechak, D. (2015). Social work as a value-based profession: Value conflicts and implications for practitioners' self-concepts. *Journal of Social Work Values and Ethics, 12*(2), 41–48. https://jswve.org/archives/

Cochran-Smith, M., & Lytle, S. L. (2001). Beyond certainty: Taking an inquiry stance on practice. In A. Lieberman & L. Miller (Eds.), *Teachers caught in the action: Professional development that matters* (pp. 45–60). Teachers College Press.

Cook, S. A., & Borkovitz, D. K. (2017). Student perception of a mathematics major for prospective elementary teachers with an inquiry-based philosophy. *Problems, Resources, and Issues in Mathematics Undergraduate Students, 27*(1), 125–147. https://doi.org/10.1080/10511970.2016.1194341

Cooner, T. S. (2011). Learning to create enquiry-based blended learning designs: Resources to develop interdisciplinary education. *Social Work Education, 30*(3), 312–330. https://doi.org/10.1080/02615479.2010.482983

Cooper, T., Bailey, B., Briggs, K., & Holliday, J. (2017). Assessing student openness to inquiry-based learning in precalculus. *Problems, Resources, and Issues in Mathematics Undergraduate Studies, 27*(7), 736–753. https://doi.org/10.1080/10511970.2016.1183155

Coplin, B. (2012). *10 things employers want you to learn in college, revised: The skills you need to succeed.* Random House.

Council on Social Work Education. (2015). *Educational policy and accreditation standards.* https://cswe.org/Accreditation/Accreditation-Process/2015-EPAS

Cranston, J. (2011). Relational trust: The glue that binds a professional learning community. *Alberta Journal of Educational Research, 57*(1), 59–72. https://doi.org/10.11575/ajer.v57i1.55455

Cranton, P. (1994). *Understanding and promoting transformative learning.* Jossey-Bass.

Cranton, P., & Carusetta, E. (2004). Perspectives on authenticity in teaching. *Adult Education Quarterly, 55*(1), 5–22. https://doi.org/10.1177/0741713604268894

Crenshaw, K. (1989). Mapping the margins: Intersectionality, identity politics, and violence against women of color. In M. A. Fineman (Ed.), *The public nature of violence: The discovery of domestic abuse* (pp. 93–117). Routledge.

Creswell, J. W., & Plano Clark, V. L. (2011). *Designing and conducting mixed methods research* (2nd ed.). SAGE.

Csikszentmihalyi, M. (2014). *Applications of flow in human development and education.* Springer. https://doi.org/10.1007/978-94-017-9094-9

Cuneo, C., Harnish, D., Roy, D., & Vajoczki, S. (2012). Lessons learned: The McMaster inquiry story from innovation to institutionalization. In V. S. Lee (Ed.), *Inquiry-Guided Learning* (New Directions for Teaching and Learning, no. 129, pp. 93–104). Jossey-Bass. https://doi.org/10.1002/tl.20010

Curzon-Hobson, A. (2002). A pedagogy of trust in higher learning. *Teaching in Higher Education, 7*(3), 265–276. https://doi.org/10.1080/13562510220144770

D'Olimpio, L. (2018). Trust as a virtue in education. *Educational Philosophy and Theory, 50*(2), 193–202. https://doi.org/10.1080/00131857.2016.1194737

Daloz, L. (1986). *Effective teaching and mentoring: Realizing the transformational power of adult learning experiences.* Jossey-Bass.

Damianakis, T., Barrett, B., Archer-Kuhn, B., Samson, P., Matin, S., & Ahern, C. (2019). Teaching for transformation: Master of social work students identify teaching approaches that made a difference. *Journal of Transformative Education,* 1–22. https://doi.org/10.1177/1541344619865948

Damnjanovic, A. (1999). Attitudes toward inquiry-based teaching: Differences between preservice and inservice teachers. *School Science and Mathematics, 99*(2), 71–76. https://doi.org/10.1111/j.1949-8594.1999.tb17450.x

Deci, E. L., & Ryan, R. M. (1992). The initiation and regulation of intrinsically motivated learning and achievement. In A. K. Boggiano & T. S. Pittman (Eds.), *Achievement and motivation: A social-developmental perspective* (pp. 9–36). Cambridge University Press.

Dede, C. J., & Richards, J. (2020). *The 60-year curriculum: New models for lifelong learning in the digital economy.* Routledge.

Dewey, J. (1980). Democracy and education. In J. A. Boydston (Ed.), *The middle works of John Dewey, 1899–1924* (pp. 87–106). Southern Illinois University Press. (Original work published in 1916)

Dill, K., Montgomery, L., Davidson, G., & Duffy, J. (2016). Service-user involvement in social work education: The road less traveled. *Practice Digest, 6*(2), 1–11. https://fieldeducator.simmons.edu/article/service-user-involvement-in-social-work-education-the-road-less-traveled/

Dirkx, J. M., Mezirow, J., & Cranton, P. (2006). Musings and reflections on the meaning, context, and process of transformative learning: A dialogue between John M. Dirkx and Jack Mezirow. *Journal of Transformative Education, 4*(2), 123–139. https://doi.org/10.1177/1541344606287503

Dominelli, L. (2004). New directions for social work: Interdependence, reciprocity, citizenship, and social justice. In L. Dominelli (Ed.), *Social Work: Theory and Practice for a Changing Profession* (pp. 230–248). Polity Press.

Drewery, D. W., Sproule, R., & Pretti, T. J. (2020). Lifelong learning mindset and career success: Evidence from the field of accounting and finance. *Higher Education, Skills and Work-Based Learning, 10*(3), 567–580. https://doi.org/10.1108/HESWBL-03-2019-0041

Dunleavy, J., & Milton, P. (2009). *What did you do in school today? Exploring the concept of student engagement and its implications for teaching and learning in Canada.* Canadian Education Association.

Dweck, C. S. (2008). *Mindset: The new psychology of success.* Random House.

Elbow, P. (1997). Grading student writing: Making it simpler, fairer, clearer. In M. D. Sorcinelli & P. Elbow (Eds.), *Writing to Learn: Strategies for Assigning and Responding to Writing Across the Disciplines* (New Directions for Teaching and Learning, no. 69, pp. 127–140). Jossey-Bass. https://doi.org/10.1002/tl.6911

Elia, G., & Margherita, A. (2018). Can we solve wicked problems? A conceptual framework and a collective intelligence system to support problem analysis and solution design for complex social issues. *Technological Forecasting and Social Change, 133*, 279–286. https://doi.org/10.1016/j.techfore.2018.03.010

Ellis, R. A. (2016). Qualitatively different university student experiences of inquiry: Associations among approaches to inquiry, technologies and perceptions of the learning environment. *Active Learning in Higher Education, 17*(1), 13–23. https://doi.org/10.1177/1469787415616721

Elo, S., Kääriäinen, M., Kanste, O., Pölkki, T., Utriainen, K., & Kyngäs, H. (2014). Qualitative content analysis: A focus on trustworthiness. *SAGE Open.* https://doi.org/10.1177/2158244014522633

Engel, R., & Schutt, R. (2016). *The practice of research in social work* (4th ed.). SAGE.

England, B. J., Brigati, J. R., & Schussler, E. E. (2017). Student anxiety in introductory biology classrooms: Perceptions about active learning and persistence in the major. *PLOS One, 12*(8), 1–17. https://doi.org/10.1371/journal.pone.0182506

Enwere, J. O., Ezenwafor, J. I., & Eze, T. I. (2020). Relative effectiveness of just-in-time teaching and peer instructional strategies on students' retention in financial accounting in colleges of education. *International Journal of Scientific and Technology Research, 9*(4), 955–957. https://www.researchgate.net/publication/340815381_Relative_Effectiveness_Of_Just-In-Time_Teaching_And_Peer_Instructional_Strategies_On_Students%27_Retention_In_Financial_Accounting_In_Colleges_Of_Education

Feldt, J. E., & Petersen, E. B. (2021). Inquiry-based learning in the humanities: Moving from topics to problems using the "humanities imagination." *Arts and Humanities in Higher Education, 20*(2), 155–171.

Fook, J., Collington, V., Ross, F., Ruch, G., & West, G. (2016a). A research agenda for critical reflection in the professions. In J. Fook, V. Collington, F. Ross, G. Ruch, & L. West (Eds.), *Researching critical reflection: Multidisciplinary perspectives* (pp. 183–191). Routledge.

Fook, J., Collington, V., Ross, F., Ruch, G., & West, L. (2016b). *Researching critical reflection: Multidisciplinary perspectives.* Routledge.

Fook, J., Psoinos, M., & Sartori, D. (2016). Evaluation studies of critical reflection. In J. Fook, V. Collington, F. Ross, G. Ruch, and L. West (Eds.), *Researching critical reflection: Multidisciplinary perspectives* (pp. 90–106). Routledge.

Fougner, A. (2012). Exploring knowledge through peer tutoring in a transitional learning community: An alternative way of teaching counseling skills to students in social work education. *Social Work Education, 31*(3), 287–301. https://doi.org/10.1080/02615479.2011.557431

Freire, P. (1984). *Pedagogy of the oppressed.* Continuum.

Frey, R., & Shadle, S. (2019). The guided inquiry. In S. Simonson (Ed.), *POGIL: An introduction to process oriented guided inquiry learning for those who wish to empower learners* (pp. 69–84). Stylus.

Friedman, D., Crews, T., Caicedo, J., Besley, J., Weinberg, J., & Freeman, M. (2010). An exploration into inquiry-based learning by a multidisciplinary group of higher education faculty. *Higher Education, 59*(6), 765–783. https://doi.org/10.1007/s10734-009-9279-9

Friesen, S., & Scott, D. (2013). *Inquiry-based learning: A review of the research literature.* https://galileo.org/focus-on-inquiry-lit-review.pdf

Froehle, K., Phillips, A. R., & Murzi, H. (2021). Lifelong learning is an ethical responsibility of professional engineers: Is school preparing young engineers for lifelong learning? *Journal of Civil Engineering Education, 147*(3). https://doi.org/10.1061/(ASCE)EI.2643-9115.0000045

Fry, S. W., & Villagomez, A. (2012). Writing to learn: Benefits and limitations. *College Teaching, 60*(4), 170–175. https://www.jstor.org/stable/23525114

Fuentes, M., Alvarado, A., Berdan, J., & DeAngelo, L. (2014). Mentorship matters: Does early faculty contact lead to quality faculty interaction? *Research in Higher Education, 55,* 288–307. https://doi.org/10.1007/s11162-013-9307-6

Funston, A., & Lee, N. (2014). The Graduating Project: A cross-disciplinary inquiry-based capstone in arts. In P. Blessinger & J. F. Carfora (Eds.), *Inquiry-based learning for faculty and institutional development: A conceptual and practical resource for educators* (pp. 223–241). Emerald. https://doi.org/10.1108/S2055-364120140000001012

Furmedge, D. S., Iwata, K., & Gill, D. (2014). Peer-assisted learning—beyond teaching: How can medical students contribute to the undergraduate curriculum? *Medical Teacher, 36*(9), 812–817. https://doi.org/10.3109/0142159X.2014.917158

Gappa, J. M., Austin, A. E., & Trice, A. G. (2007). *Rethinking faculty work: Higher education's strategic imperative.* Jossey-Bass.

Gehring, K. M., & Eastman, D. A. (2008). Information fluency for undergraduate biology majors: Applications of inquiry-based learning in a developmental biology course. *CBE—Life Sciences Education, 7*(1), 54–63. https://doi.org/10.1187/cbe.07-10-0091

Ghosh, A. K., Whipple, T. W., & Bryan, G. A. (2001). Student trust and its antecedents in higher education. *The Journal of Higher Education, 72*(3), 322–340. https://doi.org/10.1080/00221546.2001.11777097

Gilardi, S., & Lozza, E. (2009). Inquiry-based learning and undergraduates' professional identity development: Assessment of a field research-based course. *Innovative Higher Education, 34*(4), 245–256. https://doi.org/10.1007/s10755-009-9109-0

Gino, F. (2018, September–October). Why curiosity matters. *Harvard Business Review,* 47–61. https://hbr.org/2018/09/curiosity

Gleason, N. W. (2018). *Higher education in the era of the fourth industrial revolution.* Springer. https://doi.org/10.1007/978-981-13-0194-0

Goguen, L. M. S., Hiester, M. A., & Nordstrom, A. H. (2010). Associations among peer relationships, academic achievement, and persistence in college. *Journal of College Student Retention: Research, Theory & Practice, 12*(3), 319–337. https://doi.org/10.2190/CS.12.3.d

González-Sanmamed, M., Muñoz-Carril, P. C., & Santos-Caamaño, F. J. (2019). Key components of learning ecologies: A Delphi assessment. *British Journal of Educational Technology, 50*(4), 1639–1655. https://doi.org/10.1111/bjet.12805

Gordon, R. (1994). Keeping students at the center: Portfolio assessment at the college level. *Journal of Experiential Education, 17*(1), 23–27. https://doi.org/10.1177/105382599401700106

Gormally, C., Brickman, P., Hallar, P., & Armstrong, N. (2009). Effects of inquiry-based learning on students' science literacy skills and confidence. *International Journal for the Scholarship of Teaching and Learning, 3*(2), 1–24. https://doi.org/10.20429/ijsotl.2009.030216

Gottfried, A. E. (1985). Academic intrinsic motivation in elementary and junior high school students. *Journal of Educational Psychology, 77*(6), 631–645. https://doi.org/10.1037/0022-0663.77.6.631

Gottfried, A. E. (1990). Academic intrinsic motivation in young elementary school children. *Journal of Educational Psychology, 82*(3), 525–538. https://doi.org/10.1037/0022-0663.82.3.525

Gray, K. (2022). *Perceptions of new grad proficiency in competencies.* https://www.naceweb.org/career-readiness/competencies/recruiters-and-students-have-differing-perceptions-of-new-grad-proficiency-in-competencies/

Gray, M., Coates, J., Yellow Bird, M., & Hetherington, T. (2013). *Decolonizing social work.* Ashgate. https://doi.org/10.4324/9781315576206

Green, L., & Wilks, T. (2009). Involving service users in a problem based model of teaching and learning. *Social Work Education, 28*(2), 190–203. https://doi.org/10.1080/02615470802112985

Groccia, J. E. (2018). What is student engagement? In J. E. Groccia & W. Buskist (Eds.), *Student Engagement: A Multidimensional Perspective* (New Directions for Teaching and Learning, no. 154, pp. 11–20). Jossey-Bass. https://doi.org/10.1002/tl.20287

Grover, S., Sood, N., & Chaudhary, A. (2017). Reforming pathology teaching in medical college by peer-assisted learning and student-oriented interest building activities: A pilot study. *Education for Health, 30*(2), 126–132. https://doi.org/10.4103/efh.EfH_267_16

Guberman, D. (2021). Student perceptions of an online ungraded course. *Teaching and Learning Inquiry, 9*(1), 86–98. https://doi.org/10.20343/teachlearninqu.9.1.8

Haber-Curran, P., Everman, D., & Martinez, M. A. (2017). Mentors' personal growth and development in a college access mentorship program. *Mentoring & Tutoring: Partnership in Learning, 25*(4), 485–503. https://doi.org/10.1080/13611267.2017.1403558

Hairida, H. (2016). The effectiveness using inquiry based natural science module with authentic assessment to improve the critical thinking and inquiry skills of junior high school students. *Journal Pendidikan IPA Indonesia, 5*(2), 209–215. https://doi.org/10.15294/jpii.v5i2.7681

Hanstedt, P. (2018). *Creating wicked students: Designing courses for a complex world.* Stylus.

Hanusch, S. (2020). Summative portfolios in undergraduate mathematics courses. *PRIMUS, 30*(3), 274–284. https://doi.org/10.1080/10511970.2019.1566185

Harris, P. L. (2012). *Trusting what you're told.* Harvard University Press.

Hart, M., Sinclair, R., & Bruyere, G. (2009). *Wícihitowin: Aboriginal social work in Canada.* Fernwood.

Harvie, L., Harper-Travers, S., & Jaeger, A. (2017). Assessment within ILP: A journey of collaborative inquiry. *Journal of Educational Leadership, Policy and Practice, 32*(1), 133. https://search.informit.org/doi/10.3316/informit.021979664120138

Hauhart, R. C., & Grahe, J. E. (2010). The undergraduate capstone course in the social sciences: Results from a regional survey. *Teaching sociology, 38*(1), 4–17.

Hauhart, R. C., & Grahe, J. E. (2015). *Designing and teaching undergraduate capstone courses.* Wiley.

Haynes, F. (2018). Trust and the community of inquiry. *Educational Philosophy and Theory, 50*(2), 144–151. https://doi.org/10.1080/00131857.2016.1144169

Hays, J. (2015). *Chaos to capability: Educating professionals for the 21st century.* https://www.unitec.ac.nz/epress/index.php/chaos-to-capability-educating-professionals-for-the-21st-century/

Hays, J., & Reinders, H. (2018). Critical learnership: A new perspective on learning. *International Journal of Learning, Teaching and Educational Research, 17*(1), 1–25. https://doi.org/10.26803/ijlter.17.1.1

Hays, J., & Reinders, H. (2020). Sustainable learning and education: A curriculum for the future. *International Review of Education, 66*(1), 29–52. https://doi.org/10.1007/s11159-020-09820-7

Head, B. W. (2019). Forty years of wicked problems literature: Forging closer links to policy studies. *Policy and Society, 38*(2), 180–197. https://doi.org/10.1080/14494035.2018.1488797

Healey, M. (2005). Linking research and teaching: Exploring disciplinary spaces and the role of inquiry-based learning. In R. Barnett (Ed.), *Reshaping the university: New relationships between research, scholarship and teaching* (pp. 67–78). McGraw-Hill/Open University Press.

Healey, M., & Jenkins, A. (2009). *Developing undergraduate research and inquiry.* Higher Education Academy.

Heen, S., & Stone, D. (2014). Find the coaching in criticism. *Harvard Business Review*, *92*, 108–111. https://hbr.org/2014/01/find-the-coaching-in-criticism

Hendry, G., & Oliver, G. (2012). Seeing is believing: The benefits of peer observation. *Journal of University Teaching and Learning Practice*, *9*(1), 1–11. https://ro.uow.edu.au/jutlp/vol9/iss1/7

Henschke, J. A. (2013). Trust in learning: Makes all the difference. In C. Boden-McGill & K. P. King (Eds.), *Conversations About Adult Learning in Our Complex World* (pp. 15–31). Information Age. https://digitalcommons.usf.edu/ehe_facpub/54

Hiller, T. B., & Hietapelto, A. B. (2001). Contract grading: Encouraging commitment to the learning process through voice in the evaluation process. *Journal of Management Education*, *25*(6), 660–684. https://doi.org/10.1177/105256290102500605

Hmelo-Silver, C. E., Duncan, R. G., & Chinn, C. A. (2007). Scaffolding and achievement in problem-based and inquiry learning: A response to Kirschner, Sweller, and Clark (2006). *Educational Psychologist*, *42*(2), 99–107. https://doi.org/10.1080/00461520701263368

Hofhues S. (2019). Inquiry-based learning with digital media. In H. A. Mieg (Ed.), *Inquiry-based learning: Undergraduate research*. Springer. https://doi.org/10.1007/978-3-030-14223-0_35

Holaday, S., & Buckley, K. (2008). Addressing challenges in nursing education: Through a clinical instruction model based on a hybrid, inquiry-based learning framework. *Nursing Education Perspectives (National League for Nursing)*, *29*(6), 353–358. PMID: 19244801.

Hudspith, B., & Jenkins, H. (2001). *Teaching the art of inquiry* [Green guide no 3]. Society for Teaching and Learning in Higher Education, University of Western Ontario.

Hughes, K. S. (2011). Peer-assisted learning strategies in human anatomy and physiology. *The American Biology Teacher*, *73*(3), 144–147. https://doi.org/10.1525/abt.2011.73.3.5

Hughes, P. W., & Ellefson, M. R. (2013). Inquiry-based training improves teaching effectiveness of biology teaching assistants. *PLoS One*, *8*(10). https://doi.org/10.1371/journal.pone.0078540

Janik, M. D., & Daniel, S. (2005). *Unlock the genius within: Neurobiological trauma, teaching, and transformative learning*. R&L Education.

Johnson-Bailey, J., & Alfred, M. V. (2006). Transformational teaching and the practices of Black women adult educators. In E. W. Taylor (Ed.), *Teaching for Change: Fostering Transformative Learning in the Classroom* (New Directions for Adult and Continuing Education, no. 109, pp. 49–58). Jossey-Bass. https://doi.org/10.1002/ace.207

Jovanovic, V., & Brdaric, D. (2012). Did curiosity kill the cat? Evidence from subjective well-being in adolescents. *Personality and Individual Differences*, *52*(3), 380–384. https://doi.org/10.1016/j.paid.2011.10.043

Jovanović, V., & Gavrilov-Jerković, V. (2014). The good, the bad (and the ugly): The role of curiosity in subjective well-being and risky behaviors among adolescents. *Scandinavian Journal of Psychology, 55*(1), 38–44. https://doi.org/10.1111/sjop.12084

Justice, C., Rice, J., Roy, D., Hudspith, B., & Jenkins, H. (2009). Inquiry-based learning in higher education: Administrators' perspectives on integrating inquiry pedagogy into the curriculum. *Higher Education, 58*(6), 841–855. https://doi.org/10.1007/s10734-009-9228-7

Justice, C., Rice, J., & Warry, W. (2009). Developing useful and transferable skills: Course design to prepare students for a life of learning. *International Journal for the Scholarship of Teaching and Learning, 3*(2), Article 9. https://doi.org/10.20429/ijsotl.2009.030209

Justice, C., Rice, J., Warry, W., Inglis, S., Miller, S., & Sammon, S. (2007). Inquiry in higher education: Reflections and directions on course design and teaching methods. *Innovative Higher Education, 31*(4), 201–214. https://doi.org/10.1007/s10755-006-9021-9

Justice, C., Warry, W., Cuneo, C., Inglis, S., Miller, S., Rice, J. & Sammon, S. (2002). *A grammar for inquiry: Linking goals and methods in a collaboratively taught social sciences inquiry course.* The Alan Blizzard Award Paper: The Award Winning Papers, Windsor. McGraw-Hill Ryerson.

Kaplan, M., Silver, N., LaVaque-Manty, D., & Meizlish, D. (2013). *Using metacognition and reflection to improve student learning.* Stylus.

Kashdan, T. (2009). *Curious? Discover the missing ingredient to a fulfilling life.* William Morrow & Co.

Kashdan, T. B., & Fincham, F. D. (2004). Facilitating curiosity: A social and self-regulatory perspective for scientifically based interventions. In P. A. Linley & S. Joseph (Eds.), *Positive psychology in practice* (pp. 482–503). Wiley.

Kashdan, T. B., Goodman, F. R., Disabato, D. J., McKnight, P. E., Kelso, K., & Naughton, C. (2020). Curiosity has comprehensive benefits in the workplace: Developing and validating a multidimensional workplace curiosity scale in United States and German employees. *Personality and Individual Differences, 155*, 109717. https://doi.org/10.1016/j.paid.2019.109717

Kashdan, T. B., McKnight, P. E., Fincham, F. D., & Rose, P. (2011). When curiosity breeds intimacy: Taking advantage of intimacy opportunities and transforming boring conversations. *Journal of Personality, 79*(6), 1369–1402. https://doi.org/10.1111/j.1467-6494.2010.00697.x

Kashdan, T. B., & Steger, M. F. (2007). Curiosity and pathways to well-being and meaning in life: Traits, states, and everyday behaviors. *Motivation and Emotion, 31*(3), 159–173. https://doi.org/10.1007/s11031-007-9068-7

Katz. C., Elsaesser. C., Klodnik. V., & Khare. E. (2018). Mentoring matters: An innovative approach to infusing mentorship in a social work doctoral program. *Journal of Social Work Education, 55*(2), 306–313. https://doi.org/10.1080/10437797.2018.1526729

Kegan, R. (2000). What "forms" transforms? A constructive-developmental approach to learning. In J. Mezirow (Ed.), *Learning as transformation* (pp. 35–70). Jossey-Bass.

Kendall, K. D., & Schussler, E. E. (2013). Evolving impressions: Undergraduate perceptions of graduate teaching assistants and faculty members over a semester. *CBE Life Science Education, 12*, 92–105. https://doi.org/10.1187/cbe.12-07-0110

Kim, K. H. (2011). The creativity crisis: The decrease in creative thinking scores on the Torrance tests of creative thinking. *Creativity Research Journal, 23*(4), 285–295. http://dx.doi.org/10.1080/10400419.2011.627805

Kim, Y. H., & Choi, N. Y. (2019). Career decision self-efficacy of Asian American students: The role of curiosity and ethnic identity. *The Career Development Quarterly, 67*(1), 32–46. https://doi.org/10.1002/cdq.12161

Kirschner, P. A., Sweller, J., & Clark, R. E. (2006). Why minimal guidance during instruction does not work: An analysis of the failure of constructivist, discovery, problem-based, experiential, and inquiry-based teaching. *Educational Psychologist, 41*(2), 75–86. https://doi.org/10.1207/s15326985ep4102_1

Kirwan, A., & Adams, J. (2009). Students' views of enquiry-based learning in a continuing professional development module. *Nurse Education Today, 29*(4), 448–455. https://doi.org/10.1016/j.nedt.2008.09.003

Kogan, M., & Laursen, S. L. (2014). Assessing long-term effects of inquiry-based learning: A case study from college mathematics. *Innovative Higher Education, 39*(3), 183–199. https://doi.org/10.1007/s10755-013-9269-9

Kohn, A. (2006). The trouble with rubrics. *English Journal, 95*(4), 12–15. https://library.ncte.org/journals/ej/issues/v95-4

Kori, K. (2021). Inquiry-based learning in higher education. In C. Vaz de Carvalho & M. Bauters (Eds.), *Technology supported active learning* (pp. 59–74). Springer. https://doi.org/10.1007/978-981-16-2082-9

Kotter, J., & Cohen, D. (2002). *The heart of change*. Harvard Business School Press.

Kramer, D., Hillman. S., & Zavala. M. (2018). Developing a culture of caring and support through a peer mentorship program. *Journal of Nursing Education, 57*(7), 430–435. https://doi.org/10.3928/01484834-20180618-09

Krathwohl, D. R. (2002). A revision of Bloom's taxonomy: An overview. *Theory Into Practice, 41*(4), 212–218. https://doi.org/10.1207/s15430421tip4104_2

Kurdziel, J. P., Turner, J. A., Luft, J. A., & Roehrig, G. H. (2003). Graduate teaching assistants and inquiry-based instruction: Implications for graduate teaching assistant training. *Journal of Chemical Education, 80*(10), 1206–1210. https://doi.org/10.1021/ed080p1206

Kyza, E. A., Golan, R., Reiser, B. J., & Edelson, D. C. (2002, January 7). Reflective inquiry: Enabling group self-regulation in inquiry-based science using the Progress Portfolio tool. *Proceedings of the Conference on Computer Support for Collaborative Learning: Foundations for a CSCL Community*, 227–236. https://dl.acm.org/doi/10.5555/1658616.1658648

Lamnina, M., & Chase, C. C. (2019). Developing a thirst for knowledge: How uncertainty in the classroom influences curiosity, affect, learning, and transfer. *Contemporary Educational Psychology, 59*, 101785. https://doi.org/10.1016/j.cedpsych.2019.101785

Land, G., & Jarman, B. (1992). Future pull. *The Futurist*, 25–27. https://www
.proquest.com/openview/7af695cc8b19e22e4e12122bb2042393/1?pq-origsite=
gscholar&cbl=47758

Lang, A. (2012). *The power of why.* Collins.

Laursen, S. L., Hassi, M., Kogan, M., & Weston, T. J. (2014). Benefits for women
and men of inquiry-based learning in college mathematics: A multi-institution
study. *Journal for Research in Mathematics Education, 45*(4), 406–418. https://doi
.org/10.5951/jresemathheduc.45.4.0406

Laursen, S. L., & Rasmussen, C. (2019). I on the prize: Inquiry approaches in undergraduate mathematics. *International Journal of Research in Undergraduate Mathematics Education, 5*(1), 129–146. https://doi.org/10.1007/s40753-019-00085-6

Lazonder, A. W., & Harmsen, R. (2016). Meta-analysis of inquiry-based learning:
Effects of guidance. *Review of Educational Research, 86*(3), 681–718. https://doi
.org/10.3102/0034654315627366

Lee, V. S. (Ed.). (2012). Opportunities and challenges in institutionalizing inquiry-
guided learning in colleges and universities. In *Inquiry-Guided Learning* (New
Directions for Teaching and Learning, no. 129, pp. 105–116). Jossey-Bass.
https://doi.org/10.1002/tl.20011

Levy, P. (2012). Developing inquiry-guided learning in a research university in the United
Kingdom. In V. S. Lee (Ed.), *Inquiry-Guided Learning* (New Directions for Teaching
and Learning, no. 129, 15–26). Jossey-Bass. https://doi.org/10.1002/tl.20003

Levy, P., & Petrulis, R. (2012). How do first-year university students experience
inquiry and research, and what are the implications for the practice of inquiry-
based learning? *Studies in Higher Education, 37*(1), 85–101. https://doi.org/
10.1080/03075079.2010.499166

Li, L. Y. (2007). Exploring the use of focused freewriting in developing academic
writing. *Journal of University Teaching & Learning Practice, 4*(1), 46–60. https://
doi.org/10.53761/1.4.1.5

Lindemann, D. F., & Harbke, C. R. (2011). Use of contract grading to improve
grades among college freshmen in introductory psychology. *SAGE Open, 1*(3),
1–7. https://doi.org/10.1177/2158244011434103

Linden. J., Ohlin. M., & Brodin. E. (2013). Mentorship, supervision and learning experiences in PhD education. *Studies in Higher Education, 38*(5), 639–662.
https://doi.org/10.1080/03075079.2011.596526

Lindholm, M. (2018). Promoting curiosity? *Science & Education, 27*(9–10), 987–
1002. https://doi.org/10.1007/s11191-018-0015-7

Linenberger, K., Slade, M. C., Addis, E. A., Elliott, E. R., Mynhardt, G., &
Raker, J. R. (2014). Training the foot soldiers of inquiry: Development and
evaluation of a graduate teaching assistant learning community. *Journal of College
Science Teaching, 44*(1), 97–107. https://www.jstor.org/stable/43631783

Lintern, A., McPhillips, L., Winfrey, B., Duncan, J., & Grady, C. (2020). Best
management practices for diffuse nutrient pollution: Wicked problems across
urban and agricultural watersheds. *Environmental Science & Technology, 54*(15),
9159–9174. https://doi.org/10.1021/acs.est.9b07511

Litmanen, T., Lonka, K., Inkenen, M., Lipponen, L., & Hakkarainen, K. (2012). Capturing teacher students' emotional experiences in context: Does inquiry-based learning make a difference? *Instructional Science, 40*(6), 1083–1101. https://doi .org/10.1007/s1121-011-9203

Litterio, L. M. (2018). Contract grading in the technical writing classroom: Blending community-based assessment and self-assessment. *Assessing Writing, 38,* 1–9. https://doi.org/10.1016/j.asw.2018.06.002

Little, S. (2010). *Inquiry-based learning in the social sciences: A meta-analytical study.* Centre for Inquiry-based Learning in the Arts and Social Sciences, University of Sheffield. www.shef.ac.uk/polopoly_fs/1.122795!/file/IBL_in_SocSci-FINAL.pdf

Liu, H., Fernandez, F., & Grotlüschen, A. (2019). Examining self-directedness and its relationships with lifelong learning and earnings in Yunnan, Vietnam, Germany, and the United States. *International Journal of Educational Development, 70,* 102088. https://doi.org/10.1016/j.ijedudev.2019.102088

Lorenzetti, D., Shipton, L., Nowell, L., Jacobsen, M., Lorenzetti, L., Clancy, T., & Paolucci, E. (2019). A systematic review of graduate student peer mentorship in academia. *Mentoring & Tutoring: Partnership in Learning, 27*(5), 549–576. https://doi.org/10.1080/13611267.2019.1686694

Love, B., Hodge, A., Corritore, C. & Ernst, D. C. (2015). Inquiry-based learning and the flipped classroom model. *Problems, Resources, and Issues in Mathematics Undergraduate Studies, 25*(8), 745–762. https://doi.org/10.1080/10511970 .2015.1046005

Luft, J. A., Kurdziel, J. P., Roehrig, G. H., & Turner, J. (2004). Growing a garden without water: Graduate teaching assistants in introductory science laboratories at a doctoral/research university. *Journal of Research in Science Teaching, 41*(3), 211–233. https://doi.org/10.1002/tea.20004

MacFarlane, B. (2009). A leap of faith: The role of trust in higher education teaching. *Nagoya Journal of Higher Education, 9*(1), 221–238. http://www.cshe.nagoya-u .ac.jp/publications/journal/no9/14.pdf

MacKinnon, S. L. (2017). "The Curiosity Project": Re-igniting the desire to inquire through intrinsically-motivated learning and mentorship. *Journal of Transformative Learning, 4*(1), 4–21. https://jotl.uco.edu/index.php/jotl/article/view/65/119

Maksum, A., & Khory, F. D. (2020). Effect of learning climate, thinking pattern, and curiosity on academic performance in higher education. *Problems of Education in the 21st Century, 78*(1), 102–113. https://doi.org/10.33225/pec/20.78.102

Maluleka, K. J. (2021). Education for self-reliance and its relevance to lifelong learning in the previously colonised countries. *International Journal of Lifelong Education, 40*(2), 129–141. https://doi.org/10.1080/02601370.2021.1899320

Mangione, L., Mears, G., Vincent, W., & Hawes, S. (2011). The supervisory relationship when women supervise women: An exploratory study of power, reflexivity, collaboration and authenticity. *The Clinical Supervisor, 30*(2), 141–171. https://doi.org/10.1080/07325223.2011.604272

Marion, A. (2013). Training teaching assistants in inquiry-based learning. *Proceedings of the Association for Biology Laboratory Education, 34,* 337–339. http://www .ableweb.org/volumes/vol-34/?art=31

Martin, L. J. (2019). Introducing components of specifications grading to a general Chemistry I course. In S. K. Hartwell & T. Gupta (Eds.), *Enhancing retention in introductory chemistry courses: Teaching practices and assessments* (pp. 105–119). American Chemical Society. https://doi.org/10.1021/bk-2019-1330.ch007

Masiello, L., & Skipper, T. L. (2013). *Writing in the senior capstone: Theory and practice.* National Resource Center for The First-Year Experience and Students in Transition. University of South Carolina.

McKinney, P. (2014). Information literacy and inquiry-based learning: Evaluation of a five-year programme of curriculum development. *Journal of Librarianship and Information Science, 46*(2), 148–166. https://doi.org/10.1177/0961000613477677

McLean, S. F. (2016). Case-based learning and its application in medical and health-care fields: A review of worldwide literature. *Journal of Medical Education and Curricular Development, 3,* 39–49. https://doi.org/10.4137/JMECD.S20377

Mezirow, J. (1990). *Fostering critical reflection in adulthood.* Jossey-Bass.

Mezirow, J. (1991) *Transformative dimensions of adult learning.* Jossey-Bass.

Mezirow, J. (2000). *Learning as transformation: Critical perspectives on a theory in progress.* Jossey-Bass.

Miller, T. (2014). How to scale inquiry-based teaching and learning through progressive faculty development. In P. Blessinger & J. M. Carfora (Eds.), *Inquiry-based learning for faculty and institutional development: A conceptual and practical resource for educators* (pp. 317–337). Emerald. https://doi.org/10.1108/S2055-364120140000001016

Miller, D. T., & McFarland, C. (1991). When social comparison goes awry: The case of pluralistic ignorance. In J. Suls & T. A. Wills (Eds.), *Social comparison: Contemporary theory and research* (pp. 287–313). Erlbaum.

Miller-Young, J., & Yeo, M. (2015). Conceptualizing and communicating SoTL: A framework for the field. *Teaching & Learning Inquiry, 3*(2), 37–53. https://doi.org/10.2979/teachlearninqu.3.2.37

Minigan, A. (2016, October 7). Cultivating curiosity by deliberately teaching students how to ask questions. *Education Week.* https://www.edweek.org/leadership/opinion-cultivating-curiosity-by-deliberately-teaching-students-how-to-ask-questions/2016/10

Minigan, A. (2017). The importance of curiosity and questions in 21st-century learning. *Education Week, 36,* 32. https://www.edweek.org/teaching-learning/opinion-the-Importance-of-curiosity-and-questions-in-21st-century-learning/2017/05

Mirsky, G. M. (2018). Effectiveness of specifications grading in teaching technical writing to computer science students. *Journal of Computing Science in Colleges, 34*(1), 104–110. https://dl.acm.org/doi/abs/10.5555/3280489.3280505

Moon, J. A. (1999). *Reflection in learning and professional development: Theory and practice.* Routledge.

Morales, D., Grineski, S., & Collins, T. (2021). Effects of mentoring relationship heterogeneity on students' outcome in summer undergraduate research. *Studies in Higher Education, 46*(3), 423–436. https://doi.org/10.1080/03075079.2019.1639041

Mullaly, B., & West, J. (2017). *Challenging oppression and confronting privilege: A critical approach to anti-oppressive and anti-privilege theory and practice* (3rd ed.). Oxford University Press.

Murthy, P. P., Thompson, M., & Hungwe, K. (2014). Development of a semester-long, inquiry-based laboratory course in upper-level biochemistry and molecular biology. *Journal of Chemical Education, 91*(11), 1909–1917.

Mussel, P. (2013). Introducing the construct curiosity for predicting job performance. *Journal of Organizational Behavior, 34*(4), 453–472. https://doi.org/10.1002/job.1809

Nadan, Y., Weinberg-Kurnik, G., & Ben-Ari, A. (2015). Bringing context and power relations to the fore: Intergroup dialogue as a tool in social work education. *British Journal of Social Work, 45*(1), 260–277. https://doi.org/10.1093/bjsw/bct116

Nadelson, L. S., Nadelson, S. G., Broyles, A., Edgar, J., Einhorn, J., Hatchett, A., Scroggins, T., Skipper, A., & Ulrich, C. (2019). Beyond the books: Teacher practices and perceptions of teaching caring and curiosity. *Journal of Curriculum and Teaching, 8*(3), 84–101. https://doi.org/10.5430/jct.v8n3p84

Nair, K. U., & Ramnarayan, S. (2000). Individual differences in need for cognition and complex problem solving. *Journal of Research in Personality, 34*(3), 305–328. https://doi.org/10.1006/jrpe.1999.2274

Narayan, L. (2000). Freire and Gandhi: Their relevance for social work education. *International Social Work, 43*(2), 193–204. https://doi.org/10.1177/002087280004300205

Narushima, M., Liu, J., & Diestelkamp, N. (2018). I learn, therefore I am: A phenomenological analysis of meanings of lifelong learning for vulnerable older adults. *The Gerontologist, 58*(4), 696–705. https://doi.org/10.1093/geront/gnx044

National Association of Colleges and Employers. (n.d.). *Home page.* https://www.naceweb.org/

Nemeth, C., Brown, K., & Rogers, J. (2001). Devil's advocate versus authentic dissent: Stimulating quantity and quality. *European Journal of Social Psychology, 31*(6), 707–720. https://doi.org/10.1002/ejsp.58

Ness, I. J., & Riese, H. (2015). Openness, curiosity and respect: Underlying conditions for developing innovative knowledge and ideas between disciplines. *Learning, Culture and Social Interaction, 6,* 29–39. https://doi.org/10.1016/j.lcsi.2015.03.001

Neumann, A., & Terosky, A. L. (2007). To give and to receive: Recently tenured professors' experiences of service in major research universities. *The Journal of Higher Education, 78*(3), 282–310. https://doi.org/10.1080/00221546.2007.11772317

Newmann, F., Bryk, A., & Nagaoka, J. (2001, January). *Authentic intellectual work and standardized tests: Conflict or coexistence.* Consortium on Chicago School Research. https://consortium.uchicago.edu/publications/authentic-intellectual-work-and-standardized-tests-conflict-or-coexistence

Newmann, F., Marks, H., & Gamoran, A. (1996). Authentic pedagogy and student performance. *American Journal of Education, 104*(4), 280–312. https://doi.org/10.1086/444136

Newton, J., Williams, M., & Feeney, D. (2020). Implementing non-traditional assessment strategies in teacher preparation: Opportunities and challenges. *Journal of Culture and Values in Education, 3*(1), 39–51. https://doi.org/10.46303/jcve.03.01.3

Newton-Calvert, Z., & Smith Arthur, D. (2018). Capstone courses and projects. In K. E. Linder & C. M. Hayes (Eds.), *High-impact practices in online education: Research and best practices* (pp. 165–181). Stylus.

Nilson, L. B. (2015). *Specifications grading: Restoring rigor, motivating students, and saving faculty time.* Stylus.

Nuebel, E., Nowinski, S. M., Hemmis, C. W., & Lindsley, J. E. (2020). A curriculum design and teaching experience created by and for bioscience postdoctoral fellows in a medical school. *Medical Science Educator, 30*(1), 97–101. https://doi.org/10.1007/s40670-019-00889-w

Obhi, H. K., Hardy, A., & Margrett, J. A. (2021). Values of lifelong learners and their pursuits of happiness and whole-person wellness. *Aging & Mental Health, 25*(4), 672–678. https://doi.org/10.1080/13607863.2020.1711868

Oliver, R. (2008). Engaging first year students using a web-supported inquiry-based learning setting. *Higher Education, 55*(3), 285–301. https://doi.org/10.1007/s10734-007-9055-7

O'Mahony, J. (2014). *Enhancing student learning and teacher development in transnational education.* The Higher Education Academy. https://www.heacademy.ac.uk/sites/default/files/resources/enhancingtne_final_080414.pdf

O'Neal C., Wright, M., Cook, C., Perorazio, T., & Purkiss, J. (2007). The impact of teaching assistants on student retention in the sciences: Lessons for TA training. *Journal of College Science Teaching, 36*(5), 24–29. https://www.jstor.org/stable/42992683

Otfinowski, R., & Silva-Opps, M. (2015). Writing toward a scientific identity: Shifting from prescriptive to reflective writing in undergraduate biology. *Journal of College Science Teaching, 45*(2), 19–23. http://www.jstor.org/stable/43631899.

Paglis, L., Green. S., & Bauert. T. (2006). Does adviser mentoring add value? A longitudinal study of mentoring and doctoral student outcomes. *Research in Higher Education, 47*(4), 451–476. https://doi.org/10.1007/s11162-005-9003-2

Parmelee, D., Roman, B., Overman, I., & Alizadeh, M. (2020). The lecture-free curriculum: Setting the stage for life-long learning: AMEE guide no. 135. *Medical Teacher, 42*(9), 962–969. https://doi.org/10.1080/0142159X.2020.1789083

Parsons, J., & Taylor, L. (2011). Improving student engagement. *Current Issues in Education, 14*(1). https://cie.asu.edu/ojs/index.php/cieatasu/article/view/745

Passon, J., & Schlesinger, J. (2019). Inquiry-based learning in geography. In H. A. Mieg (Ed.), *Inquiry-based learning—undergraduate research* (pp. 281–290). Springer.

Payne, M. (2015). *Modern social work theory* (4th ed.). Lyceum Books.

Peterson, E. G. (2020). Supporting curiosity in schools and classrooms. *Current Opinion in Behavioral Sciences, 35*, 7–13. https://doi.org/10.1016/j.cobeha.2020.05.006

Petrie, S., & Peters, P. (2020). Untangling complexity as a health determinant: Wicked problems in healthcare. *Health Science Inquiry, 11*(1), 131–135. https://doi.org/10.29173/hsi299

Pierce, J. P., Distefan, J. M., Kaplan, R. M., & Gilpin, E. A. (2005). The role of curiosity in smoking initiation. *Addictive Behaviors*, *30*(4), 685–696. https://doi.org/10.1016/j.addbeh.2004.08.014

Pittaway, L. (2009). The role of inquiry-based learning in entrepreneurship education. *Industry and Higher Education*, *23*(3), 153–162. https://doi.org/10.5367/000000009788640251

Plowright, D., & Watkins, M. (2004). There are no problems to be solved, only inquiries to be made, in social work education. *Innovations in Education and Teaching International*, *41*(2), 185–206. https://doi.org/10.1080/1470329042000208701

Pope, L., Parker, H. B., & Ultsch, S. (2020). Assessment of specifications grading in an undergraduate dietetics course. *Journal of Nutrition Education and Behavior*, *52*(4), 439–446. https://doi.org/10.1016/j.jneb.2019.07.017

Potts, G. (2010). A simple alternative to grading. *Inquiry*, *15*(1), 29–42. https://commons.vccs.edu/inquiry/vol15/iss1/4

Prasad, P. V. (2020). Using revision and specifications grading to develop students' mathematical habits of mind. *PRIMUS*, *30*(8–10), 908–925. https://doi.org/10.1080/10511970.2019.1709589

Pstross, M., Talmage, C. A., Peterson, C. B., & Knopf, R. C. (2017). In search of transformative moments: Blending community building pursuits into lifelong learning experiences. *Journal of Education Culture and Society*, *62*(2), 62–78. http://cejsh.icm.edu.pl/cejsh/element/bwmeta1.element.ojs-doi-10_15503_jecs20171_62_78

Pulliam, R. M. (2017). Practical application of critical race theory: A social justice course design. *Journal of Social Work Education*, *53*(3), 414–423. https://doi.org/10.1080/10437797.2016.1275896

Quintana, R., & Quintana, C. (2020). When classroom interactions have to go online: The move to specifications grading in a project-based design course. *Information and Learning Sciences*, *121*(7/8), 525–532. https://www.emerald.com/insight/2398-5348.htm

Raine, A., Reynolds, C., Venables, P. H., & Mednick, S. A. (2002). Stimulation seeking and intelligence: A prospective longitudinal study. *Journal of Personality and Social Psychology*, *82*(4), 663–674. https://doi.org/10.1037/0022-3514.82.4.663

Rancourt, D., & Archer-Kuhn, B. (2019, July 8). How universities can really help PhD grads get jobs. *The Conversation*. https://theconversation.com/how-universities-can-really-help-phd-grads-get-jobs-118241

Ranz, R., & Korin Langer, N. (2018). Preparing international social work students to engage with unequal power relations. *Social Work Education*, *37*(4), 535–545. https://doi.org/10.1080/02615479.2018.1444158

Reisch, M., & Garvin, C. (2016). *Social work and social justice: Concepts, challenges, and strategies.* Oxford University Press.

Reisch, M., & Jani, J. S. (2012). The new politics of social work practice: Understanding context to promote change. *The British Journal of Social Work*, *42*(6), 1132–1150. https://doi.org/10.1093/bjsw/bcs072

Richards, C. (2015). Outcomes-based authentic learning, portfolio assessment, and a systems approach to "complex problem-solving": Related pillars for enhancing the innovative role of PBL in future higher education. *Journal of Problem Based Learning in Higher Education*, *3*(1), 78–95. https://doi.org/10.5278/ojs.jpblhe .v3i1.1204

Richman, L. S., Kubzansky, L., Maselko, J., Kawachi, I., Choo, P., & Bauer, M. (2005). Positive emotion and health: Going beyond the negative. *Health Psychology*, *24*(4), 422–429. https://doi.org/10.1037/0278-6133.24.4.422

Richmond, A. S., Fleck, B., Heath, T., Broussard, K. A., & Skarda, B. (2015). Can inquiry-based instruction promote higher-level learning? *Scholarship of Teaching and Learning in Psychology*, *1*(3), 208–218. https://doi.org/10.1037/stl0000032

Risley, L. M., & Petroff, K. M. (2014). Examining the element of trust from multiple perspectives in educational environments. In C. J. Boden-McGill & K. P. King (Eds.), *Developing and sustaining adult learners* (pp. 3–15). Information Age.

Roohr, K. C., & Burkander, K. (2020). Exploring critical thinking as an outcome for students enrolled in community colleges. *Community College Review*, *48*(3), 330–351. https://doi.org/10.1177/0091552120923402

Rothstein, D., & Santana, L. (2011). *Make just one change: Teach students to ask their own questions*. Harvard Education Press.

Roy, D., Kustra, E., & Borin, P. (2003). *What is a good inquiry question?* McPherson Institute. http://cll.mcmaster.ca/resources/misc/good_inquiry_question.html

Rüber, I. E., Rees, S. L., & Schmidt-Hertha, B. (2018). Lifelong learning–lifelong returns? A new theoretical framework for the analysis of civic returns on adult learning. *International Review of Education*, *64*(5), 543–562. https://doi .org/10.1007/s11159-018-9738-6

Rushton, G. T., Lotter, C., & Singer, J. (2011). Chemistry teachers' emerging expertise in inquiry teaching: The effect of a professional development model on beliefs and practice. *Journal of Science Teacher Education*, *22*(1), 23–52. https:// doi.org/10.1007/s10972-010-9224-x

Ryan, R. M., & Deci, E. L. (2000). Intrinsic and extrinsic motivations: Classic definitions and new directions. *Contemporary Educational Psychology*, *25*(1), 54–67. https://doi.org/10.1006/ceps.1999.1020

Sandi-Urena, S., Cooper, M. M., & Gatlin, T. A. (2011). Graduate teaching assistants' epistemological and metacognitive development. *Chemistry Education Research and Practice*, *12*(1), 92–100. https://doi.org/10.1039/C1RP90012A

Sandi-Urena, S., & Gatlin, T. (2013). Factors contributing to the development of graduate teaching assistant self-image. *Journal of Chemical Education*, *90*(10), 1303–1309. https://doi.org/10.1021/ed200859e

Saunders-Stewart, K. S., Gyles, P. D. T., & Shore, B. M. (2012). Student outcomes in inquiry instruction: A literature-derived inventory. *Journal of Advanced Academics*, *23*(1), 5–31. https://doi.org/10.1177/1932202X11429860

Sawyer, K. (2006a). The future of learning: Grounding educational innovation in the learning sciences. In K. Sawyer (Ed.), *The Cambridge handbook of the learning sciences* (pp. 726–746). Cambridge University Press.

Sawyer, K. (2006b). The new science of learning. In K. Sawyer (Ed.), *The Cambridge handbook of the learning sciences* (pp. 1–16). Cambridge University Press.

Schattner, A. (2020). An antidote to burnout? Developing broad-spectrum curiosity as a prevailing attitude. *QJM: An International Journal of Medicine, 114*(11), 1–3. https://doi.org/10.1093/qjmed/hcz322

Schön, D. (1983). *The reflective practitioner: How professionals think in action.* Basic Books.

Schuman, D., Parekh, R., Fields, N., Woody, D., & Miller, V. (2021). Improving outcomes for at risk MSW students: A pilot e-mentorship program using a near peer model. *Journal of Teaching in Social Work, 41*(1), 42–56. https://doi.org/10.1080/08841233.2020.1852361

Scott, S. G. (2010). Enhancing reflection skills through learning portfolios: An empirical test. *Journal of Management Education, 34*(3), 430–457. https://doi.org/10.1177/1052562909351144

Seaman, J., & Rheingold, A. (2013). Circle talks as situated experiential learning: Context, identity, and knowledgeability in "learning from reflection." *Journal of Experiential Education, 36*(2), 155–174. https://doi.org/10.1177/105382591 3487887

Seldin, P. (1993). *Successful use of teaching portfolios.* Anker.

Seldin, P. (1997). Using student feedback to improve teaching. *To improve the academy, 16*(1), 335–345. https://doi.org/10.1002/j.2334-4822.1997.tb00333.x

Sensoy, Ö., & DiAngelo, R. (2009). Developing social justice literacy an open letter to our faculty colleagues. *Phi Delta Kappan, 90*(5), 345–352. https://doi.org/10.1177/003172170909000508

Shin, J. C., & Jung, J. (2014). Academics job satisfaction and job stress across countries in the changing academic environments. *Higher Education, 67*(5), 603–620. https://doi.org/10.1007/s10734-013-9668-y

Simonson, S. (2019). *POGIL: An introduction to process oriented guided inquiry learning for those who wish to empower learners.* Stylus.

Sinclair, R. (2004). Aboriginal social work education in Canada: Decolonizing pedagogy for the seventh generation. *First Peoples Child & Family Review, 1*(1), 49–61. https://doi.org/10.7202/1069584ar

Slater, A., Morison, V., & Rose, D. (1982). Visual memory at birth. *British Journal of Psychology, 73*(4), 519–525. https://doi.org/10.1111/j.2044-8295.1982.tb01834.x

Smallhorn, M., Young, J., Hunter, N., & da Silva, K. B. (2015). Inquiry-based learning to improve student engagement in a large first year topic. *Student Success, 6*(2), 65–72. https://studentsuccessjournal.org/article/view/459

Smith, J., Lee, V., & Newman, F. (2001). *Instruction and achievement in Chicago elementary schools.* Consortium on Chicago School Research, University of Chicago.

Smits, H., Wang, H., Towers, J., Crichton, S., Field, J., & Tarr, P. (2005). Deepening understanding of inquiry teaching and learning with e-portfolios in a teacher preparation program. *Canadian Journal of Learning and Technology, 31*(3). https://www.learntechlib.org/p/43171/

Spronken-Smith, R., & Walker, R. (2010). Can inquiry-based learning strengthen the links between teaching and disciplinary research? *Studies in Higher Education, 35*(6), 723–740. https://doi.org/10.1080/03075070903315502

Spronken-Smith, R., Walker, R., Batchelor, J., O'Steen, B., & Angelo, T. (2011). Enablers and constraints to the use of inquiry-based learning in undergraduate education. *Teaching in Higher Education, 16*(1), 15–28. https://doi.org/10.1080/13562517.2010.507300

Stokoe, R. (2012). Curiosity, a condition for learning. *The International Schools Journal, 32*(1), 63–65. https://eshop.isjournal.eu/product/isj-november-2012-curiosity-a-condition-for-learning/

Stommel, J. (2020). How to ungrade. In S. D. Blum & A. Kohn (Eds.), *Ungrading: Why rating students undermines learning* (pp. 23–41). West Virginia University Press.

Stone, D., & Heen, S. (2015). *Thanks for the feedback: The science and art of receiving feedback well even when it's off-base, unfair, poorly delivered, and frankly, you're not in the mood.* Penguin.

Stone, D., Patton, B., & Heen, S. (2010). *Difficult conversations: How to discuss what matters most.* Penguin.

Summerlee, A. J. (2018). Inquiry-based learning: A socially just approach to higher education. *Journal of Human Behavior in the Social Environment, 28*(4), 406–418. https://doi.org/10.1080/10911359.2018.1438956

Swan, G. E., & Carmelli, D. (1996). Curiosity and mortality in aging adults: A 5-year follow-up of the Western Collaborative Group Study. *Psychology and Aging, 11*(3), 449–453. https://doi.org/10.1037/0882-7974.11.3.449

Tamburro, A. (2013). Including decolonization in social work education and practice. *Journal of Indigenous Social Development, 2*(1), 1–16. http://hdl.handle.net/10125/29814

Taranto, D., & Buchanan, M. T. (2020). Sustaining lifelong learning: A self-regulated learning (SRL) approach. *Discourse and Communication for Sustainable Education, 11*(1), 5–15. https://doi.org/10.2478/dcse-2020-0002

Taylor, E. W. (2007). An update of transformative learning theory: A critical review of the empirical research (1999–2005). *International Journal of Lifelong Education, 26*(2), 173–191. https://doi.org/10.1080/02601370701219475

Taylor, E. W. (2008). Transformative learning theory. In S. B. Merriam (Ed.), *An Update of Adult Learning* (New Directions for Adult and Continuing Education, no. 119, pp. 5–15). Jossey-Bass.

Taylor, E. W. (2009). Fostering transformative learning. In J. Mezirow & E. W. Taylor (Eds.), *Transformative learning in practice: Insights from community, workplace, and higher education* (pp. 3–17). Wiley.

Teater, B. A. (2011). Maximizing student learning: A case example of applying teaching and learning theory in social work education. *Social Work Education, 30*(5), 571–585. https://doi.org/10.1080/02615479.2010.505262

Telegraph Staff and Agencies. (2013, March 28). Mothers asked nearly 300 questions a day, study finds. *The Telegraph.* https://www.telegraph.co.uk/news/uknews/9959026/Mothers-asked-nearly-300-questions-a-day-study-finds.html

Tenenberg, J. (2016). Learning through observing peers in practice. *Studies in Higher Education, 41*(4), 1–18. https://doi.org/10.1080/03075079.2014.950954

Theall, M., & Franklin, J. L. (2010). Assessing teaching practices and effectiveness for formative purposes. In K. J. Gillespie and D. L. Robertson (Eds.), *A guide to faculty development* (pp. 151–168). Jossey Bass.

Thompson, N., & Pascal, J. (2012). Developing critically reflective practice. *Reflective Practice, 13*(2), 311–325. https://doi.org/10.1080/14623943.2012.657795

Thomson, A., Smith-Tolken, A., Naidoo, T., & Bringle, R. (2010). Service learning and community engagement: A comparison of three national contexts. *International Journal of Voluntary and Nonprofit Organizations, 22*(2), 214–237. https://doi.org/10.1007/s11266-010-9133-9

Tisdell, E. J. (2003). *Exploring spirituality and culture in adult and higher education.* Jossey-Bass.

Toriz, E. (2019). Learning based on flipped classroom with just-in-time teaching, Unity3D, gamification and educational spaces. *International Journal on Interactive Design and Manufacturing (IJIDeM), 13*(3), 1159–1173. https://doi.org/10.1007/s12008-019-00560-z

Toshalis, E. (2015). *Make me! Understanding and engaging student resistance in school.* Harvard Education Press.

Trumbull, E., & Lash, A. (2013). *Understanding formative assessment: Insights from learning theory and measurement theory.* West Ed.

Tutt, G. D. (2021). *Exploring interpersonal trust in coworking spaces* [Unpublished doctoral dissertation]. Adler University.

University of Calgary. (2018). *ii' taa'poh'to'p (a place to rejuvenate and re-energize during a journey).* https://www.ucalgary.ca/indigenous-strategy/

University of New South Wales, Sydney. (n.d.). *When groups first meet.* https://www.teaching.unsw.edu.au/group-work-when-groups-first-meet

University of Prince Edward Island. (2021, October 6). *Curiosity and inquiry lab.* https://projects.upei.ca/curiosityandinquiry/

University of Sydney School of Education and Social Work. (2018). *Constructivism.* http://sydney.edu.au/education_social_work/learning_teaching/ict/theory/constructivism.Shtml

Ural, E. (2016). The effect of guided-inquiry laboratory experiments on science education students' chemistry laboratory attitudes, anxiety and achievement. *Journal of Education and Training Studies, 4*(4), 217–227. http://dx.doi.org/10.11114/jets.v4i4.1395

Vajoczki, S., Watt, S., Vine, M. M., & Xueqing, L. (2011). Inquiry learning: Level, discipline, class size, what matters? *International Journal for the Scholarship of Teaching & Learning, 5*(1), 1–11. https://doi.org/10.20429/ijsotl.2011.050110

van Woezik, T., Koksma, J., Reuzel, R., Jaarsma, D., & Jan van der Wilt, G. (2020). How to encourage a lifelong learner? The complex relation between learning strategies and assessment in a medical curriculum. *Assessment & Evaluation in Higher Education, 45*(4), 513–526. https://doi.org/10.1080/02602938.2019.1667954

von Renesse, C., & Ecke, V. (2017). Teaching inquiry with a lens toward curiosity. *Problems, Resources, and Issues in Mathematics Undergraduate Studies, 27*(1), 148–164. https://doi.org/10.1080/10511970.2016.1176973

Wall, K. P., Dillon, R., & Knowles, M. K. (2015). Fluorescence quantum yield measurements of fluorescent proteins: A laboratory experiment for a biochemistry or molecular biophysics laboratory course. *Biochemistry and Molecular Biology Education, 43*(1), 52–59. http://dx.doi.org/10.1002/bmb.20837

Wang, P. H., Wu, P. L., Yu, K. W., & Lin, Y. X. (2015). Influence of implementing inquiry-based instruction on science learning motivation and interest: A perspective of comparison. *Procedia: Social and Behavioral Sciences, 174*, 1292–1299. https://doi.org/10.1016/j.sbspro.2015.01.750

Ward, W. A. (n.d.). *William Arthur Ward quotes.* AllAuthor. https://allauthor.com/quotes/author/william-arthur-ward/

Wasniewski, E., Munro, T., & Tandon, T. (2021). Exploring online specifications grading: An undergraduate course case study. In T. Bastiaens (Ed.), *Proceedings of EdMedia + Innovate Learning* (pp. 179–184). Association for the Advancement of Computing in Education. https://www.learntechlib.org/primary/p/219655/

Weaver, P. M. (1989). *An assessment of the skills needed in a college art and design curriculum to facilitate student involvement and competence with computers in artistic applications* [Unpublished doctoral dissertation]. University of Maryland at College Park.

Weber, E. P., Lach, D., & Steel, B. S. (2017). *New strategies for wicked problems: Science and solutions in the 21st century.* Oregon State University Press.

Wheeler, L. B., Maeng, J. L., Chiu, J. L., & Bell, R. L. (2017). Do teaching assistants matter? Investigating relationships between teaching assistants and student outcomes in undergraduate science laboratory classes. *Journal of Research in Science Teaching, 54*(4), 463–492. https://doi.org/10.1002/tea.21373

Wheeler, L. B., Maeng, J. L., & Whitworth, B. A. (2017). Characterizing teaching assistants' knowledge and beliefs following professional development activities within an inquiry-based general chemistry context. *Journal of Chemical Education, 94*(1), 19–28. https://doi.org/10.1021/acs.jchemed.6b00373

White, B., & Frederiksen, J. (2005). A theoretical framework and approach for fostering metacognitive development. *Educational Psychologist, 40*(4), 211–223. https://doi.org/10.1207/s15326985ep4004_3

Wood, W. (2003). Inquiry-based undergraduate teaching in the life sciences at large research universities: A perspective on the Boyer commission report. *Cell Biology Education, 2*(2), 112–116. https://doi.org/10.1187/cbe.03-02-0004

Woolf, J. (2017). An analytical autoethnographical account of using inquiry-based learning in a graduate research methods course. *Canadian Journal for the Scholarship of Teaching and Learning, 8*(1). https://doi.org/10.5206/cjsotl-rcacea.2017.1.5

World Economic Forum. (2016). *The future of jobs: Employment, skills and workforce strategy for the fourth industrial revolution.* http://www3.weforum.org/docs/WEF_Future_of_Jobs.pdf

Wright, G. (2011). Student-centered learning in higher education. *International Journal of Teaching and Learning in Higher Education, 23*(1), 92–97. https://www.isetl.org/ijtlhe/ijtlhe-issue.php?v=23&n=1&y=2011

Wright, L. L., Lange, E., & Da Costa, J. (2009). Facilitating adult learning and a researcher identity through a higher education pedagogical process. *US-China Education Review, 6*(11), 1–16. https://eric.ed.gov/?id=ED511184

Wright, W., Knight, P., & Pomerleau, N. (1999). Portfolio people: Teaching and learning dossiers and innovation in higher education. *Innovative Higher Education, 24,* 89–103. https://doi.org/10.1023/B:IHIE.0000008148.71650.e6

Yamashita, T., López, E. B., Stevens, J., & Keene, J. R. (2017). Types of learning activities and life satisfaction among older adults in urban community-based lifelong learning programs. *Activities, Adaptation & Aging, 41*(3), 239–257. https://doi.org/10.1080/01924788.2017.1310583

Yang, M. (2015). Promoting self-sustained learning in higher education: The ISEE framework. *Teaching in Higher Education, 20*(6), 601–613. https://doi.org/10.1080/13562517.2015.1052785

Yesudhas, R., Lalit, P., Josy, A., & Impana, S. (2014). Water and sanitation in Mumbai's slums: Education through inquiry-based learning in social work. *The Qualitative Report, 19*(45), 1–12. https://nsuworks.nova.edu/tqr/vol19/iss45/1

Yorks, L., & Kasl, E. (2006). I know more than I can say: A taxonomy for using expressive ways of knowing to foster transformative learning. *Journal of Transformative Education, 4*(1), 43–64. https://doi.org/10.1177/1541344605283151

Zammitti, A., Magnano, P., & Santisi, G. (2020). "Work and surroundings": A training to enhance career curiosity, self-efficacy, and the perception of work and decent work in adolescents. *Sustainability, 12*(16), 1–14. https://doi.org/10.3390/su12166473

Ziegler, M., Paulus, T., & Woodside, M. (2006). Creating a climate of engagement in a blended learning environment. *Journal of Interactive Learning Research, 17*(3), 295–318. https://www.learntechlib.org/primary/p/6286/

Zorn, I., & Seelmeyer, U. (2017). Inquiry-based learning about technologies in social work education. *Journal of Technology in Human Services, 35*(1), 49–62. https://doi.org/10.1080/15228835.2017.1277913

Zubaroglu, P., & Popescu, M. (2015). Preparing social work students for international interdisciplinary practice: A teaching model and its impact on self-efficacy. *Advances in Social Work, 16*(2), 214–232. https://doi.org/10.18060/18504

Zubizarreta, J. (2004). *The learning portfolio: Reflective practice for improving student learning.* Wiley.

Stacey L. MacKinnon, PhD, is an associate professor with the Department of Psychology at the University of Prince Edward Island. Stacey has spent the last 12 years designing and implementing The Curiosity Project and the past 6 years developing and coordinating UPEI 1020, "First Year Inquiry Studies." She is the recipient of the 2022 Janet Pottie Murray Award for Excellence in Educational Leadership, 2016 UPEI Professor of the Year, 2012 Hessian Award for Excellence in Teaching, and the 2012 President's Award of Merit for Teaching. As a lifelong and life-wide learner herself, Stacey strives to inspire her students and colleagues to fully engage their curiosity mindset and inquiry skills to explore all the possibilities our world has to offer. She is currently developing a new approach to reading nonfiction that incorporates active inquiry to improve students' ability and willingness to engage in deeper critical understanding, academic discussion, and quality of both informal and formal writing. She strongly believes that learning should be both enjoyable and challenging for both the students and professor. By harnessing our curiosity or "desire to inquire" much can be done to achieve that goal.

Beth Archer-Kuhn, PhD, is an associate professor with the Faculty of Social Work at the University of Calgary and was named a Teaching and Learning Scholar with the Taylor Institute for Teaching and Learning. She is the recipient of the Teaching Excellence Award from the Faculty of Social Work. Beth has spent the last 10 years learning about IBL-HE through implementation and SoTL research with undergraduate, graduate, and doctoral students within courses on campus, study abroad, and online. She believes IBL-HE is a socially just and inclusive pedagogy that aligns with the values of social work education, can support students with varied learning preferences, and allows students the necessary choice and agency to inspire lifelong learners. Beth's website for her Teaching Scholars project provides a number of resources for implementing IBL-HE (https://live-ucalgary .ucalgary.ca/node/339351).

POGIL

An Introduction to Process Oriented Guided Inquiry Learning for Those Who Wish to Empower Learners

Edited by Shawn K. Simonson

"This collected wisdom of the POGIL community is immense, reflecting both practical classroom strategy and strong ties to theoretical frameworks in science education, sociology, and the learning sciences. With origins in undergraduate chemistry education, the ideas contained in this guide are relevant to any instructor—in any discipline and at any cognitive level—who aspires to structure an engaging and equitable classroom environment that also challenges students to be architects of their own learning."
— *Kimberly Tanner, San Francisco State University*

Process Oriented Guided Inquiry Learning (POGIL) is a pedagogy that's based on research on how people learn and has been shown to lead to better student outcomes in many contexts and in a variety of academic disciplines. Beyond facilitating students' mastery of a discipline, it promotes vital educational outcomes such as communicational thinking and critical thinking. Its active international community of practitioners provides an accessible educational development and support for anyone developing related courses.

Having started as a process developed by a group of chemistry professors focused on helping their students better grasp the concepts of general chemistry, The POGIL Project has grown into a dynamic organization of committed instructors who help each other transform classrooms and improve student success, develop curricular materials to assist this process, conduct research expanding what is known about learning and teaching, and provide professional development and collegiality from elementary teachers to college professors. As a pedagogy it has been shown to be effective in a variety of contexts and at different educational levels. This is an introduction to the process and the community.

POGIL

An Introduction to Process Oriented Guided Inquiry Learning for Those Who Wish to Empower Learners

Edited by Shawn R. Simonson

"This collected wisdom of the POGIL community is immense, reflecting both practical classroom strategies and strong ties to theoretical frameworks in science education, sociology, and the learning sciences. With origins in undergraduate chemistry education, the ideas contained in this guide are relevant to any instructor—in any discipline and at any cognitive level—who aspires to structure an engaging and equitable classroom environment that also challenges students to be architects of their own learning."
—**Kimberly Tanner**, *San Francisco State University*

Process-oriented guided inquiry learning (POGIL) is a pedagogy that is based on research on how people learn and has been shown to lead to better student outcomes in many contexts and in a variety of academic disciplines. Beyond facilitating students' mastery of a discipline, it promotes vital educational outcomes such as communication skills and critical thinking. Its active international community of practitioners provides accessible educational development and support for anyone developing related courses.

Having started as a process developed by a group of chemistry professors focused on helping their students better grasp the concepts of general chemistry, The POGIL Project has grown into a dynamic organization of committed instructors who help each other transform classrooms and improve student success, develop curricular materials to assist this process, conduct research expanding what is known about learning and teaching, and provide professional development and collegiality from elementary teachers to college professors. As a pedagogy it has been shown to be effective in a variety of content areas and at different educational levels. This is an introduction to the process and the community.

High-Impact ePortfolio Practice

A Catalyst for Students, Faculty, and Institutional Learning

Bret Eynon and Laura M. Gambino

Foreword by George D. Kuh

Published in Association with AAC&U

"Drawing on years of work with campuses nationwide, the authors provide excellent analyses of best practices in ePortfolio use, and they situate their examples in critical contexts that demonstrate the role ePortfolios play in facilitating reflection and integration, essential elements of impactful education. This book will be an indispensable resource for colleges and universities."
—*Natalie McKnight, Dean, College of General Studies, Boston University*

At a moment when over half of U.S. colleges are employing ePortfolios, the time is ripe to develop their full potential to advance integrative learning and broad institutional change.

The authors outline how to deploy the ePortfolio as a high-impact practice and describe widely applicable models of effective ePortfolio pedagogy and implementation that demonstrably improve student learning across multiple settings.

Drawing on the campus ePortfolio projects developed by a constellation of institutions that participated in the Connect to Learning network, Eynon and Gambino present a wealth of data and revealing case studies. Their broad-based evidence demonstrates that, implemented with a purposeful framework, ePortfolios correlate strongly with increased retention and graduation rates, broadened student engagement in deep learning processes, and advanced faculty and institutional learning.

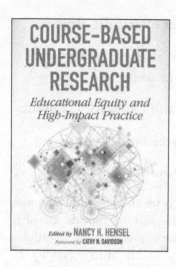

Course-Based Undergraduate Research

Educational Equity and High-Impact Practice

Edited by Nancy H. Hensel

Foreword by Cathy N. Davidson

"If you are an educator who believes in the importance of all students engaging in undergraduate research as a way to develop the competencies needed to thrive in an innovation-driven economy, then this book is a must-read. Course-based research provides practical, equitable, and inclusive strategies for making undergraduate research accessible and engaging for every student."—*Tia Brown McNair*, *Vice President; Office of Diversity, Equity, and Student Success; Association of American Colleges and Universities*

Undergraduate research has long been recognized as a high-impact practice (HIP) but has unfortunately been offered only to juniors and seniors, and to very few of them (often in summer programs). This book shows how to engage students in authentic research experiences, built into the design of courses in the first 2 years, thus making the experience available to a much greater number of students.

Delivering on the Promise of High-Impact Practices

Research and Models for Achieving Equity, Fidelity, Impact, and Scale

Edited by John Zilvinskis, Jillian Kinzie, Jerry Daday, Ken O'Donnell, and Carleen Vande Zande

Epilogue by Shaun Harper

Afterword by George D. Kuh

Research shows that enriching learning experiences such as learning communities, service-learning, undergraduate research, internships, and senior culminating experiences—collectively known as High-Impact Practices (HIPs)—are positively associated with student engagement; deep and integrated learning; and personal and educational gains for all students – particularly for historically underserved students, including first-generation students and racially minoritized populations.

While HIPs' potential benefits for student learning, retention, and graduation are recognized and are being increasingly integrated across higher education programs, much of that potential remains unrealized; and their implementation frequently uneven.

The goal of *Delivering on the Promise of High-Impact Practices* is to provide examples from around the country of the ways educators are advancing equity, promoting fidelity, achieving scale, and strengthening assessment of their own local high-impact practices. Its chapters bring together the best current scholarship, methodologies, and evidence-based practices within the HIPs field, illustrating new approaches to faculty professional development, culture and coalition building, research and assessment, and continuous improvement that help institutions understand and extend practices with a demonstrated high impact.

For proponents and practitioners this book offers perspectives, data, and critiques to interrogate and improve practice. For administrators it provides an understanding of what's needed to deliver the necessary support.

Specifications Grading

Restoring Rigor, Motivating Students, and Saving Faculty Time

Linda B. Nilson

Foreword by Claudia J. Stanny

In her latest book, Linda Nilson puts forward an innovative but practical and tested approach to grading that can demonstrably raise academic standards, motivate students, tie their achievement of learning outcomes to their course grades, save faculty time and stress, and provide the reliable gauge of student learning that the public and employers are looking for.

She argues that the grading system most commonly in use now is unwieldy, imprecise and unnecessarily complex, involving too many rating levels for too many individual assignments and tests, and based on a hairsplitting point structure that obscures the underlying criteria and encourages students to challenge their grades.

This new specifications grading paradigm restructures assessments to streamline the grading process and greatly reduce grading time, empower students to choose the level of attainment they want to achieve, reduce antagonism between the evaluator and the evaluated, and increase student receptivity to meaningful feedback, thus facilitating the learning process—all while upholding rigor. In addition, specs grading increases students' motivation to do well by making expectations clear, lowering their stress and giving them agency in determining their course goals.

Student-Led Peer Review

A Practical Guide to Implementation Across Disciplines and Modalities

Kimberly A. Lowe, Liv Cummins, Summer Ray Clark, Bill Porter, and Lisa Spitz

Foreword by Peggy Maki

Student-led peer review can be a powerful learning experience for both giver and receiver, developing evaluative judgment, critical thinking, and collaborative skills that are highly transferable across disciplines and professions. Its success depends on purposeful planning and scaffolding to promote student ownership of the process. With intentional and consistent implementation, peer review can engage students in course content and promote deep learning, while also increasing the efficiency and effectiveness of faculty assessment.

Based on the authors' extensive experience and research, this book provides a practical introduction to the key principles, steps, and strategies to implement student peer review—sometimes referred to as "peer critique" or "workshopping." It addresses common challenges that faculty and students encounter. The authors offer an easy-to-follow and rigorously tested three-part protocol to use before, during, and after a peer review session, and advice on adapting each step to individual courses.

The process is applicable across all disciplines, content types, and modalities, face-to-face and online, synchronous and asynchronous. Instructors can guide students in peer review in one course, across two or more courses that are team-taught, or across programs or curriculums. When instructors, students, and university stakeholders create a culture of peer review, it enhances learning benefits for students and allows faculty to share pedagogical resources.